NORMANDY, PICARDY & PAS DE CALAIS

PASSPORT'S REGIONAL GUIDES OF FRANCE
Series Editor: Arthur Eperon

Auvergne & the Massif Central
Rex Grizell

Brittany
Frank Victor Dawes

Champagne-Ardennes & Burgundy
Arthur and Barbara Eperon

The Dordogne & Lot
Arthur and Barbara Eperon

Languedoc & Roussillon
Andrew Sanger

The Loire Valley
Arthur and Barbara Eperon

Paris
Vivienne Menkes-Ivry

Provence & the Côte d'Azur
Roger Macdonald

The Rhône Valley & Savoy
Rex Grizell

South West France
Andrew Sanger

Also available:
Passport's Regional Guides of Italy
Passport's Regional Guides of Portugal

NORMANDY PICARDY & PAS DE CALAIS

Barbara Eperon

Second Edition

Photographs by Joe Cornish

PASSPORT BOOKS
a division of *NTC Publishing Group*
Lincolnwood, Illinois USA

This edition first published in 1997 by
Passport Books, a division of NTC
Publishing Group, 4255 West Touhy
Avenue, Lincolnwood (Chicago), Illinois
60646–1975, U.S.A.
Originally published by Christopher Helm
(Publishers) Ltd, a subsidiary of A & C Black
(Publishers) Ltd, 35 Bedford Row, London,
England.

Photographs by Joe Cornish.
Line illustrations by David Saunders.

ISBN 0–8442–9943–X

Library of Congress Catalog, Card Number:
95–71159

The author and the publishers have done
their best to ensure the accuracy of all the
information in this guide. They can accept
no responsibility for any loss, injury or
inconvenience sustained by any traveller as
a result of information or advice contained
in this book.

Printed and bound in Italy by Printer Trento.

Contents

Maps and Plans

NORMANDY, PICARDY & PAS DE CALAIS

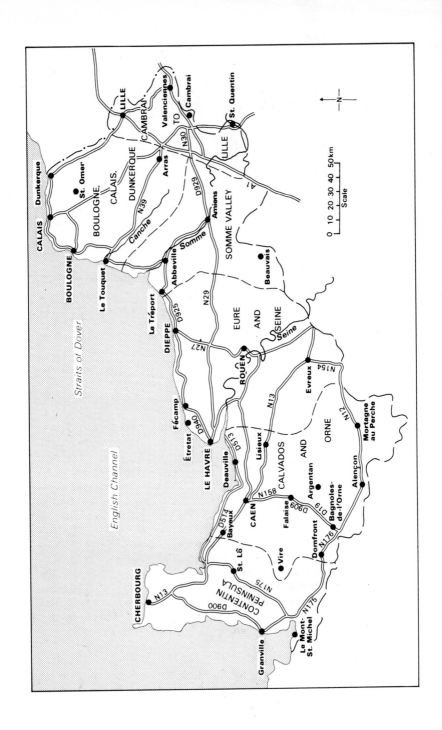

1. Introduction

Normandy is a lush and prosperous land whose people are so self-sufficient that they have turned their back often on the politics of Paris. Only the EU has managed to alter that with its farm production quotas and fishing regulations. The lands to the north — Pas-de-Calais and Flanders — have not been quite so blessed and have seen much poverty and destruction over the centuries. Often they have been a political football. The great beauty of Normandy comes from its soft fertility rather than grandeur. There are rocks and cliffs washed by mountainous winter seas on the west coast of the Manche and the white chalk cliffs from Dieppe to near Le Havre — Côte d'Albâtre (the Alabaster Coast). But go a short distance inland and you are in the rich countryside of meadows where brown and white cows with rings round their eyes munch luscious grass, rivers with sheep grazing on their banks, of apple and pear orchards, fine woods and forests of beech and oak, and patchwork fields of the *bocage* protected by hedges and criss-crossed with narrow lanes, often sunk below the fields. When the US forces landed on the Manche and Calvados coasts in 1944, they had to learn a new way of fighting. Their tanks and armoured vehicles simply could not get through the *bocage* country and they had to learn to fight on their feet like the British Commandos. Where they could use tanks they progressed literally hedge by hedge. They fitted bulldozer blades to the fronts of their tanks to chop down the hedges.

Normandy is still rich in old black and white half-timbered farms, barns and town houses, in medieval and Renaissance churches, in old castles and villages. Only in the Manche and Calvados where the heavy fighting took place in 1944 has much of the old been destroyed, and even there a lot has been restored. Through history wars have treated Normandy lightly compared with the rest of France. Even the First World War hardly touched it and though Upper Normandy was occupied in the Franco-Prussian War of 1870–1, the Normans kept the Prussian soldiers quiet with a ration of a litre of calvados, the fiery apple spirit, per man per day. The Second World War was a different matter. During the German advance to the coast in 1940 many towns and villages in Upper Normandy were bombed or burned almost to the ground, much was knocked down by the occupying Germans building their West Wall — Fortress Europe — and then the Allied landings in 1944 left hardly a town in Lower Normandy except Bayeux intact. Pas-de-Calais and Flanders in the north have been constantly ravaged by wars through history.

Normandy is divided between open countryside and the wooded *bocage,* but nearly all of it is very attractive. The dullest area is possibly the almost treeless windswept arable land in the Caen–Falaise area — flat and monotonous. The most enduring crop this land has produced is the whitish Caen stone used for building medieval to modern churches and châteaux not only in Normandy itself but in England. Westminster Abbey is of Caen stone. Iron is found here, too, making it the most industrialised part of Normandy after the Seine estuary ('Petrol-land') and Rouen. Yet to the north-east of this countryside is Pays d'Auge, the wooded land with pastures and orchards which produces the best cider and calvados and some of the best cheeses. The village of Camembert itself is here. And west of Falaise in the Orne river country is the beautiful if fancifully named Suisse Normande, a delightful land of rocky cliffs, twisting and looping rivers, waterfalls, ravines and woodland, all lovely to explore on foot or slowly by car. This almost secretive land hidden among the lushness of Lower Normandy was hardly known except to walkers, rock climbers and canoeists until quite recently. The Paris–Rouen–Caen motorways have brought some Parisians, the useful Brittany Ferries route from Portsmouth to Caen has brought more British. But it is certainly not crowded.

Despite a few coastal nuclear energy plants, which don't worry the French as they do the Americans and British, little extra industry has opened up in Normandy. The 'technological revolution' in France has passed it by, partly because the Normans are proud of being farmers and working on the land. Even the young have not been tempted by high wages into city factories as they have in many other agricultural areas.

Another lesser-known area is the Cotentin Peninsula, despite the fact that there are ferries from Britain to Cherbourg. The coastline is rocky and spectacular but with many little sand beaches in between, and further down the Manche coast are the vast beaches of the Bay of Mont-St. Michel, where the tide can go out 15km!

Also little known is the *bocage* countryside between St. Lô and Vire. This is one of the areas of horse studs. Ste. Mère-Église is the main centre for horse breeding, with national studs nearby at St. Lô and at Pin-au-Haras east of Argentan. Normandy has bred thoroughbred horses since the 18th century. Trotters are now popular, too. Percherons were the great French dray and farm horses. They are still bred for show purposes or special ceremonies, but, alas, many are bred for meat. The Percheron was said to be rather like the Norman people — strong, hard-working, slow, dogged.

The forests are very pleasant. Écouves, Brotonne, the beautiful beech woodland of Eawy near Dieppe are all a delight for walking, for picnics and for driving through. Perhaps Lyons Forest, east of Rouen, is the most attractive. Mainly beech, it still covers 10,700 hectares and has some delightful hamlets. It can be part of a most pleasant wandering route from the Loire or the south to the Channel ports, missing out Rouen's horrific traffic. Normandy's scenery may not be spectacular, but it is calming and relaxing.

The coastlines are more invigorating. The notorious Alderney Race sweeps past the granite rock west of Cherbourg. On the other coast the seas are kinder around Barfleur and St. Vaast, which provides some of the best oysters in France.

If the Seine has become 'the River of Petrol' as the French call it, it is only so in a few places, especially the estuary around Le Havre. Apart from inevitable industrial development at Rouen, the major port for the massive Seine barges, and the huge petroleum installations at Port-Jérome, the river banks have succeeded in staying surprisingly attractive. Some old-style rural scenes have survived, like the little village of La Bouille which Monet loved and its *bac* (small ferry) across to the Forest of Roumare through which you can take a rural drive into Rouen. The stretch from Vernon to Rouen runs through farmlands with massive meanders past rocky escarpments with fine views over the Seine valley, like those at Les Andelys and Côte des Deux Amants. Napoleon said that Le Havre, Rouen and Paris were one city with a common main road, the Seine. If new bridges and motorways carrying heavy lorries have made it slightly less important, it is certainly not dead as a major highway.

The Calvados coast of the D-Day landing beaches was always one of small family beach resorts. Despite almost total destruction in 1944 they are back, rebuilt, and enjoying something of a boom because of nearby motorways linking them with Paris and the Portsmouth–Caen ferry. This docks at Ouistreham, a port-resort joined to Caen by river and canal. Films and publicity about D-Day landings have brought not only veterans of the landings and their families but younger people wanting to discover more about the war which is history to them.

Deauville may not have quite the same standing in the fashionable world as it had before the jet age but its Grand Prix horse-racing season in August still attracts the 'top people' and those who like to be close to them. Little old ports and resorts like Honfleur, Étretat, Fécamp and St. Valery-en-Caux are enjoying a new popularity with Parisians, many of them young families, who can get there fast by car for summer weekends. Many own flats and studios for weekends and school holidays. Dieppe is once again popular with the British, who almost colonised it at the end of the last century.

Technically, the frontier of Normandy is at the seaside resort and fishing port of Le Tréport, marked by the river Bresle, but Mers-les-Bains across the river, though in the Somme Département, is virtually a suburb of Le Tréport.

All three areas of the North which this book covers, Picardy, Artois and Flanders (the Départements of Somme, Pas-de-Calais, Nord and part of Aisne), remain mainly peaceful and rural despite some ugly industrial patches, and the scars of wars. There are stretches of rather dull, flat but fertile farmland, but there is also a lot of beautiful scenery with quiet lanes winding through gentle hills to tranquil hamlets and villages and green wooded valleys. Despite the important ports of Dieppe, Boulogne, Calais and Dunkerque, and a few thriving seaside resorts such as Le Touquet, Berck, Hardelot and Malo-les-Bains, the coast is little developed and attractive, especially from the sea from where you can truly appreciate its white cliffs

3

with broad sands between. In the little towns inland, the Flemish and French cultures meet in architecture and art, with exuberant Gothic buildings beside Flemish churches and town halls with tall belfries. The further north you go, the more the Flemish influence takes over. Most of these towns are more Flemish than French in their history.

The importance of the Channel ports as the gateway to England has been the major reason why these lands have suffered the devastation of war for centuries. The worst has been in this century. The country north from Amiens and the river Somme to the Belgian border (and beyond, of course) was almost literally flattened in the First World War. Lovely old towns were destroyed, villages totally wiped out and many of the people, as well as hundreds of thousands of soldiers, died to prevent the Germans occupying northern France. Deaths were fewer but devastation even more widespread in the Second World War when the Germans did occupy France in 1940 and the Allies drove them out in 1944–5. Towns and villages which had not had time to recover from one destruction were hit as hard a mere 20 years later.

It is surprising how it has all settled down — villages are prosperous and tranquil, towns busy and often crowded. But motorways have taken away so much of the traffic heading for Belgium or Britain through the Channel ports and tunnel that the countryside is now as peaceful and rural as it has been at any time in the last century. Few Frenchmen, and even fewer Britons speeding down to the Mediterranean, ever see, for instance, the peaceful and beautiful countryside behind Calais and Boulogne — a fertile, varied land of hills, forests, streams still rich in trout, hamlets with tiny old churches, narrow lanes and old-fashioned farmyards with pecking chickens. Even towns once streaming with traffic, like the medieval hilltop town of Montreuil-sur-Mer, or St. Quentin, which was rebuilt after terrible destruction in the First World War, have been so successfully bypassed that most of their traffic is local. Their hotels and Logis have become hideouts for Britons who have extended the 'great British weekend' to northern France on a considerable scale. The completion of the Channel Tunnel from near Folkestone in Kent to Coquelles, inland 6km south of Calais, has cleared the coast area of much commercial traffic, bringing back Britons on short-break holidays to coastal villages like Wimereux, Hardelot and Le Touquet, where their grandparents might have spent holidays.

Calais has lost cross-channel traffic to the 'Chunnel' but has been compensated with extra ferry traffic switched from Boulogne. At present Boulogne has only the Seacats and Hovercraft of Hoverspeed landing British visitors. It was hit hard by the loss of ferry boat traffic and boatloads of day-trippers, from schoolchildren to pensioners ('Troisième Âge' the French call us). But a new motorway brings British visitors from Calais. The streets are more pleasant, the town is more French again and Britons are re-discovering it for shopping and gastronomic weekends or last nights before going home.

2. History

The recorded history of what is now Normandy, goes back to Roman times. The Gauls of this area put up the last great stand against Julius Caesar's armies in 52 BC. Nevertheless, they fared well under the Romans, with many of them finding it profitable to support Roman rule. They set up ports at Rouen, Honfleur and Lillebonne as military bases and to trade with England.

Then in the 4th century AD invaders from the north and east, Alamans, Goths and Franks, destroyed the rule of Rome. Clovis, King of the Franks, came to power. He had become a Christian and he introduced the religion to the area.

The 'modern' history of Normandy, however, begins in 911 when Earl Rollo, on one of the annual Norse raids to pillage, rape, destroy and make away with loot back to Norway, surprisingly made a peace treaty with the Frankish King Charles the Simple, was baptised as a Christian and settled down as Robert Patrician (ruler) of Normandy with his followers to breed cattle and children. The title Duke of Normandy was not adopted for two generations. But Robert did adopt the French language and defended his territory against other invading Norsemen and Vikings. He gave Normandy a stability which it has maintained through history.

For two centuries the area had suffered the terrible raids each spring when the Norsemen arrived in their longboats. They could take these boats up rivers and they sacked and looted right up the Seine, the Somme, the Orne and rivers southwards to the Loire. Each autumn when they departed they took as many slaves as their boats could hold and killed most of the rest. But it was inevitable that sooner or later at least some of them would prefer life in this lush land to the hard winters with near-starvation in the northern countries.

The Frankish kings mistakenly believed that the dukes would be their vassals. In fact, part of the treaty between Robert and King Charles was that the former should do homage to Charles by kneeling and kissing his feet. This he refused to do and ordered one of his followers to do it for him. The Norseman, instead of bending down to the King's feet, pulled the foot up to his lips and tilted the King onto his back. Norsemen did not bend the knee to any man.

William the Bastard, later called the Conqueror, became Duke of Normandy as a baby despite opposition from the barons and by the time he was 19 was having to fight Norman enemies determined to destroy him and the French who were equally determined to take over his troublesome dukedom. His defeat of the French King Henry and his ally Geoffrey Martel of Anjou at Varaville, a little place north-east of Caen, in 1058 left him free to invade England.

The story of William's claim to the English throne is told completely differently in France to the way it's told in England. In both cases, of course, the historians of the time were just propagandists. King Edward the Confessor of England had been brought up almost entirely in Normandy by monks. French was his language and he was more French than English. He took Norman advisers to England when he became King. His Normans became very unpopular in England, and Harold, Earl of Wessex, Edward's right-hand man, led the fight for power against the Normans at court in London.

There is no doubt that at some time about 1051 Edward had promised the crown of England to William of Normandy. By a quirk of fate, when Harold was sailing off the south coast of England from Bosham one day, a storm drove him across to Ponthieu and he fell into William's hands. William treated him with honour and respect but prevented him from returning to England until he agreed to William's terms. They obviously got along fairly well because Harold helped William to reconquer Brittany. But in England the Northumbrians had revolted and Harold, who was virtual 'prime minister' to the dying monarch, had to get back. He could not leave without swearing to support William's claim to the English throne. Afterwards he said that he had sworn under threat and repudiated his oath.

King Edward died on 5 January 1066, appointing Harold as king on his deathbed. He had no legal right to do this any more than he had earlier had to promise the throne to William. The new king had to be elected by the Witan, a sort of Privy Council of very important citizens. The Witan chose Harold, so he was legally king. He was crowned by the Archbishop of York. To William, this was an insult — a breach of an oath. To the Pope, Harold was an impudent usurper, seizing a crown which did not belong to him, and a perjurer who had broken an oath. Moreover, many of the churchmen in England were Normans and supporters of William.

When William sailed for England, it was not under the flag of the Duke of Normandy but that of the Pope. And by no means were all his followers Normans. Behind all the claims of legal and moral right was the promise of power, lands and wealth, and when he had won, William distributed all three to his followers, for England was a rich country.

When William was killed fighting the King of France, his eldest son Robert became Duke of Normandy, and his second son William Rufus King William II of England. There was also a younger brother Henry, born in England. And when William Rufus was killed by an arrow while hunting in the New Forest in 1100 (probably murdered by his enemies) Henry, who had helped Robert defend Normandy, seized the English royal treasury and was elected King Henry I by the Witan. Then he made war against Robert, defeated him and kept him prisoner until he died 28 years later.

The Battle of Hastings

When Edward died and Harold was appointed his successor by the Witan, a council of important citizens, he had the support of most of the English, who did not like the Normans Edward had brought with him when he was crowned. Harold refused William's claim to the throne categorically. William had the support of the Pope because Harold had sacked the Norman Archbishop of Canterbury. The Pope not only encouraged William but allowed him to sail under the papal banner. There was more than church discipline involved — there was the prospect of wealth. It was also the promise of profit in loot and land which persuaded the Norman barons to follow William. They were the descendants of the Norsemen and Vikings, and looting was a way of life.

William's followers were not all Normans. Any fighting man or bandit who wanted to come was welcome. The Duke of Brittany took a huge force. The French were there in number, so were the men of Anjou, Maine and many Flemings. Adventurers came from Italy, Hungary and Germany. The Normans in England could not wait for William's arrival, and acted as spies for him. Furthermore, Harold's brother Tostig, King of Norway, who had started an unsuccessful insurrection in Northumberland, invaded England in the north to divert Harold's army. Harold marched north and defeated Tostig at Stamford Bridge, only to learn that William's forces had crossed the Channel and landed near Pevensey on the south coast of England.

Harold made a forced march south. The armies met near Hastings on 14 October 1066. Harold's army must have been extremely fit to have fought at all so soon after another battle and a long march. But their discipline finally broke down and Harold was outwitted. He had chosen a very good position for his defence and William was unable to penetrate it. Towards dusk when it seemed that the weary armies had reached stalemate the Normans started to retreat towards their boats. The delighted Anglo-Saxons charged out of their strong positions to move in for the kill. William's forces turned and slaughtered them. Harold died with an arrow through his eye. The Bastard had become the Conqueror, and his band of mercenaries were fully rewarded. Their leaders were given the Anglo-Saxon lands and noble titles. Even William's cook, William de Percy, who is said to have fought at Hastings wielding a huge spoon like a cudgel, was given lands in Yorkshire, Lincolnshire, Hampshire and Essex and made a baron. He was the founder of the great Percy family, and one of his descendants distinguished himself fighting for England at Crécy!

William dealt cruelly with the Anglo-Saxons, for whom years of misery and near-slavery had begun. London, with its eye on profit and privileges, received William like a hero and he was crowned there on Christmas Day 1066. Then he went back to Normandy and gave a great party at Fécamp to show off his loot of gold, silver and jewellery. He rarely returned to England, except to put down revolts. He died in 1087 of burns received when he burned down the town of Mantes. Within two generations, under Henry II of England, Normandy was a dukedom under the English crown.

When Henry I died, the English crown was seized by Stephen, his nephew. But his daughter Matilda, married to the Count of Anjou, had inherited Normandy, and at 18 her son Henry Plantagenet became Duke, then with his father's death, Count of Anjou. Next he married Eleanor of Aquitaine, divorced wife of King Louis VII of France, and so added her lands of Poitou and Guyenne to his empire. Then he landed in England and made Stephen agree to make him his heir. Stephen died a year later, in 1154, and Henry was crowned King of England. Even William the Conqueror had not achieved such power. The role of Duke of Normandy had become very much secondary to that of King of England.

A series of rebellions by his sons and wars against the new strong French king, Philippe-Auguste, ended in defeat and death for Henry. One of his sons, Richard the Lionheart, had helped Philippe-Auguste defeat him. So had his weaker, and favourite, son John.

Philippe-Auguste and Richard went on a Crusade. Having promised not to touch Richard's territories, Philippe returned to France, and no sooner was he back than he made a pact with John, Richard's brother, to carve them up. On Richard's return, there was a fierce war over them, particularly Normandy. Richard was largely successful, but he was killed by a stray arrow at a minor siege, and Philippe soon overcame the weak John, taking Richard's superb Château Gaillard at Les Andelys in 1204, then the whole of Normandy the same year.

But the French had by no means secured Normandy. In 1328 Edward III of England claimed the French throne by heredity through his mother. In 1346, with his son the Black Prince, he invaded France and conquered most of Normandy, then totally defeated the French at Crécy, where 1,300 French knights were killed. It was the beginning of the terrible Hundred Years War between England and France. In the fighting most of Normandy became French again, then in 1415 Henry V of England landed at Harfleur, won one of the most remarkable victories in history at Agincourt in old Picardy and two years later successfully besieged Rouen. Normandy was back under the English crown. Henry then married the French king's daughter, Margaret of Valois, and in 1420 was made Regent of France and heir to the throne. However he died after a sudden illness the next year.

Joan of Arc recovered Orléans for France, and roused the frightened Dauphin, the hereditary heir to the French throne, persuading him to be crowned Charles VII. Normandy remained English, but after Joan's death, her great companion-in-arms, Jean Dunois, gradually drove the English out of France and the area became French once more in 1450. The dukedom disappeared in 1469.

Meanwhile the Normans had become very much a seafaring people. Their ships ranged far to go fishing and adventuring, often as corsairs preying on merchantmen. The seamen of Dieppe, Honfleur and Le Havre sailed to the New World and opened up regions of North and South America. Samuel Champlain of Dieppe founded a Norman colony in Quebec in 1608. In 1635 Pierre Belain d'Esnambuc took over Martinique, and Guadaloupe followed. The little isle of St. Bartholomé near Guadaloupe was taken over by Normans and is to this day peopled by white blondes with blue eyes. In 1682 Robert Cavalier, Sieur de La Salle, from Rouen, descended the Ohio and Mississippi rivers to the sea, taking possession of Louisiana.

In the Wars of Religion Normandy was mainly Protestant, especially in Caen with its university and in the seaports, influenced by contact with Holland and England. Henri of Navarre, the Protestant leader who became King Henri IV by announcing his conversion to Catholicism, made Protestantism legal in much of France, and won important battles against the extremist Catholic League armies at Arques- and Ivry-la-Bataille. When Henri died, Protestantism was made illegal and there was a mass emigration of Protestants both from Flanders and from Normandy. Since many were skilled artisans, Normandy's economy was in tatters for a while and this rich land knew poverty while England and Holland, who took many of the refugees, prospered. Dieppe alone lost 14,000 men. Le Havre dropped from the leading port in France to the fifth most important.

The Revolution brought the destruction of beautiful churches, abbeys and some castles but Normandy was not as badly hit as many parts of France because it was a peasant economy with fewer big landowners.

In the Franco-Prussian War of 1870–1 the Prussian occupation was softened not only by the ration of a litre of calvados per Prussian soldier each day (see Chapter 9) but by warnings from the British that they would intervene if the Prussians occupied the Channel ports.

Even the First World War left Normandy fairly unharmed by the standards of most of northern France. Some of the heaviest and biggest destruction came on the Somme, just north of Normandy's border.

The effects of the Second World War, however, were devastating. In the three months following the D-Day landings in 1944, two million men fought in and over Normandy. Not only the coastal towns and villages near landing beaches but dozens of small towns inland and near other coasts were virtually wiped out. Caen, Falaise and Cherbourg were nearly obliterated. Of Le Havre's 180,000 civilians, 5,000 were killed, and most of the rest left homeless. The destruction in Normandy was horrific; the post-war rebuilding and recovery, from villages to ports and cities, was almost miraculous. So many lovely old buildings, like William and Matilde's two abbeys at Caen, have been superbly restored.

The old provinces of Picardy, Artois and Flanders, stretching from the Norman border and the Île-de-France to the Belgian border, have a few hills but are mostly flat plain and their story has inevitably been one of invading armies. The French kings, the dukes of Normandy, the kings of England and Spain, have all invaded it and ruled it, mostly for their own benefit rather than that of the local people.

The ancient countship of Flanders included the area from Dunkerque to the Ardennes, with Belgian and Dutch Flanders. In 1419 Duke Philip the Good of Burgundy also became Count of Flanders and ruled until 1467, consolidating Burgundian power. After the death of his son, Charles the Bold in battle at Nancy in 1477, the French seized much of Burgundy and Artois (the area around Arras) but did not get hold of most of Flanders. Mary of Burgundy, who had become ruler of Flanders on Charles's death, married the Hapsburg Archduke Maximilian of Austria and Flanders became part of the Hapsburg Empire. This empire spread to Spain and what is now French Flanders became with Belgian and Dutch Flanders the Spanish Netherlands under the Spanish King Charles VI. His son was the Catholic bigot Philip II, who sent the Armada to try to conquer Protestant England and whose ruthless persecution of so-called 'heretics' in Flanders led to constant uprisings over 30 years, and the spread of Protestantism in Holland. The Dutch in the north separated from the south in 1579 when the Catholics of Walloon Flanders and of Artois signed a treaty supporting Catholicism and Spain.

In 1663 Louis XIV of France married the Infanta of Spain, Maria-Theresa, daughter of Philip IV. When Philip died, Louis claimed the whole of the Netherlands. In 1667 he took Catholic Flanders but was stopped from advancing further by the Protestant countries of England, Holland and Sweden.

Louis finally took Artois in 1676 and was able to establish the frontier of France, fortified by Vauban, the great military architect, along a line running from Dunkerque to Bergues, Lille, Valenciennes and Le Quesnoy. Another fortified line ran from Gravelines (just south of Dunkerque) to St. Omer, Aire-sur-la-Lys, Béthune, Arras, Douai and Cambrai. It became official in 1713 under the Treaty of Utrecht.

The coastal ports had very different histories. They were constantly at war with the English. Boulogne was the port used by Julius Caesar to invade England in 55 BC. The English from Calais ravaged Boulogne and the surrounding country, a Duke of Burgundy took it when he ruled Flanders and Artois. Henry VIII of England took it in 1554, stripped it of everything movable, and then sold it back to Henry II of France for 400,000 gold écus six years later.

After Edward III of England's victory over the French at Crécy in 1346 he besieged Calais and took it. The English held it for 210 years, and battles took place in all the surrounding countryside involving the English, French, Burgundians and Spanish. In Mary Tudor's reign the English were driven out of Calais by François de Guise in 1558. Mary was so upset that she said that when she died they would find 'Calais' written on her heart.

Dunkerque went through all the problems and change of rulers suffered by the rest of Walloon Flanders, although it was once given by the Flemish

Protestants to Oliver Cromwell of England in return for the help of Oliver's famous Ironside troops in fighting the Spanish. When Charles II came to the English throne he sold Dunkerque to Louis XIV for 5,000,000 livres.

The Protestant Dutch were prone to attacking Dunkerque boats, so the Dunkerque sailors under the famous Jean Bart turned corsairs (pirates licensed by the king) and preyed on Dutch, English and Spanish ships. Bart was so successful that he was made Squadron Commander of the Royal Fleet. All these ports were the lairs of corsairs on and off from the 14th century to the end of the Napoleonic Wars in 1815. Their fishermen ran a lucrative trade in smuggling to England and the English did the same to France. Smuggling became big business, run by Mafia-like gangs in the Napoleonic Wars when Napoleon introduced his Continental System to kill all England's trade with Europe and make it bankrupt.

The whole of Flanders was so devastated in the First World War that in some places every village, house, barn, fence and tree was destroyed. Occasionally human bones and shells are still found in fields. From the time the German armies crossed into northern France from Belgium in 1914 the war raged over the countryside and cities as far as the Marne and the Somme, from which Marshal Foch of France and General Haig of Britain launched the counter-attack. The carnage lasted until the German retreat and surrender in 1918.

Again in 1940 the Germans came through Belgium and bombed and shelled many towns and villages as their mechanised forces rushed to the Channel ports. The British 51st Highland Division stood at St. Valery en-Caux and some men got away but most were killed or wounded. This time the Somme proved no line of defence against modern armour and dive-bombers, though General Weygand tried to hold it. Meanwhile German panzers swept towards Dunkerque where a British rearguard held them long enough for the remarkable evacuation. Three hundred and fifty thousand men, mostly British but many French too, were taken off the beaches under massive artillery fire and constant dive-bombing, to safety in England. Battleships, fishing boats, merchantmen, yachts and amateurs' little sailing boats from England went back and forth ferrying men to safety.

Dunkerque, Calais and Boulogne were heavily bombed by the RAF throughout 1940–4. The Germans expected the Allied invasion to come through these ports but the Allies carried their own prefabricated port, Mulberry Harbour, with them and landed in Calvados and Manche. However, Dunkerque suffered again severely when the Germans held out there from September 1944 until May 1945. Eighty-five per cent of Boulogne was destroyed — but not its walled old town.

All these ports have new industries, all have fishing fleets. Boulogne's fishing fleet is one of the biggest in Europe. And by a twist of history all are prospering because of lorries going backwards and forwards on ferries to England and because of the millions of British tourists who pass through — or even go over for the day for shopping and a French meal. The Channel Tunnel may well hit all three, but the ferries will inevitably still carry much of the traffic.

3. Food and Drink

Normandy

If a restaurant in Normandy serves nouvelle cuisine dishes or modern meals with colourful décor but tiny portions, its customers will be visiting Parisians or British followers of the Gault-Millau guide. Certainly no Norman farmer will pay 200F for décor on a plate. They work hard and eat and drink heartily in Normandy. The days of cream on everything — even ladled into soup — are over, but cream is still used extensively. Normandy butter is the best in France and Isigny butter from around the little port in Calvados is considered the best of all. Butter is used for cooking in most dishes but traditionally Normans used graisse normande for cooking meat (pork fat and suet flavoured with herbs and vegetables). Cheese is a must at every main meal, and apples, cider and calvados are part of many Norman dishes as they have been for centuries. Lamb from the salt marshes around Mont-St. Michel is regarded as some of the best in France. Pigs fed on skimmed milk and windfall apples and pears are made into superb ham, bacon and charcuterie. Cows are almost the symbol of Normandy and cattle breeding is an industry, so is the fattening of bullocks and calves on the pasturelands of the Cotentin Peninsula. Beef is very succulent and veal is milk- and pasture-fed out in fields. Tripe is a delicacy in Calvados. Chickens feed in the open on hillsides and so do the famous Normandy ducks. Most of the prized Rouen ducks now come from Yvetot and Duclair.

Fish is freshly landed at many ports, including Dieppe, Barfleur, Carteret, Grandcamp-les-Bains, Port-en-Bessin and Pourville. Sole is excellent and very popular. Turbot and *barbue* (brill — a lesser turbot) are much more highly prized in France than in Britain. So are whiting. Dieppe is known for mackerel (*lisette* or *maquereau*). Its scallops (*coquilles St. Jacques*) are famous, too. Every self-respecting shellfish platter has to include a lot of winkles (*bigorneaux*). Outside little restaurants near fish quays you can see people sitting at tables working their way through mounds of *crevettes grises* (shrimps) or *crevettes roses* (prawns). But the most popular shellfish are oysters, mussels, clams (*praires*) and lobsters for those who can afford them. Excellent oysters come from St. Vaast-la-Hougue and Courseulles-sur-Mer. Cherbourg has delicious young lobsters (*demoiselles*).

Fine bigger lobsters are landed at Carteret. Good fish markets are at

A cheese stall in an open market

Cherbourg, Fécamp, Honfleur, Caen, Rouen and especially Dieppe, but none compare with the superb market at Boulogne.

Gastronomes and would-be gastronomes who follow fashions have long underestimated the cooking of Normandy. Meals are normally for trenchermen and traditional dishes are still preferred to anything 'inventive' or eccentric simply because the ingredients from land and sea are so superb, fresh and wholesome. Young chefs may lighten these dishes somewhat but to lure local customers they must keep them on the menu. One problem is that lesser chefs outside Normandy have given many of these regional classics a bad name by cutting corners or calling almost any dish with cream in it '*dieppoise*' or '*normande*'. Cooking sole in wine then adding cream to make a sauce is not '*sole à la normande*'. The true traditional way is to poach the sole in cider and cream and thicken the sauce with cream and eggs. Many chefs add mushrooms, prawns or mussels.

A dish which each chef does his own way is duck or chicken *Vallée d'Auge*, but the bird must be *flambéd* in calvados and there must be plenty of cream. Old chefs used to baste the bird with cider.

For *sole à la dieppoise* the old way was to cook the fish in cider with shallots, thicken the sauce with cream and butter, with mussels cooked in. Now even Normans sometimes use wine instead of cider and poach the mussels in wine to serve as a garnish. The name *sauce normande* is now used for any

The Norman Specialities

Tripe   .
Norman tripe is the stomach of ox and a famous recipe is *tripes à la mode de Caen*. It is very rarely home-cooked now — you buy it ready-cooked in jars or tins.

The pieces of stomach are put in layers with leeks, onions, carrots, cloves, pepper and a bouquet garni of herbs (usually thyme, parsley and bay). It is cooked with two split calves' feet. It used to be cooked in cider and calvados, but it then goes yellowish in colour so it is now usually cooked in water and a big glass of calvados. The pot is sealed with flour and water and cooked slowly for anything up to 24 hours. The farming tradition is to eat it as a mid-morning snack with cider or calvados.

Rouen Duck
Rouen ducks, bred these days in Yvetot and Duclair, are a cross between wild and domestic ducks, which gives them a reddish flesh and a more gamey taste. To preserve the game image for the dish *caneton rouennais*, they are strangled to keep in the blood, which may upset modern Britons but bothers very few Normans. It is stuffed with liver of duck and chicken, roasted very lightly and served with red wine sauce. If the carcase is put in a press to take out the blood, this is used to thicken the sauce (*caneton à la presse*).

Calvados
To make a litre of calvados spirit, it takes 30 litres of cider. The cider is left in the cask on the lees. A year or two later it is cleared and distilled in pot stills like cognac. Then the apple cores are kept in the distilled liquid, which matures in oak casks. Age makes as much difference to taste as it does with single malt whisky. The cheapest, which should not be called calvados, is really *eau de vie de cidre*.

Fine calvados is 2–3 years old. *Vieux* or *VSOP* is at least 5 years old. *Hors-âge*, *Âge Inconnu* or *Napoléon* are at least 6 years old, possibly 12–15 years.

Benedictine Liqueur
A Venetian monk named Vincelli, sent to the monastery of Fécamp in 1510, sought an elixir to fight winter illness brought on by the winds of the Normandy coast. So he distilled a spirit using 27 herbs and spices, many of which grew wild on local cliffs. When the abbey was closed during the French Revolution, the formula was lost. In 1863 a local historian Alexander Legrand, going through old abbey papers, found recipes for menthe, a healing ointment, and Vincelli's elixir. Legrand started to make the drink again, and later built an ostentatious Gothic-Renaissance distillery at Fécamp which looks more like a château.

thick sauce with real cream, cider or calvados or both. For fish a fish *fumet* is used. Turbot or sole *au cidre* means cooked whole in cider with parsley and chopped shallots — no cream.

Marmite dieppoise, stew with fish and shellfish, leeks and cream in cider, is also cooked sometimes now in white wine. It should have the herb chervil (*cerfeuil*) in it. Some chefs put in tomato, which is not traditional, or lobster, which is a waste of lobster, as it is in *bouillabaisse* from southern France.

For six centuries at least Fécamp has been salting cod (*morue*) and herrings and also smoking them. By the 16th century Honfleur was selling salt cod to the Far East in return for spices.

Charcuterie, including many pâtés and terrines, are very popular in Normandy. Mortagne-au-Perche claims to be the capital of the black pudding (*boudin*) and a Brotherhood of Pudding Tasters (*Confrérie des Chevaliers du Goûte-Boudin*) runs an annual contest for the best black puddings. Pudding tasting goes on for three whole days, with puddings brought from all over Western Europe. Lancashire puddings have won awards and the Scots are well represented, too. The record for black pudding eating was set in 1969 — 1.25 metres in 15 minutes.

Caen and Vire are known for *andouille* and *andouillette* (chitterling sausages), beloved by modern French gastronomes but not by all foreigners. Smoked versions are most palatable. Vires' big sausage is served sliced as a starter.

Game is fairly rare in Normandy except in the Suisse Normande, where trout is plentiful, and pheasant, wild duck, partridge and woodcock are all obtainable. Pheasant and wild duck are superb cooked *à la normande* — casseroled with apples and calvados, with cream stirred in. You can cook chicken this way too.

Apples are inevitably used a lot in desserts and *tarte normande* is still the great favourite — apple tart cooked many different ways, but always with the apples softened in calvados before cooking, and with shortcrust. Apricot jam is often used as a glaze and the tart is served with lots of cream. *Bourdelos* are apples baked in suet crust (baked apple dumplings) and *douillens* are the same but with pears instead of apples. A dessert Normans buy from *pâtisseries* is *mirliton* (puff pastry tart filled with almond paste, egg yolks and sugar). Chocolates can be flavoured with calvados or given cream fillings flavoured with Benedictine (made in Fécamp).

Normandy has more than 30 fairly well-known cheeses. Many are still made on farms and sold direct or in local markets. Most are soft though washed-rind cheeses are made particularly in Bray.

Camembert is now produced in more than 60 départements of France but it was first made in the Calvados village of Camembert and marketed in nearby Vimoutiers. The best is still made in Normandy. Made from cow's milk and cured for three weeks, it is often eaten in France when firm and chalky but most people prefer it soft and just a little runny. It was certainly made on farms in the 16th century but improved and marketed first in 1790 by a farmer's wife from Camembert, Marie Harel, with the help of a priest

she was hiding during the French Revolution. It became fashionable under Napoleon III, who ate it, and then a Paris company packed it in its characteristic wooden boxes to export it.

Pont l'Évêque, made on many farms in the old days, dates from the Middle Ages, when it was called *angelot*. It is matured in humid caves for 1–2 months, tastes sweetish, has an orangy-coloured rind, criss-cross crust from drying on mats and is sold in rectangular boxes. It should be slightly soft. A farm-made version is called Trouville as it comes from near that resort.

The third really great cheese of Normandy, Livarot, is not to everybody's taste. It is very strong and pungent after maturing in a cave for at least a month. The rind is coloured to a shiny red-brown. Smaller versions are called Petits Lisieux.

You can see good Camembert, Pont l'Évêque and Livarot being made, and taste them, in the town of Livarot at the little Conservatoire des Techniques Fromagères. Here the Livarot is wrapped traditionally in the sedge-reeds from the Vie river, not in strips of coloured paper — the usual modern practice.

Among the other Normandy cheeses, the following are the best known:

Brillat-Savarin — a nice mild cheese but made with triple cream and very fatty. It was first marketed in the 1930s and named after the great gastronome and writer on food. The best is made in Rouvray-Catillon in Bray. Smaller

A panoramic view of Cherbourg and its docks from Fort Roule

versions, not quite so creamy or fatty, are Excelsior and Fin-de-Siècle.

Demi-sel — very well-known uncured cheese; moist, low in salt, so used for fruit-cream dishes. Sold foil-wrapped. Invented last century in Gournay-en-Bray, it is now made in many parts of France.

Neufchâtel — delicately flavoured, moussy. When fresh (*fleuri*) it is eaten with fruit. When ripe (*affiné*) it is strong. Dates back to the 10th century. A farm-made version is Carré de Bray (small, salty, rather tart and smells of mushrooms). Coeur de Bray is a soft, fruity cheese.

Pavé d'Auge — super strong spicy cheese. Pavé de Moyaux is similar.

Petit-Suisse — soft, fresh, unsalted. Often mixed with sugar and served with fruit or used in desserts. Wrapped in paper tubes. Invented by a Bray farmwife and her Swiss cowherd in 1850, it is now made all over France.

Other lesser-known cheeses well worth tasting are:

Fromage de Monsieur — firm, fruity but smelly. It comes from Roumois (between Caux and Auge) and was invented by a farmer named Monsieur Fromage.

Lucullus — fatty triple-cream factory cheese with lovely nutty flavour. From Evreux. Also made in Brie (Île-de-France) where Brie itself was first made.

Trappiste de Bricquebec — made by monks at Bricquebec on Cotentin Peninsula. Soft, yellow, mouth-filling.

Picardy and the North

The Flemish influence on the cooking of Picardy and the North has led many French to dismiss it as 'peasant'. Certainly, it is hearty and filling and owes more to the farmhouse kitchen than to cookery schools, but it is very tasty, satisfying and particularly appealing on a winter's day.

Pork is good and plentiful, and leads to the making of some of the best charcuterie in France, with splendid sausage, usually smoked. Arras is famous for *andouillettes* (chitterling sausages). Lille has vast charcuterie factories. *Boudin* (blood sausage or black pudding) is common. Valenciennes is known for sheep's tongues — *langues fourrées* (stuffed sheep's tongue) and *langues fumées* are smoked sheep's tongues. There are many local pâtés, too. Péronne produces eel pâté. *Potje flesh* (or *vleesch*), sometimes called *terrine flamande*, is a superb pâté of veal, chicken and rabbit. Alas, Belgian factories now swamp shops with mediocre pâté and terrines, as they do Britain's super-markets, but you can still find charcuterie shops which make their own, and even some restaurants. You can often spot these by their simple white bowls and terrines and lack of such unnecessary decorations as cherries, pieces of peel or coloured gelatine. Chef-made duck pâtés and ballottines can be deli-cious. Amiens's *pâte de caneton* is a great gastronomic dish. The duck is fried whole, surrounded by a forcemeat of duck and chicken livers, fat bacon, onion and herbs, wrapped in pastry, baked and served cold in slices.

The North is beef country and in Flemish style much beer is used in cooking, also juniper berries (*genièvre*) and Dutch gin which is heavily perfumed with juniper berries. The great Flemish dishes include *flamiche* (or *flamique*) (leek tart), *carbonade flamande* (beef braised in beer), *chou rouge à la flamande* (red cabbage with apples) and *soupe à la bière* (beer soup). *Hochepot* is a 'soup-stew' with many versions, but it is usually made with brisket of beef, bacon, pig's ears, breast and shoulder of mutton or lamb, cooked with mixed sliced vegetables such as cabbage (almost compulsory), onions, carrots, leeks and potatoes. It is served like a *pot au feu*, with the liquid served as a soup, the meat and vegetables as a separate course. *Ficelles picardes* are pancakes stuffed with mushrooms and ham in cream, or sometimes with cream cheese.

The vegetables grown in the market gardens around the waterways near St. Omer are some of the finest in Europe, which is why the people of Picardy and Flanders prefer old-style cooking to modern cuisine where vegetables are often confined to a few slices for decoration. Leeks, cauliflowers, sprouts (picked young), chicory (which the French call *endive*) are all plentiful, and asparagus is very good in season. The Flemish way is to serve it hot with melted butter and hot hard-boiled eggs cut in half. You mash your own egg into the butter. It is called inevitably *asperges à la flamande*. An unusual vegetable is *jets de houblon* (hop shoots). The male flower shoots which are no good for beer are broken away from the stems, boiled in salt water with a squeeze of lemon, then tossed in butter. Sometimes they are then simmered in cream. Modern sexing methods for hops are making this vegetable rare. Sometimes they are served with poached eggs and fried bread croutons.

Fine fresh fish is landed, especially at Boulogne and Dunkerque. A third of all fish landed in France goes through Boulogne. It has a large fleet and Mediterranean ships bring in fish from the south — *rascasse*, the ugly fish regarded as essential for *bouillabaisse*, red mullet (*rouget*), and *violets de Toulon* (a small sea creature which looks like a knobbly potato; its edible inside looks like scrambled egg). Boulogne is a superb place to buy or eat fish. The boats land it alongside stalls on the harbour's edge in a car park — and the stalls keep open until lunchtime every day except Sunday. The sole is superb and each restaurant has its own special way of cooking it, usually including shellfish garnish or sauce, mushrooms and cream. Cod (*cabillard*) is usually very good and so is ling (*lingue*) — a long thin fish of the cod family. Mussels (*moules*) can be excellent. They are usually cooked the most popular way in France — *à la marinière* (stewed in wine with chopped onion, parsley and bay leaf). Those tender little mussels are called *bouchots* after the posts on which mussels are often cultivated. Cockles, a speciality of the Picardy coast, are usually called *hénons* here, *coques* elsewhere. Fish stews are popular under various names, like *bouillabaisse du nord* or *chau-drée à la boulognaise* (or some other town). One of the finest fish soups in France is made in Le Touquet by Serge Perard, who keeps a wonderful fish shop and good fish restaurant. He bottles his fish soup and it goes all over France. Many a well-known restaurant serves it as a house product! His crab bisque is excellent.

Recipes (all recipes serve four)

Sole à la dieppoise

INGREDIENTS

Cleaned sole (or turbot, plaice or
 John Dory)
1 onion or 3 shallots finely chopped
¼ litre very dry cider
 (or Muscadet wine)

butter
½ litre thick cream
mussels
shrimps

METHOD

Allow about 300–400g per person.
Butter fireproof dish generously, sprinkle shallot, put in fish seasoned
with salt and pepper. Pour on cider. Cover with buttered paper, put in
oven (190°C, 375°F, Mark 5), basting every 5 minutes, for 15 minutes.
Remove paper, stir in 300ml of cream, replace paper and cook a
further 15 minutes. Poach mussels and shrimps in cider or wine for
garnish. Remove fish to hot dish, pour sauce into saucepan, add rest
of cream and knob of butter, heat until reduced to a smooth, velvety
sauce. Pour over fish and garnish.

Faisan à la normande

INGREDIENTS

Brace of pheasant
1½kg cooking apples
1½kg dessert apples
 (preferably green)

¾ litre double and soured
 cream mixed
salt, pepper
small wineglass of calvados

METHOD

Any game birds or duck can be used as an alternative to pheasant.
Turn pheasants in butter until golden all over. Put in fairly tight casserole. Peel, core and quarter apples and turn in butter until well
covered. Pack apples round the pheasants, season with salt and
pepper. Cook in moderate oven (190°C, 375°F, Mark 5) for 50–60
minutes. Whisk cream and calvados and stir gently into apple mixture.
Return to oven uncovered for 5 minutes. (Chicken can be substituted.)

Boeuf bouilli à la crème

INGREDIENTS

600–700g cooked beef cut into
 thin slices
300g mushrooms
4 shallots
a good knob of butter
tablespoon flour

1dl cider
1dl well-flavoured stock
2dl cream
salt
freshly ground black pepper
lemon

METHOD

Arrange meat slices in a buttered oven dish, sprinkle with some of the cider and stock, cover with foil and put in a low oven to warm without cooking. Chop shallots finely and soften in melted butter, add the sliced mushrooms and a few drops of lemon juice. When shallots are soft, stir in flour and cook for a few minutes, then add rest of cider and stock. Stir and cook until thick, season to taste, and pour over the meat. Return to oven for a few minutes to allow flavours to blend and then top with the cream Warm in oven for a few minutes longer before serving.

Tarte normande

INGREDIENTS

2 or 3 large cooking apples
  (Bramleys or similar)
4 medium-sized hard eating apples
  (Coxes, golden delicious)
8″ tart case (sweet or savoury)
2 dessertspoons of sugar

knob of butter
cup of cider
wineglass of calvados
squeeze of lemon juice
dessertspoon of apricot jam

METHOD

Peel and core cooking apples, cook until soft in cider and 1 dessertspoon of sugar. Beat into a mousse with butter and lemon juice. Spread mixture into pastry case. Peel, core and slice eating apples and arrange slices over the mousse in circles to cover it. Pour calvados evenly over the slices. Sprinkle with rest of sugar. Melt apricot jam with a little water. Pour jam over tart as a glaze. Bake in medium oven for about 40 minutes until pastry is golden. Serve with lots of cream.

Chou rouge flamande
(Red cabbage)

INGREDIENTS

I red cabbage
3 large (tart) cooking apples
1 teaspoon brown sugar

vinegar
butter
salt, pepper

METHOD

Cut a red cabbage into quarters, wash and shred, cutting out hard core and stem. Season with salt, pepper and sprinkle with a little vinegar (preferably cider). Put into a casserole with butter (no water). Cook on gentle heat with lid on. When cabbage is three-quarters cooked, add cooking apples, peeled and cut into thick slices, and brown sugar. Finish cooking on low heat. Probable total cooking time 2 hours.

Carbonade de boeuf à la flamande (Beef in beer)

INGREDIENTS

750g of lean beef (skirt or chuck)	lard
250g sliced onions	3 tablespoons beef stock
600ml of beer	1 tablespoon brown sugar
3 tablespoons of roux	bouquet garni
(125g each of butter and flour)	2 cloves crushed garlic

METHOD

In Flanders this is served with onions, turnips, carrots and potatoes, not mushrooms and tomatoes, as for most beef cooked in wine.

Cut beef into thick strips 1½cm x 10cm x 5cm. Season them and brown both sides in lard; remove beef; fry onions in same fat. Put beef and onions in casserole in layers with bouquet garni and garlic. Dilute pan juices with beer and stock, thicken with roux, add sugar, stir for some minutes, strain into casserole. Bring to boil, cover with lid and cook in moderate oven (160°C, 325°F, Mark 3) for about 2½ hours.

Harengs calaisienne (Stuffed herrings)

INGREDIENTS

8 fresh herrings, approximately	50g parsley
250g each, with roes	100g butter
250g soft herring roes	salt, pepper
50g shallots	1 tablespoon oil
50g mushrooms	

METHOD

Scale the fish, then split them down the back, cut the backbone just behind the head and in front of the tail, and pull it out. Gut the fish as cleanly as possible, saving any roes, wash and wipe.

Put the shallots, mushrooms, parsley, soft roes, butter, and salt and pepper through a blender. Dice any hard roes and add to this mixture. Stuff the herrings with this, rub the outside with salt and pepper, and wrap each one in oiled foil. Cook in a very hot oven for 15 minutes.

Flan de carottes (Sweet carrot flan)

INGREDIENTS

Pastry	carrots (enough to fill the flan case)
butter	sugar to taste
custard	icing sugar

METHOD

Line buttered tart tin with pastry. Fill with finely chopped carrots boiled in very little water and mixed with butter, sugar, and several tablespoons of thick custard. Bake in moderate oven. Just before taking it out, sprinkle with icing sugar and leave in to glaze.

Herrings and mackerel are part of the way of life in Picardy and Flanders — salted, pickled or smoked. Both fishes are smoked in Boulogne and Dunkerque. They are called craquelot (or bouffi) and are more like the British bloater than kipper. In Dunkerque on the Sunday before Mardi Gras, as a finale to the Mardi Gras Festival, the Mayor throws them from the Town Hall. Kippers are smoked much more lightly than in Scotland, England or the Isle of Man. Harengs saurs are salted and smoked (sometimes called gendarmes). In Calais you can still buy hareng à la calaisienne (herrings stuffed with roes and herbs and ready baked in paper cases).

Sprats, called harengs de Bergues around Dunkerque, harenguet elsewhere in Flanders and esprot in most of France, are smoked and eaten as snacks.

Freshwater fish stews (matelotes) usually include any coarse fish available — carp, perch, pike with herbs. The Flemish waterzooi adds vegetables and cream. But the same name waterzooi is used for chicken stewed with leeks and served with cream sauce made from the stock. Trout is cooked with black pepper.

Eels are regarded as a delicacy in the North. Anguilles au vert (or à la flamande) are jellied eels cooked in wine and herbs. They are also cooked in beer to counter the fattiness.

The lovely Vallée de la Course, between Desvres and Montreuil-sur-Mer, produces excellent trout. On the D127 is a riverside trout farm where you can buy them absolutely fresh or catch your own.

Quenelles, little mousses, are made locally with pike (quenelles de brochet) and can be bought in bottles, tins or fresh. You can also buy cervelais de brochet — a thin sausage of pike and potatoes.

Dunkerque produces many cakes and biscuits, including kokeboterom, a sweet brioche dotted with raisins. Lille is known for its biscuits (petits beurres and gauffres fourrés), Amiens and Douai make macarons (almond macaroons). Open tarts of apples, prunes or pears are everywhere. Picardy has an interesting conserve called raisiné picard (pear jam cooked in grape juice, eaten with a spoon). Cambrai makes bêtises (mint humbugs).

There are no really famous cheeses in this area, but several well worth trying. For a really low-fat cheese, try Bergues from the village of that name near Dunkerque. It is washed with beer daily to remove fat.

A nice strong Flemish cheese flavoured with herbs is called Boulette d'Avesnes when made in farmhouses, Le Dauphin when factory made. Boulette de Cambrai is fresher but herby. Rollot from around Arras has a rich smell and flavour.

Mimolette, made around Lille, is a cousin of Gouda and Edam. Gris de Lille, made mostly by small dairies and farms, is an acquired taste. In a slab with a sticky pink-grey rind, it is cured in brine and beer and has a very strong taste and smell. It is not surprisingly known also as gris puant (grey stinky) or puant de Lille.

A very good cheese you may find in good restaurants is Belval (or Fromage d'Hesdin) developed quite recently at Belval Monastery.

The Markets

Abbeville — Thurs, last Wed in month.
Alençon — Fri, Sun.
Amiens — Daily except Sun.
Les Andelys — Mon.
Arras — Thurs, Sat, Sun am.
Avranches — Sat.
Barneville-Carteret — Sat in summer.
Bayeux — Daily pm (fish).
Blangy-sur-Bresle — Fri am, 3rd Wed of month.
Boulogne — Wed, Sat.
Caen — Daily except Mon.
Calais — Wed, Sat, Sun.
Cambrai — Daily except Mon.
Caudebec-en-Caux — Sat am.
Cherbourg — Daily except Sun (fish).
Coutances — Mon.
Deauville — Daily am.
Dieppe — Tues, Wed, Thurs am, Sat (great street market).
Domfront — Sat.
Douai — Daily.
Dunkerque — Wed, Sat.
Fécamp — Sat, big market last Sat of month.
Gisors — Mon, Fri, Sun.
Harfleur — Thurs am.
Le Havre — Tues, Thurs, Sat mornings.
Hesdin — Thurs.
Honfleur — Sat.
Isigny-sur-Mer — Every 2nd Sat.
Louviers — Wed, Sat.
Lyons-la-Fôret — Thurs.
Montreuil — Sat am.
Mortagne-au-Perche — Sat.
Neufchâtel-en-Bray — Tues, Sat mornings.
Péronne — Fri (fish), Sat.
Pont-l'Évêque — Mon.
St. Lô — Tues.
Ste. Mère-Église — Thurs.
St. Omer — Wed, Sat.
St. Vaast-la-Hougue — Sat.
St. Valery-en-Caux — Fri, Sun am June–Sept.
Le Touquet — Thurs, Sat (Mon in summer), Easter Mon, Whitsun.
Yvetot — Wed am.
Thury-Harcourt — Tues.
Villedieu-les-Poêles — Tues.
Vire — Fri.

The weekly open markets are still very popular with French shoppers, especially for fruit and vegetables

The great Maroilles cheese still comes from the north-east in Aisne, roughly between the Ardennes and Hainault. It has been made for 1,000 years and sometimes tastes as if it has been kept that long, especially when soaked in beer and brine. It is then called puant (smelly). Matured in crocks, and masked with herbs, it becomes Fort Béthunes.

Drink

Not much wine was ever produced in Normandy and none has been made so far as records go for well over a century. Cider is, of course, the wine of Normandy, Picardy, Artois and Flanders, and very good cider it is, too. It has become fashionable to drink it *bouché* — fizzy, from wired-cork bottles where it is still fermenting. That is all right for a reviver on a hot day but not to accompany creamy Norman dishes or heavier Flemish stews. It is made in factories, and no Norman farmer would offer it. The best cider comes from Pays d'Auge and has a label to prove it (*Appellation Contrôlée Pays d'Auge*). Usually still, it is sometimes *pétillant* (slightly bubbling). It can be sweetish, dry or very dry indeed. The best centres are Pont l'Évêque, Livarot, Vimoutiers, Cambremer, Lisieux and Bonnebosc, though good cider is produced in many other places, including Thury Harcourt, and Gournay and Neufchâtel in Bray. Any cider marked '*Cru de Cambremer*' has been chosen at an annual tasting as one of the best of the Auge.

Cider is made from a chosen mixture of varieties of apple with lovely old names like 'fieldmouse red' and 'tranquil'. As the pure apple juice matures, it clouds over, then clears, sugar turns to alcohol (5%) and it becomes sharper. Farm cider is still better than that from a factory on the whole.

Pear-cider (perry) made still or *pétillant*, has survived better in Normandy than in England's West Country, and is still very popular there. A fashionable new drink, made in Livarot, is a fizzy cider made from apple and peach juice, called Deauville.

A new aperitif, Pommereau, is a calvados and apple juice mixture, like the marc and grape juice ratafia of Champagne and Burgundy.

Calvados, the spirit made from apple juice, dates back at least until the 10th century. It varies enormously in quality and price, with the cheapest fit only for 'flaming' (*flambé*) or for preserving fruit, and the smooth, old very expensive calvados fit for drinking as a liqueur after any meal. You need something in between the two for the *trou normand* (the Norman hole) — the slug of calvados swallowed in the middle of a big meal to aid the digestion. This is the only true *trou*. Many Normans still take a *café-calva* (black coffee with a slug of calvados) for breakfast.

Beer is made in the North — and not just the cheap 'factory' beer with which the French and the British visitors fill the boots of their cars at hypermarkets. There are still small breweries left producing good bottled beer, though not as good as the best from Belgium. Belgian Trappiste, still made in monasteries, is in a class of its own. A good French beer is St. Leonard, made in the village of that name, now virtually a suburb of Boulogne.

Benedictine liqueur is produced now in a huge factory at Fécamp, which crowds tour in summer — with tasting, of course (Easter–mid-November 9–11.15, 2–6; winter Monday–Friday only).

Part One
Normandy

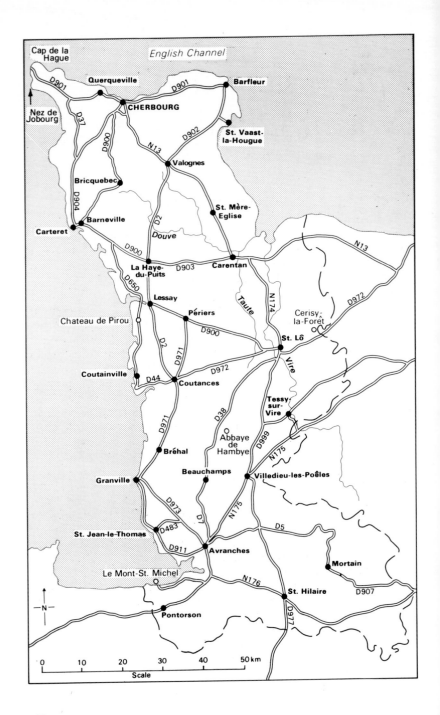

4. The Cotentin Peninsula

Cherbourg to Coutainville and St. Lô

Cherbourg has had a very chequered existence since Vauban, the great military engineer, fortified the fishing village 300 years ago. It has been important at times, then ignored when it has not been useful to the rest of France. It has only very recently emerged totally from a traumatic period as the Allies' main port in 1944. Its heyday was in the 1930s when the big Atlantic liners docked here on romantic journeys and the rich and famous were driven to and from its port and customs sheds. Now the main traffic is in car ferries from Britain and yachts, often sheltering from Atlantic gales or the Alderney Race, the dangerous off-shore currents. It is a fishing port, too, with an excellent fish market. And it has grown into a pleasant little place for shopping — not at the hypermarket built mostly for ferry passengers but in the little shops in shopping precincts in or near the tree-shaded place Général-de-Gaulle, where a food and clothes market is held on Tuesdays, Thursdays and Saturday mornings. In the pedestrian-only streets by the square are expensive shoe shops and clothes boutiques. Grand' Rue has some good food shops. The old town has been well restored and there is a new yacht marina among its several port basins.

A road winds up to Fort du Roule (112 metres high) from where you have fine views over town and harbour. The Germans made their last stand against the US Army here in June 1944. Now it has a Liberation Museum which includes maps showing the progress of the war from D-Day (6 June 1944) to the German capitulation (7 May 1945).

The Musée Thomas-Henry has an 18th-century Italian masterpiece, Fra Angelico's 'Conversion of St. Augustin', but for most people visiting Cherbourg the 30 paintings and drawings of local country life by the great local artist Jean-François Millet are more interesting. The son of a peasant, born in nearby Gruchy in 1814, he brought the Norman countryside and its people to life and is still genuinely popular with all sorts of people, from connoisseurs to birthday-card buyers. He lived later in Jersey.

Emmanuel Liais gardens have some interesting tropical plants.

Cherbourg is pleasant enough but there are so many charming little fishing villages and inland towns within easy driving range, and Cherbourg's hotels are so often full of business people in the week, that I would stay outside.

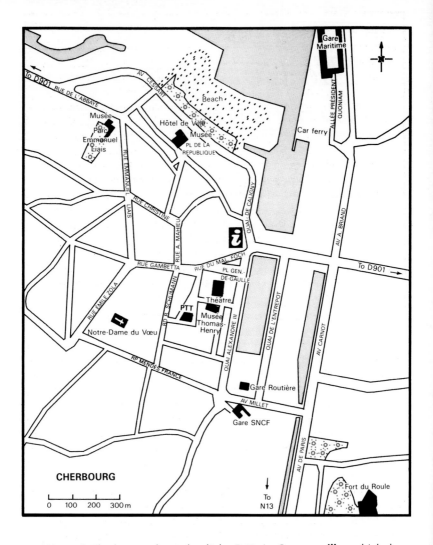

CHERBOURG

0   100   200   300 m

West of Cherbourg along the little D45 is **Querqueville**, which has possibly the oldest religious building in western France — the shamrock-shaped Chapelle St. Germain, built in the 6th–8th centuries. From between the chapel and the church you get views along the whole coastline from Pointe Jardeheu in the west to Cap Lévy in the east.

Next is Port Racine, the smallest port in France, with a tiny little harbour used by the odd fishing boat, and a charming little restaurant with ten rooms and a garden far above the sea, L'Erguillère. This is the rugged, savage Cap de la Hague. Overlooking the bay to the south the long barren rocky cape, Nez de Jobourg, is a seabird reserve. Views both to the Channel Isles and over

Les Hommes Grenouilles

The capture of Cherbourg by the US 7th Corps on 26–27 June 1944 was a turning point in the battle for Normandy. The Mulberry Harbour off the American beach of Omaha had broken up in a storm. The Arromanches Mulberry in the British sector still brought in supplies until December 1944, but was sanding up and battered. Much heavier loads needed to be landed. And 'Pluto' was waiting — Pipe Line Under The Ocean, the pipe built in Britain the previous winter to pump oil all the way from the Isle of Wight. The petrol came through on 12 August 1944, saving having to use dozens of oil tankers.

The Germans realised the importance of Cherbourg and before they lost the port they blew up the installations, heavily mined the harbours and approaches and sank wrecks. It was all cleared incredibly quickly, however, by divers of the Royal Navy — *Hommes Grenouilles* the French called them (Frog Men).

During the Battle of the Ardennes in December 1944, Cherbourg handled twice the tonnage that New York handled in its shipping heyday of 1939.

Vauville Bay to Flamanville Cliffs are really spectacular. Alas, the scene of unspoiled nature ends at Flamanville, where there is a monstrous nuclear power plant, with towers, roadways and concrete blocks behind electric fences.

The most interesting route to the resorts of the west coast from Cherbourg is along the D900 to Bricquebec. This pleasing little town is built around a 14th-century castle of which the remains include a keep. You must climb 160 steps for fine views of the countryside. Within the castle close is an 11th-century château now the Vieux Château Hotel. Queen Victoria stayed in it in 1857. Henry V gave it to the Duke of Suffolk after Agincourt. An interesting market is held outside the castle gates on Mondays.

The road continues to **Barneville-Carteret**, twin family beach resorts. Barneville has the bigger beach, Carteret is livelier and more interesting. Carteret has a working fishing fleet and you can watch fish being landed and packed, and nets drying, then taste the absolutely fresh fish at the cheap if unprepossessing restaurants on the quay or in the elegant dining room of the well-run Marine Hotel, where fish is superbly cooked. Barneville's 11th-century church was given a fortified tower in the 15th century. The decoration of the church's Romanesque arches is lovely. On the way out of Barneville is a memorial commemorating the cutting of the Cotentin Peninsula by US forces on their way to Cherbourg.

Continue along the D903 to La Haye-du-Puits. Take the D900 to **Lessay**, a pleasant agricultural town with an abbey built in 1056 by monks from Bec-Hellouin. It is a masterpiece of Norman architecture. The beautiful abbey-church was mined by Germans in 1944, the lantern tower and vaults

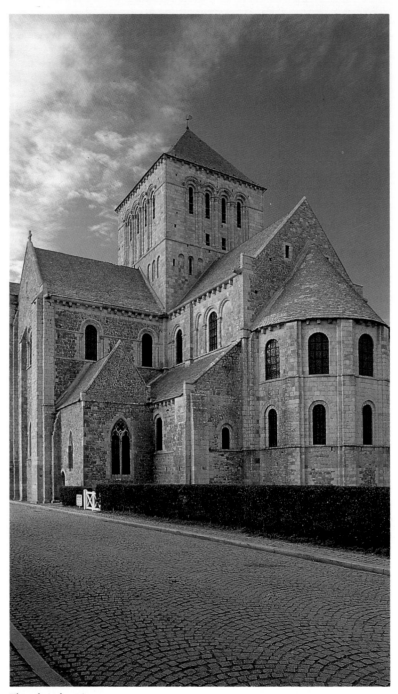

The church at Lessay

collapsed and the church was ruined. It was painstakingly restored, using old stone and as far as possible medieval methods of building. The stained glass is modern but based on old illuminated manuscripts from Ireland. A huge fair, Foire Ste. Croix, has been held here for nearly 1,000 years. It was started by Benedictines, and is still held in mid-September when cattle and colts are sold in hundreds. Tents and a funfair cover the moorland and for three days and nights sausages, beef and lamb are spitroasted to be eaten with cider.

Go west on the D652 to join the D650 along the coast past a series of little-known seaside villages with little beaches. Just off the road to the left is the Château de Pirou, originally Coutance's advance defence against sea raiders. You enter over a stone bridge (replacing a drawbridge) to the guard room and bakery, with kitchens and dining rooms above and a staircase to the ramparts, with good views from the tower. The legend of the castle tells of the days when it was a wooden fort and the invading Norsemen were attacking it. One night they saw a great flock of wild geese fly from the ramparts. Everything seemed to go silent within, and when they entered they found only a bedridden old man. He told them that the family and retainers had been turned magically into geese and had escaped. The geese returned the following year to look for the book of magic so that they could return to human form. Alas, the Norsemen had burned down the castle and the book had perished. But still every year the wild geese fly in over the coast to look for the book. The stone castle of the 12th century was remodelled in the 17th century.

Coutainville has been a popular summer resort since the last century and until recently it had hardly changed. It became popular because of its 7km of fine sand beach and dunes, and the railway was brought there. The resort went through a lean patch a few years back and has now tried to modernise a little, with a casino, theatre, racecourse, swimming pools, water-skiing and scuba-diving, and its superb *fin-de-siècle* beach huts have been replaced by straw huts in South Seas style. But its promenade still has a *fin-de-siècle* air, with its pseudo-Gothic, ornate houses.

Just over 10km inland is **Coutances**, a delightful town on a hill crowned with a beautiful cathedral. By AD 161 it was mentioned as a Roman city, Cosedia, and by AD 300 was a larger Roman city, and its name had become Constantia. The Roman temple on the hill was replaced by a church in the 15th century. It became a bishopric and its fighting bishop Geoffrey de Montbray went with William to conquer England. More important, the incredible de Hauteville family came from these parts. They went to Italy and several became kings there. They poured money into the building of a Romanesque cathedral in the 11th century. Parts of it that were left after a terrible fire in 1218 were incorporated into a new cathedral of superb soaring columns, including a magnificent 41-metre high octagonal lantern. Chapels extending from the apse were added in the 14th century. One is dedicated to St. Thomas à Becket. The 14th-century statue of Notre Dame is much venerated.

Though the town was destroyed in 1944, the cathedral was almost miraculously saved. The new town is very pleasant, with good shops and beautiful

The little Vieux Château inn at Bricquebec is built into the courtyard of a 14th-century castle

public gardens on three levels, with pools, rare flowers and trees, and benches to rest and admire it all. Son-et-Lumière performances are given from 1 July to 15 September on Thursdays, Saturdays and Sundays.

The D972 eastwards from Coutances to St. Lô passes Marigny, a little market town with a busy Wednesday market. It is known especially for the unassuming-looking Restaurant de la Poste in the market square. Patron chef Joël Meslin has been described as 'the most solid chef in the Manche département'. He cooks some of the most copious and satisfying meals for their price, too.

St. Lô is lively and seemingly prosperous but I find it a sad town — an uninspired exercise in concrete which took 20 years to make. The only asset St. Lô possessed at the end of the Second World War was the chance to rebuild imaginatively and beautifully. The authorities muffed it.

Two mutilated towers of the 13th–14th-century church of Notre-Dame were saved from the bombardment of the town in 1944, so was the unusual open-air pulpit. They have been well incorporated into the new church and a green shale façade has three lovely contemporary bronze doors by Jean Bernard. By the choir is a large 18th-century Christ. In the chapel dedicated to St. Thomas (à Becket) of Canterbury is a magnificent great window by Max Ingrand.

The museum in the town hall has good 18th-century paintings by Boudin, Millet, Gros, Jordaens and Corot and some superb and jolly 16th-century tapestries with pastoral scenes.

St. Lô's Haras is, with Haras Le Pin (also in Normandy), the most important French national stud. There are about 150 stallions but many are away between mid-February and mid-July. You can visit during that time but from mid-July to February there are guided tours (½ hour). At 10 am on Thursdays from the last Thursday in July to the first in September, team-driving shows are given.

The border of Manche swings out eastward to the edge of the Cerisy Forest then returns west to follow the Vire river to its estuary near Isigny, which is in Calvados. **Cerisy-la-Fôret** is on the forest edge and a centre for forest drives and walks. The 11th-century abbey-church of pale stone is a fine example of Norman Romanesque architecture. Alas, only three of its eight bays are left. Last century the others were destroyed to sell the stone for house building. Over 60 years restoration has continued slowly. What is left is still impressive.

The main road north from St. Lô, the N174, joins the N13 just east of **Carentan**. This is an old town, certainly here in the 5th century, and an attractive place despite being damaged in 1944. Its port was silted up long ago by silt from the three rivers which converge at the coast — the Douve, the Vire and the Taute, which runs alongside the town. The long stretch of waterway which joins the little old port to the sea is tree-lined and very pleasant. The silt has produced rich pastures, as it has around Isigny, and the town thrives as a cattle and butter market. The massive 14th-century church of Notre-Dame is one of the finest Gothic churches in North France.

The huge market place of Carentan with ancient houses above 15th-century arcades makes you forget the drama of June 1944, when the US parachute troops landed early on D-Day. It was at Carentan that the British forces from Gold Beach linked up with the Americans from Utah. A museum of the 101st Parachute Brigade tells the story.

Four kilometres north of Carentan the D913 road forks right off the N13 and takes you to the coast at La Madeleine where the Americans landed on D-Day. On the way you pass Ste. Marie-du-Mont with a Landing Museum. It has arms, military equipment, models and a film, and there is a memorial crypt.

The coastal road, the D421, is hidden from the sea by dunes. It is a scruffy area of assorted beach houses, concrete poles and old German gun-sites. At Quettehou it is joined by a road from Valognes. There are good sea views from Quettehou's church cemetery over Morsalines Bay. Roads north-west from Quettehou into the Saire valley are attractive for walking or driving. The D26 climbs through apple orchards to the pretty village of Le Vast. The low hills, woodlands, orchards and pastures were compared by Ruskin to Worcestershire in England.

At Le Vast turn right along the river to Valcanville. On the D125 to the right you can see the sea and the tall white Gatteville lighthouse. Left just off this pretty road is La Pernelle. At a German blockhouse is a viewing table and magnificent panoramic views right along the nearby coast. Return onto the D125 for an attractive road back to Quettehou.

The D1 east from Quettehou leads to **St. Vaast-la-Hougue**, a truly delightful

Country Star

Finding La Verte Campagne, the 1717 grey stone farmhouse at Trelly which Madame Meredith, the French widow of a Royal Navy Commander, had turned into a cosy country hotel, was like a treasure hunt through the maze of narrow track-like lanes deep in the Normandy *bocage*. The reward was simple home cooking and complete calm, disturbed only by clucking chickens and mooing. Then Madame retired and we heard nothing from the hotel but plenty from disappointed readers. Suddenly in the 1994 *Michelin* we saw it again — with a star!

It was grey and wet when we reached Trelly, and our thoughts were gloomy: there would be a big board outside and a macadam car park and a computer for check-in. Caroline Bernou met us in the lobby, just as Mme Meredith had done, and showed us to our room — a true farmhouse room with no frills except a modernised bathroom. The chickens were with sheep in a field alongside.

Pascal Bernou left his cooker to tell us that he had known Trelly as a child on holiday with his grandmother, and had snapped up the hotel after training with Roger Vergé at Moulin de Mougins, Fernand Arrambibe in St. Jean-Pied-de-Port and Gérard Bonnefoy in Honfleur. So much for our beloved Normandy cooking, we thought. We were wrong again. His dishes ranged from local ham in cider and Normandy tart, made of apples and raisins, to ragout of lobster in sweet wine spiced with ginger and old English gooseberry crumble. And his variation of *trou normand* called 'grog au Calvados' was calvados in cold tea. M. Bernou deserves his Michelin star but we hope that he keeps to his own dishes and to reasonable prices — and that he keeps his chickens, lambs and cows. A long, gentle moo makes a much better awakening background than tinny bells or pop music.

old fishing village famous for oysters. It has become almost as popular with yachtsmen as nearby Barfleur since a marina was made in the old port, though at some tides the sea goes out a long way. La Hougue is joined to St. Vaast (pronounced 'St. Va') by an isthmus with a kilometre-long sand beach. La Hougue's fort, designed by Vauban, is still a military post. St. Vaast's streets can get crowded in midsummer, but it is still pleasant and the beach is big enough to absorb crowds. A 15-minute walk north on the little D1 is Saire Point, near Réville, with a good all-round view of the bay.

Barfleur was an important fishing port until quite recently, but pleasure boats have taken over, with many summer yachtsmen on its quayside and streets, and summer holiday-makers. History has been changed there, especially English history. The ship which carried Duke William to conquer

England in 1066 came from there, with a Barfleur pilot. In 1120 the great *White Ship* floundered in the shallow waters and tricky currents just off Barfleur, drowning Henry I of England's son and heir William, his half-sister the Countess of Mortagne and at least 100 young noblemen of his court. It is said that William could have got away in a small boat but insisted upon returning for his sister. In 1152 after Stephen's death, Henry Plantagenet (his heir) arrived in Barfleur in mid-November to sail to England to claim the throne. In 1194 Richard Coeur de Lion sailed from there to be crowned King of England.

At Gatteville 2.5km to the north is a seafarers' church, built in the 12th century and rebuilt in the 17th, but keeping its original belfry. Bits of old wall paintings and a 15th-century altar were found during repairs over 30 years ago. The lighthouse on the nearby point is one of the highest in France (71 metres). Its light can be seen for 56km and its radar guides ships as far as Le Havre. The panoramic view from the top is quite awesome (open every day from spring holidays to September; Sundays only the rest of the year).

The main road from Carentan to Cherbourg, the N13, skirts Ste. Mère-Église, the centre of a great breeding area for horses and cattle. This little town received a brutal shock at 2.30 am on 6 June 1944, when parachutists landed in and all round it. The 11th–12th-century church still bears the scars of bullets aimed at dislodging German snipers firing machine guns from the church tower. An unusual but effective memorial to the Americans is the effigy of a parachutist dangling from the church roof, his 'chute caught round a pointed corner. Stained glass in the church tells the story. In front of the Town Hall is the first of the Liberty Stones, marked 'O' which the US forces laid as they advanced every mile across Europe to Metz. Beneath a para-chute-shaped dome in a park is an interesting Airborne Troops Museum, including Douglas C147 dropping aircraft, weapons, models and very good photographs.

Valognes, 10km up the N13, is a pleasant modern place, mostly in concrete, lively on market days (Tuesdays and Fridays). It was very attractive until those terrible battles of 1944. In the 18th century it was a centre of fash-ionable society in Normandy and fine houses (*hôtels*) were added to its already attractive churches and ornate gardens. A few have survived or been restored, notably Hôtel de Beaumont, 50 metres long, overlooking a fine terraced garden, and Hôtel de Granval-Caligny, a 17th–18th-century house with a fine salon and alcoved bedrooms. The house is finely furnished (open afternoons 1 July–mid September).

In an attractive 15th-century *logis* is the Musée Regional du Cidre, tracing the history of apple-growing and cider-making. A museum of *eau-de-vie* (distilled spirits) is in the 17th-century Hôtel de Thieuville.

Îles de Chausey (Granite Isles)

Boats make day trips from Granville to the rugged Îles de Chausey. Only one of these, La Grande Île, is now inhabited. A hundred fishermen and their families live there, though many leave in midwinter. The island is 2km long by 700 metres at its widest point. There is a fort built in the 1860s against the possibility of British attack — rather odd considering the British and French were allies in the Crimean War only about 6 years before.

Vieux Fort, which dates 1558, was reconstructed as a safe hideout by Louis Renault, the car manufacturer. The little fishermen's church has six modern stained-glass windows showing the lives of fishermen.

On the uninhabited isles are abandoned quarries which supplied the brown granite for Mont-St. Michel and other fine old buildings.

Manche — South of Cotentin Peninsula and the Bay of Mont-St. Michel

The road leading from Coutances to **Granville** passes some quite pleasant scenery. At Hyenville, where an ancient bridge crosses the Sienne river, a road to the right leads to Montmartin-sur-Mer, a little market town with vast sands nearby. The D971 from Coutances and the D20 from Coutainville meet at Bréhal. Just to the east is the Renaissance Château Chanteloup.

Granville has long been an established seaside resort, as well as a busy commercial and fishing port. But it came into being as a fortress and even in the Second World War the Germans realised its importance and fortified it heavily. It was started by the English in 1440 as a fort to counter the threat of French-held Mont-St. Michel just down the coast. But the Knights of Mont-St. Michel took it two years later and continued to fortify it. Later it was a lair of pirates.

The old upper town (Haute Ville) is still encircled by ramparts and, being built of granite, does look rather grim, but there are some fine old houses and a great square, place de l'Isthme, with views across to Brittany, and steps down to the casino. The way into Haute Ville is over a drawbridge through Grand' Porte into a warren of narrow streets with arches. From the north side of the ramparts the sea views can be spectacular in rough weather. At the west end is the rather squat church of Notre-Dame in browny-red granite, much of it built in the 15th century, though the nave itself is from the 17th. The inside is plain because you can't sculpture granite but interesting modern glass brightens it. The Vieux Granville museum in the Grand' Porte retells interestingly the story of the town, its privateers and fishermen. Beyond the church is Pointe du Roc, which is the top limit of Mont-St. Michel Bay.

The roads down to the port and commercial part of the town are steepish. The port has scalloped concrete walls to the harbour which is used by a fishing fleet. There is a large marina for pleasure boats and a yachting centre. The route to the casino and the little narrow beach with a swimming pool at the foot of the cliffs is by Tranchée aux Anglais, a trench dug by the English in the 15th century and now widened. Above the beach is the very attractive Christian Dior garden which once belonged to his family. Dior was born in Granville in 1905. A cliff path from the garden leads to the huge beach at Donville-les-Bains, almost part of Granville. There is a safe beach of golden sands with a promenade 3.5km south at St. Pair-sur-Mer. It has a very old church, too, believed to have been founded in the 6th century.

Each side of Granville are small seaside resorts where French families spend summer holidays. Past Donville northwards is Bréville-sur-Mer, then Coudeville-Plage, with a hotel (shut in winter) and a campsite. South of Granville is St. Pair with two hotels and campsite, then Jullouville, which is a pleasant little superior resort with a hotel and houses among pine trees, many of them second summer houses of the French. Its neighbour Carolles is on the last headland of the west coast of the Cotentin Peninsula. Past the headland in Mont-St. Michel Bay are huge stretches of sand at low tide. There are some attractive roads from Carolles inland to Sartilly on the Avranches road and along the coast to St. Jean-le-Thomas a popular resort with a big sand beach. The view to Mont-St. Michel so impressed General Eisenhower that he mentioned it in his memoirs.

Avranches above the river Sée estuary has been an important town through the centuries. It was St. Aubert, Bishop of Avranches, who founded nearby Mont-St. Michel in the 8th century. It seems that St. Michael himself appeared twice to the bishop commanding him to build a chapel on Mont Tombe rock, and to stress the point dug an angelic finger into his head. His head with the hole in it can be seen in St. Gervais and St. Protais Basilica in Avranches.

From Avranches on 31 July 1944, the American 3rd Army began the advance to smash the German counter-attack on this front. The monument to the advance stands on the spot where General Patton stayed before the offensive and the square where it stands is American territory, with trees brought from America and soil from each state in the USA.

Avranches is a pleasant, busy place where traffic can be formidable, especially in summer with visitors on their way to Mont-St. Michel and Brittany. A peaceful place is the Jardin des Plantes, the botanical gardens once belonging to a monastery, with a waterfall and lovely trees on land sloping down from the town. From the terrace there is a superb panorama of Mont-St. Michel Bay.

From the airfield (4km south-west on the coast) between mid-April and mid-September you can take an air trip over Mont-St. Michel (phone 33.58.02.91).

The abbey of **Le Mont-St. Michel** is called by the French 'la Merveille de l'Occident' (the Marvel of the Western World), and it is officially 'Le Premier Site de France' — France's top tourist site. It scrapes into Normandy by 2km, to the annoyance of the Bretons, but its founding and its history are pure Norman. It rises spectacularly from the sea at high tide where the river Couesnon flows into a 22km-wide estuary. On its pointed granite rock are a town, fortress, ramparts, and an abbey clinging to its side, all capped with an 11th-century abbey-church with a spire added in the 19th century, and a gilded statue of St. Michael himself brandishing a sword. When the tide goes out vast stretches of sand appear — dangerous quicksands, which could swallow an army. The monks knew the paths through them; their enemies did not. That was how the abbey survived for centuries. Now there is a three-lane causeway to a car park at the rock's base. Bare-foot, or in sandals which can take the wet, you can walk round the base of the rock, but be sure to check tides, for the sea comes in at a metre a second.

A little chapel on the rock was built by the Bishop of Avranches in AD 709, but the great abbey was not begun until 966 by Benedictine monks under Duke Richard of Normandy, grandfather of the Conqueror. It was built of granite brought across from the isles of Chausey and incredibly hauled up the sides of the rock. The church was added between 1017 and 1144.

Pilgrims of all types from barons to beggars flocked from all over Christendom to the rock. A town grew up, and the abbey was fortified. Souvenir sellers were rife even in the Middle Ages, selling emblems of St. Michael and lead caskets filled with sand from the beach.

You enter through Porte l'Avancée into a 16th-century fortified courtyard then through Porte du Roi into the steep Grande Rue, the single street of the town with side passages, stairways and changing levels. It is lined with restaurants, hotels, cafés, bars, shops, many selling immemorable souvenirs. All are in buildings spanning centuries. Steps lead up to ramparts with fine sea views.

The abbey-church is quite remarkable when you realise that only the transept crossing is built on the rock summit. The rest of the Romanesque nave is on built-up foundations. The chancel was rebuilt in 1421 in decorated Gothic. The vast monks' refectory is lit incredibly well with just two obvious windows. Look more carefully and you see narrow windows cut cunningly at the top.

The cloisters are truly superb, seemingly suspended between sea and sky. Two hundred and seventy-seven graceful columns support the arches which surround a garden. There is a pleasant walk to the old abbey gardens, which you can visit for a small extra fee.

Museums can be confusing. There's the Musée Historial du Mont, showing in pictures, wax figures and dioramas the Mount's story. The Musée Historique has much the same, plus 25,000 old clock balance cocks. The Musée de la Mer shows the Mount and the sea with video cassettes and also a film of the Mount's history (rather good) and model ships, including a collection of America's Cup yachts. A favourite show of the town is watching pancakes being made (and eating them) at Mère Poulard's just as Annette Poulard made them well over a century ago.

Do not attempt to walk across Mont-St. Michel Bay at low tide without a guide. Guides are provided at Genêts, a tiny resort across the bay

The Knight's Hall at Mont-St. Michel

(apply at Maison de La Baie, Genêts, 33.70.83.42). A mass pilgrimage crosses in July. St. Michael's Autumn Festival and Fair in September is splendid but hotel rooms are hard to come by, as they are for the May Spring Fair.

A more peaceful spot to stay is Pontorson (9km south) where the church was founded by William the Conqueror in gratitude for the saving of his army from Mont-St. Michel quicksands. It is the last Norman village before you enter Brittany. Pontaubault (15km east on the Avranches road) has hotels, too, including the 13 Assiettes with good food (33.58.14.03).

There are some very attractive roads through charming countryside east of Avranches to the Calvados border. Follow the D911 to Brécey, cut down the main D999 south to just past a hamlet called Le Gué Bottrel, then turn left along the D5 to Juvigny-le-Tertre onto the D51 and the D33 right into Mortain. This little town in the valley of the little river Cance is attractive despite rebuilding after its destruction by a violent German counter-attack against Patton's forces in 1944. It stands on a rock hillside in hilly, wooded country at the western edge of the Parc Régional Normandie-Maine. It is rather dominated by its 13th-century Gothic limestone church of St. Evroult, but its little waterways make it delightful.

Two kilometres north stands the 12th-century former Abbaye Blanche which isn't white. It was named after the habits of the Cistercian monks. The remains are mostly 19th century. But below it in a wooded gorge reached by paths well marked is the river Cance. You can see it among boulders and trees, and then you come to Grande Cascade, where the water tumbles 25 metres down natural slopes — a delightful scene. The paths are on the great GR22 footpath from Paris to Mont-St. Michel and are marked in red and white paint. There's another charming waterfall, Petite Cascade, which is actually higher (35 metres) but not so steep.

The D907 south-east passes the Forest of Mortain to the village of Barenton — a lovely 9km road. Nearby is a Maison de la Pomme et de la Poire, showing the history and growing techniques of apples and pears, production of cider, perry and calvados — and you can taste them.

The N175 road, which runs right across Normandy from Rouen and into Brittany to Rennes, reaches Avranches through **Villedieu-les-Poêles**, a likeable town which got its strange name ('God's Town of the Frying Pan') by graduating from a 12th-century commandery of the Knights of St. John of Jerusalem to the leading producer of copper pans in France in the 17th century. It still is, though it no longer finds a market for its *cannes* — copper milk churns. Aluminium cooking pans are also made today, but the superb heavy copper pans are the town's pride and are well worth their price. In France they are passed from generation to generation. There is an interesting copperware museum, and also a bell foundry. It's an active little town with little shops where the owner or his wife will probably serve you.

Little copper workshops are hidden away in alleys left from the days of the knights and with evocative names like 'Court of the Three Kings', 'Court of Lilies' and 'Court of Hell'! Old houses line the banks of the river Sienne.

The 18th-century flamboyant church has a square tower ornamented with heraldic emblems of the knights. Every fourth year since 1655, on the second or third Sunday of June, the members of the Order of St. John have marched in regalia to the church for an old ceremony called Grand Sacré. The next processions will be in 1999, 2003, etc.

The D9 north-west from Villedieu leads to the town of Gavray, the centre of delightful roads and lanes through lovely countryside. North-eastwards the roads lead to the village and old abbey of Hambye. The ruins of the abbey are in a very beautiful setting, and are still impressive, especially the roofless but tall and majestic abbey-church from the 12th century, when the abbey was founded. You can see the old kitchens with their monumental chimney, *la salle des morts*, a 14th-century wooden Christ, the refectory with 17th-century Rouen tapestries and period furniture, and the dormitories still used for conferences.

Eastward the little D258 reaches Percy on the D999 and crosses onto the attractive D98 and then little roads finally crossing the N175 to reach Ste. Marie-Outre-l'Eau. This is another area of delightful lanes, eastward into Calvados or north up the D21 to Tessy-sur-Vire. From here take the D359 north to Troisgots and La Chapelle-sur Vire, whose church has been a place of pilgrimage since the 12th century. This is the true *bocage* countryside of woods, tall hedges around pasture and lanes often sunk within banks, which stretches into Calvados. Two kilometres south of Troisgots on the D359 is the Château de L'Angotière, a charming 15th–19th-century manor in a picturesque setting with a terrace overlooking the Vire and Javre valleys. There is a view from the 400-year-old *pigeonnier*. Inside is a good collection of ceramics from Delft and the East. In the large park are beautiful oaks, limes and cedars, with woods divided romantically into *bois des amours* (lovers' wood), *bois des soupirs* (wood of sighs) and *bois des regrets* (wood of regrets).

Roches de Ham, 4km north-east of Troisgots, is a magnificent rocky escarpment with two platforms above the Vire river. From the lower platform you look down 80 metres to a deep bend of the river. From the upper platform is a wide view along the valley of the Vire.

Small roads east take you onto the D13, 2km south of Torigni-sur-Vire, a little town which suffered severely in 1944. The 17th-century château of the Matignon family has been rebuilt from a shell. It has a lovely collection of 17th-century tapestries of Brussels and Aubusson and furniture of Louis XIII, XV and XVI periods.

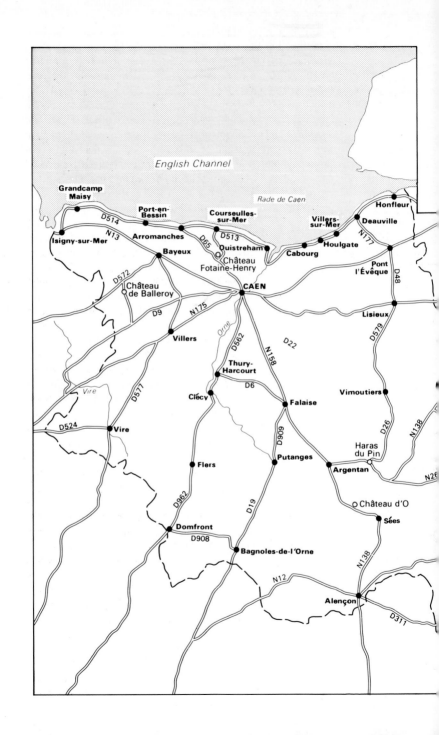

5. Calvados and Orne

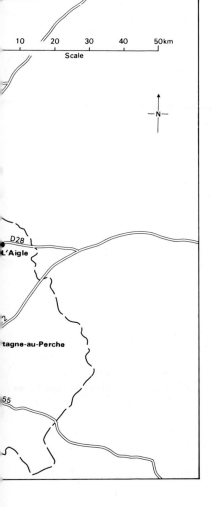

Calvados Landing Beaches and Resorts to Ouistreham

Isigny-sur-Mer, where Manche ends and Calvados begins is not quite on the sea any longer. The bay has silted up, and it is joined to the Vire estuary by the little Aure river in which a few fishing boats still tie up. It shares with Carentan the rich pastures which support enough cattle to make it a butter and cheese-making town of such repute that Isigny butter is regarded as the best in Normandy — most Frenchmen admit that Normandy butter is the best in France. Some famous hotels and restaurants serve no other. From the salt meadows, too, comes *pré-salé* lamb, with that special flavour that Britons get from the lamb of Romney Marsh.

Isigny was damaged when the Americans freed it on 9 June 1944, but the 13th-century tower and choir of the church survived, as did the 18th-century château, home of the Bricquerville family, which is now the town hall. In the main square, where a very good food market is held every other Saturday, is a memorial to the Allied troops who freed the town. It is a jolly little place with good small food shops and reasonably priced restaurants.

The N13 takes you direct to the delightful town of Bayeux. But although the little resorts on the coast were destroyed in the fighting in 1944, they are much more interesting than you might expect and very attractive in many places. So I would take the coastal D514 left to **Grandcamp-Maisy**, where the visitors are almost entirely French and come here to sail, to watch the fishing boats return and to eat the fish. It is not a pretty place but a genuine working port with atmosphere. Pleasure boats mix with fishing boats in the harbour, the quays still have genuine old-style ships' chandlers offering a higgledy-piggledy choice of ships' equipment including the genuine old blue fishermen's jerseys and the old-fashioned hemp ropes. On the port quay are stalls with blackboards which tell you the name of each boat expected that day, its estimated time of arrival and what fish it has caught. It makes planning dinner much easier for the holidaymakers who stay in the new low-built flats overlooking the harbour.

Shellfish are prolific among Roches de Grandcamp, a huge expanse of rocks which you can see off the coast at low tide, especially scallops, mussels and oysters. There is a choice of quayside fish restaurants from very cheap to the dearer simple-looking La Marée, whose *bouillabaisse* is renowned in Normandy.

Along the coast past Pointe du Hoc, the scene of a major D-Day battle, you pass Château D'Englesqueville (17th-century) on the right, then you reach the little resort of Vierville on Omaha Beach where the Americans landed on D-Day. There is an exhibition '6 June 1944' (open daily April–September) and a memorial on a blockhaus to the American National Guard. The new maritime boulevard follows the coast almost to St. Laurent. It replaces the destroyed promenade under which the first US soldiers who landed on Omaha Beach sheltered until they mounted the first assault. Three and a half kilometres south of here alongside the N13 is Formigny. Here 500 years ago in 1450 the French defeated the English, who were driven out of Normandy, and so ended the Hundred Years War. There is a Commemoration Chapel. During the battle, Sir Thomas Kyriel, the English commander and veteran of Agincourt, took too little notice of the vastly superior French forces and attacked the army of the Comte de Clermont. He was attacked in the rear by Constable de Richemont and his army defeated.

From St. Laurent the road stays just inland to Colleville-sur-Mer. The last Germans were not driven from the church of this little town until the day after D-Day. The church has been completely rebuilt. Off the coast here on Omaha Beach the second Mulberry prefabricated harbour

Above the D-Day Omaha Landing Beach at Colleville-St. Laurent, 9,386 marble crosses mark the graves of US servicemen

Mulberry Harbour

The costly Dieppe raid of 1942 taught the British that taking a highly fortified major port from the sea was almost impossible, and if it were taken after severe fighting, the port installations would be unusable. They found also that landing tanks on shingle beaches under fire was disastrous. If an invasion was to succeed, the Allies would have to take their harbour with them, and land on sand.

A prefabricated harbour was designed, the parts of which could be towed across. It was made in sections in many different parts of Britain under many guises during the winter of 1943–4. German Intelligence had no idea what was happening. Nor did they know about the Pluto undersea oil pipe later laid from the Isle of Wight right across to Cherbourg. They believed after Dieppe that the Allies would try to take a port. Two Mulberries were made, one to be taken to Omaha Beach to be set up near Vierville for the Americans and the other to be set up at Arromanches in the British Gold sector.

The harbour sections were towed across the Channel at four knots. There were 146 Phoenix caissons filled with 600,000 tons of concrete, which were sunk in the sea bed as breakwaters, 33 jetties made of vertical pillars (fixed by suction to the sea bed) on which floating steel pontoons could rise and fall with the tide, and 16km of floating roads (piers made of light metal stages on floats). Arromanches Mulberry could take 9,000 tons of material landed each day. By the end of August 500,000 tons had been landed. But by then the big ports of Cherbourg and Antwerp had been freed and were in use and Mulberry was sanding up. The Mulberry on Omaha Beach only lasted until 19 June, when it was blown away by a storm.

was built. Unlike the one at Arromanches, it was made useless by a storm on 19 June — the worst for 40 years. On the clifftop above Colleville is one of the most dramatic and beaut-ifully kept war cemeteries in Europe. It is the US forces cemetery. Over acres of carefully mown grass lie 9,386 graves — most marked with a cross in white Carrara marble, but some with the Star of David. Some sadly are marked 'Known only to God'. Above it all on the clifftop is a monumental bronze figure with a massive cross. From a belvedere are views out to sea. Monuments just outside the cemetery are to the 1st US Division and the 5th Engineer Special Brigade who cleared the beach of mines and obstacles and kept contact between the units which had landed and the ships offshore.

Port-en-Bessin is the first fairly lively seaside resort along the coast. It is picturesque, too, hidden in a hollow in the cliffs, and as it is only 9km from Bayeux, it has obvious advantages. A half-circle granite jetty forms an outer fishing harbour from which boats sail to catch mainly scallops, or white fish

As each boat lands at Grandcamp-Maisy, its catch is sold direct to housewives

off the south-west coast of England. The fish is auctioned on the quayside in the early morning. The quayside scene is well worth seeing as the boats prepare for sea. On cliffs above the end of the harbour is a tower-fortress built by Vauban, the great military architect of the 17th century. There are good coastal views from the outer jetty.

Port-en-Bessin is on the edge of Gold and Omaha Landing Beaches and was freed on 7 June by No. 47 Royal Marine Commando after a remarkable 20-hour march through enemy territory.

Past the tumbled rocks of Le Chaos reached from Longues is **Arromanches**, most important of the Landing Beaches. Mulberry Harbour was built here. Without it the Allied landings would certainly have failed. It was a little seaside resort with a good beach popular with French families. Now it has another invasion — of tourists from round the world arriving in thousands every day to see the historic beach, the remains of Mulberry Harbour at sea and the big Invasion Museum on the promenade showing models, photographs, equipment and the Royal Navy film of the landing. There are queues to get in. The promenade is a big car-park, the cafés, bars and little restaurants do good business, but the sands never seem anywhere near crowded. Families still spend holidays there. You can see

A monumental bronze figure stands over the graves of 9,386 American war dead at Colleville cemetery

the remains of the concrete and steel jetties of Mulberry most clearly through telescopes from an observation post at the east end of the town. Up the hill from the beach, Arromanches is a pleasant place once the cars and coaches have gone.

Asnelles, at the east end of Mulberry Harbour, where part of the 50th Northumberland Division landed, has a rebuilt promenade with views of Arromanches. There is a memorial on the beach to the British 231st Infantry Brigade. Ver-sur-Mer at the east end of Gold Beach was a major point on D-Day for the Northumberland's landing. The village itself is 2km inland. It has a huge 11th-century Romanesque belltower, with blind arcades. The seaside part of the village has been rebuilt but you can still see some remains of the German 'Atlantic Wall'. A landing memorial stands in avenue Colonel-Harper.

Courseulles-sur-Mer is in the Juno Beach sector where the Canadians landed. So on 12 June did Winston Churchill. On 14 June General de Gaulle, commander of the Free French forces, arrived and on 16 June, King George VI. The little port sheltered by the mouth of the Seulles river was very useful until Mulberry Harbour arrived. Now it is a fishing harbour again, and a marina too. It is growing as a resort, with holiday apartments springing up but its business is still fishing and especially oyster farming. Oysters are brought here from St. Vaast in Manche and the Île de Ré off La Rochelle to mature. A museum on the Arromanches road called Marvels of the Sea is mostly about shellfish.

Château Fontaine-Henry (6km south) is medieval with Renaissance lacy stonework and carvings added later. It is outstandingly graceful. It is set in an English-style park and has fine furniture, a splendid François I period staircase, and tableaux paintings by Nicolas Mignard, the portrait painter of Louis XIV's reign, Rigaud and the romantic landscape painter Hubert Robert. The 13th-century chapel was much altered after the Renaissance. Opening times are very complicated, so ring 31.80.00.20 or ask at Courseulles information office, boulevard de la Plage (open Easter–September, tel: 31.37.46.80).

Bernières-sur-Mer is known for shrimps and crabs, netted from boats among the reefs which show at low tide. It has long been a little family resort. The French Canadian Chaudière Division landed here on D-Day. So did the press and radio correspondents. The French headquarters has been restored. The beautiful church survived with a superb 13th-century spire 67 metres tall. A Romanesque tower has survived wars and storms since the 11th century. It has four storeys which recede so that in times of danger the people could climb up storey by storey on a rope ladder, then haul it up after them.

St. Aubin-sur-Mer is always described by the French, who like it, as *climat tonique*, which we would call bracing. It is very much an old-style French seaside resort with a holiday atmosphere. It, too, has a reef for shrimping and crab fishing. The Canadian 8th Brigade landed here. Langrune is one of the oldest resorts, with several hotels, pensions and café-bars. Its 13th-century church has a fine two-storey belfry. This is in the Sword Beach sector where the British 51st Highland Division landed. Southwards you can see the tall spires of Notre Dame-de-la-Délivrande, a neo-Gothic 19th-century basilica which contains a highly venerated Black Madonna. Pilgrimages take place in

August and September. At the edge of the village on the D35 is the Convent of Notre-Dame-de-Fidélité (ring the bell). Its chapel has three windows in crystal and chrome by René Lalique (1931) and a modern lacquer Stations of the Cross. At the nearby village of Couvres is a small shady British cemetery with 1,000 graves.

Luc-sur-Mer is another resort with bracing air. It is a pleasant little place with a 2km promenade above a sandy beach and rocks at low tide covered with seaweed. Hydrosodium iodate (sea water) treatment is given at the Thalasso Thérapie. There's a prominent white casino. At low tide you can reach low cliffs with caves.

Lion-sur-Mer, the next little family resort, was one of the main British landing places on Sword Beach. Extensive rocks (Les Roches de Lion) are uncovered at low tide. The 16th-century château with Renaissance pavilion in a park is not open to the public. As they were so badly damaged in 1944 and had to be rebuilt, most of these little resorts have lost their old atmosphere, but they are happy places in summer. Hermanville-sur-Mer was the headquarters of the British Sword Beach fighting.

Colleville-Montgomery-Plage added the name of Montgomery in honour of General Montgomery, the Commander of Allied Land Forces and victor of the desert Battle of Alamein. His ancestors came from this part of Normandy. The village itself is 3km inland. There is a statue to the general. This was the beach where the 4th Anglo-French Commando under French Commandant Philippe Kieffer landed at 8.45 am on D-Day and put the very strongly fortified German position at Riva-Bella out of action while Lord Lovat's commando carried on to fight its way inland and join up with the British airborne troops who had the night before D-Day landed and taken the bridges over the Caen Canal and River Orne at Bénouville and Ranville — '2½ minutes late on schedule', as the plaque by the new bridge tells us.

Riva-Bella is the beach of the port of Ouistreham at the estuary of the river Orne. It has grown as a seaside resort out of the ruins produced by German occupation, fortification and evacuation. The superb 2km beach of fine sand lures not only holidaymakers but at weekends the people of Caen 14km away. The river Orne and the Caen Canal reach the sea here. There is a casino, bars and cafés, as well as a memorial to the 4th Commando and a museum of their landing and successes. But otherwise all that remains from the war is a solitary German blockhouse.

Ouistreham is a lively little port these days. Since the building of the marina, with both the Orne and the canal meeting the sea here, it has become an international yachting centre. Inevitably many boats are from Britain and the Channel Isles. But the big awakening has come to Ouistreham with the Brittany Ferries car ferry service, called the Portsmouth — Caen route. It has led to more hotel accommodation, more and better restaurants and shops and, inevitably, a huge supermarket on the Caen road.

The invading Norsemen destroyed St. Samson's church in the 9th century, so it was rebuilt in the 12th century as a fortress-church. The inside

was remodelled in the 19th century and the building was restored after war damage. There are guided visits to the 30 metre-high lighthouse in the afternoons from early April to mid-September.

The bridges at Bénouville and Ranville taken by British airborne troops on the night of 5 June 1944 can be reached on the D514 south. Alas, the Bénouville bridge has been replaced by one more modern. The local authorities chose to knock it down in 1994, a few weeks before the British survivors of that vital and extremely dangerous operation were due to hold a ceremony there as part of the celebration of the 50th anniversary of the Normandy landings. A small but good museum stands beside the new bridge.

Bayeux, Caen and the Bocage

The great Bayeux Tapestry, telling the story of William the Conqueror's invasion of England

The Bayeux Tapestry showing the story of William's Conquest of England and the beautiful cathedral have filled **Bayeux** with tourists for centuries, but the little town has a charm and atmosphere which makes it worth visiting anyway. Since some streets in the centre were made traffic-free, it has become easier and safer to walk around but not easy to find parking.

The Bayeux Tapestry, shown now behind bullet-proof glass in a 17th-century house, is one of the most famous surviving works of art from the Middle Ages. The fabric is in remarkable condition for its age and the colours seem hardly to have faded.

Parts of the prefabricated Mulberry Harbour left from the invasion remain off Arromanches

Seventy metres in length, it tells in 58 scenes, at quite a fast pace, of William, Duke of Normandy's dispute with Harold about who had the right to the throne of England, and his victory at Hastings in 1066. It is told strictly from the Norman viewpoint, of course, William is the hero from whom the villain Harold has stolen the English crown.

The main story is in the central strip. The top and bottom bands show scenes from Norman life at the time, some quite erotic, symbols and inscriptions clarifying the main story, and scenes from Aesop's fables.

Strictly speaking, it is not even a tapestry. It is embroidery. But it is a superb work, intriguing and entertaining. It was made to hang in Bayeux Cathedral and did so for some centuries. During the Revolution, it was put away in a trunk. Napoleon, spotting its propaganda value, took it to Paris to raise enthusiasm for the invasion of England that never happened. You can hire a listening tape in English or French to help follow the tapestry's story.

Bayeux's splendid Gothic cathedral was built originally between 1050 and 1077 though the central lantern tower is 15th-century and the top was added in the 19th century to save this lantern tower from collapsing. A worn tympanum shows the murder of Thomas à Becket at Canterbury.

The inside is most impressive. A marriage of Romanesque and Gothic styles, it has tall windows with 13th-century vaulting, sturdy pillars in the Romanesque nave contrasting with funny grotesque carvings of primitive bishops and apes, jugglers and dragons. The chancel, rebuilt in 1230, has soaring slender columns lit by rose windows. The 16th-century carved choir-stalls are delightful. The tiled chapter house floor is set out as a maze.

Bayeux Cathedral was built in the 12th century, but alterations through the centuries have made a harmonious blend of architectural styles

The Musée Baron Gérard in the old Bishop's Palace shows old and new Bayeux lace, excellent porcelain from the early 19th century to the mid-20th century when the town was a well-known producer, and an extensive collection of paintings, many of them 19th-century French. There are very interesting pictures by François Boucher, the prolific 18th-century rococo artist who specialised in scenes of gallantry and mythology, David, the neo-classical artist who, during the Revolution, was virtual dictator of arts and who became Napoleon's official painter, and his pupil Baron Gros, whose painting here of Sappho is in poor shape but is still an excellent example of romantic art.

In the 1944 Allied invasion, Bayeux was incredibly lucky. The 50th Northumberland Division made such a successful landing on Gold Beach that they were able to free Bayeux on the day after D-Day, with hardly any damage. Their memorial is fittingly placed outside the Bayeux Tapestry museum. Bayeux was the first major town in France to be freed, but 6,000 British soldiers are buried in the cemetery off boulevard Fabian Ware.

As a result of this quick freedom, many more old houses survived in Bayeux than in other towns in Calvados, and shopping streets are delightfully 'old France'.

Along the D572 south-west from Bayeux you reach the delightful Cerisy Forest which stretches to the Manche border. At L'Embranchement the D8 forks right for a charming forest drive to Cerisy-la-Forêt in Manche (see page 35). But first take the D13 left for 2.5km to **Balleroy**. Here an avenue at right angles, lined with elegant old houses, leads to the gates of the superb Château de Balleroy. Though its grey and pink stone and brick exterior is a little faded, it is almost perfectly proportioned. It looks most impressive with its two pavilions on a terrace at the end of a drive through neat gardens designed by Le Nôtre, who laid out the gardens of Versailles. It was built between 1626 and 1636 for Jean de Choisy, Chancellor to Gaston d'Orléans, by François Mansart, the man who made the high-pitched roof fashionable and who designed many great châteaux, including Blois. Choisy's descendants, the Marquis de Balleroy, lived in his chateau for three centuries. Then it was bought by the American Forbes family. The last owner, Malcolm Forbes, who died in 1990, was the first man to cross the USA by balloon — hence the balloon museum in the old stables at Balleroy and the annual International Balloon Rally held there in June.

The balloon museum shows balloons in war and peace from the hot air balloon of the Montgolfier brothers, which carried men for the first time over Paris in 1783, to the present day. It is unusually interesting.

Northward from L'Embranchement a road through the forest leads to Le Molay-Littry, an old mining town. It has a mining museum showing the 18th-century equipment and a reconstructed mine gallery. Just outside the village is the massive luxurious 18th-century Chateau du Molay in beautiful grounds with a river running through and deer. It is a well-run hotel with excellent cuisine.

Take the D6 south from Bayeux and the little D33 right, then onto the D178 and you find Mondaye Abbey, where the abbey of 1200 and the parish church were both rebuilt and decorated in the 18th century. The organ loft, high altar and woodwork are all worth seeing.

Go left off the D6 on the D187 and you find at Audrieu another historic château turned into an hotel. A white house with a grey roof on three sides of a carriage courtyard, it is a fine example of the elegance of Louis XV's France.

Tilly-sur-Seulles has the unenviable fame of having been taken and retaken

The same family lived in the 17th-century Château de Balleroy for 300 years

by the British and the Germans 23 times between 7 and 30 June 1944. Not surprisingly, it was terribly destroyed, yet by some near-miracle its 11th-century church survived. A museum of the bloody battle is open in summer.

This is *bocage* countryside, even to the names of its villages — Villy-Bocage, Tracy-Bocage and Villers-Bocage.

The N175 and D577 south-west from Villers passes Le Bény-Bocage to the ancient town of **Vire** on a hill overlooking the rolling Bocage Virois. It was nearly obliterated in 1944 but some old buildings survived enough to be restored. Among them was the granite Gothic church of Notre-Dame (13th–15th centuries) which had only part of its east end left standing but is now completely restored. Another survivor was the strong granite twin-towered 13th-century gateway, Tour de l'Horloge, to which a belfry was added in the 15th century, which acted as a curfew and a sort of musical clock. It is now the centre of the modern main square.

A very attractive road, the D524, runs westward to the big market town of the *bocage*, St. Sever and its forest of 1,550 hectares of beech, pine and firs where game roam in semi-freedom. There are several small forest roads and footpaths. A chapel remains from a hermit monastery of Louis XIII's reign. St. Sever has a Saturday market.

The N13 south-east from Bayeux to Caen is busy and rather dull. It is worth taking the little D12 to Creully, a town with an interesting war history. The Canadians took it by 5 pm on D-Day. The 11th-century château has a 16th-century tower. On the tower door is still a notice 'BBC — Silence — No entry'. Here immediately after D-Day the BBC set up its studio to tell the world of the landings and the battle. Inside you can see photographs by British, Canadian and French war photographers. From the château terrace you can see Château de Creullet on the north-west outskirts of the town. In its park General Montgomery parked the caravan headquarters which he had used in the Western Desert when commanding the 8th Army. He camou-

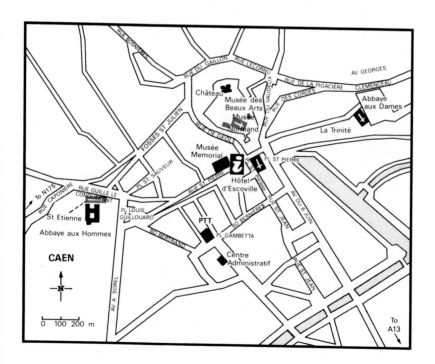

flaged it with straw. In the grand salon of the château, on 12 June 1944, he received King George VI and Winston Churchill. Just south is the beautiful 17th-century château at Lantheuil which was built for one of the Turgot family. The family still own it. It has its original décor, panelling and furniture, and an interesting collection of ancestral portraits.

Caen is truly a new town — centuries away from the old pre-Second World War town. Three-quarters of it was destroyed in the battle between the Canadians and the Germans from 9 to 20 July 1944. But the change is not simply that the town had to be rebuilt. It has been rebuilt very much as a modern town. Furthermore, it has become very industrialised. Yet it is a pleasant place, very good for shopping and for eating, and enough of its historical buildings have been restored to keep a strong link with William the Conqueror.

The first Norman settlers fortified an island at the meeting of the Orne and Odon rivers but it was William who built the town. His capital was Rouen, but that was vulnerable to attacks from the Franks, and there was always the danger from Brittany. So he built up Caen as a strong second capital. William built the great castle but his son Henry I of England built the keep, and it was enlarged over centuries.

The English sacked Caen in 1346 and 1417, and ruled for 33 years. They left behind the first university in France, founded in 1432 by the Duke of Bedford, Regent in France of Henry VI of England. Now Caen has one of the most modern universities in Europe, with more than 12,000 students.

The castle has been much restored and a pleasant public garden has been laid out between its walls, which are mostly 15th century, though some are 12th. The ramparts are 11th–15th century. They enclose buildings of different styles and centuries, the Romanesque chapel of St. Georges, the Hall of the *Echiquier* (Exchequer) and the 17th-century Governor's House. There are two museums inside. The Musée des Beaux Arts, in a modern building, has some fine paintings spanning five centuries. There is an exceptional collection of 50,000 engravings of such masters as Mantegna, Rembrandt, Dürer and Goya, which are shown in rotation. Furniture, tapestries, Limoges enamels, porcelain miniatures and 18th-century snuff boxes are all superb. The Normandy Museum in the old Governor's House of the château has tools used by Norman households and on farms.

At the foot of the castle are many of the old buildings which survived the war, especially in rue aux Fromages, place St. Sauveur and place St. Pierre, where the early Renaissance mansion Hôtel d'Escoville, built around 1535, is now the Tourist Office.

The church of St. Pierre, built in 1308 by rich merchants and luxuriously ornamented, had a 78-metre belfry which was a model for many Norman and Breton belltowers. All is now restored. The east end of the church (1518–45) is a famous example of Renaissance architecture.

The Musée de la Poste et Communications in rue St.

William the Conqueror's tomb still rests in Caen in the abbey-church which he built

Pierre follows the history of post, telegraph and telephone with horse-drawn mail coaches, early telephones and postage stamps.

Abbaye aux Hommes has the original St. Étienne church built for William the Conqueror. When the abbey was consecrated before William and his wife Matilda in 1077 it was in Romanesque style but by the time building ended in the 13th century the east end, spires and chancel were in Gothic. The spires were added to two lovely tall, slim 11th-century towers. William was buried in the church. A marble slab marks his tomb but the bones were scattered in the Revolution, when the abbey was closed. The cloisters are beautiful.

Matilda's Abbaye aux Dames was badly damaged in 1944, but the buildings have been admirably restored and are used as an administrative centre for Lower Normandy. The abbey-church of La Trinité is Romanesque apart from a 13th-century chapel in the transept. The huge nave with nine bays is pure Romanesque. Two towers lost their spires in the Hundred Years War and were replaced in the 18th century by balustrades that still don't look right. Matilda's tomb, a slab of black marble, is in the chancel.

Caen has many old churches. One of the prettiest is the original Vieux St. Étienne, at the opposite end of Abbaye aux Hommes from William's St. Étienne. All that is left is the choir, the lantern tower and some pointed arches in a single wall but it looks charming from the gardens alongside.

The new Memorial Museum of Peace and the Battle of Normandy is remarkable not only in its awesome modern blockhouse design and use of the most modern audio-visual techniques but also in its modern research and documentation section which the public can consult without charge. It opened in June 1988. It follows the story of war and peace in France from 1918 to the Second World War, through Nazi occupation of Western Europe to the Allied landings in 1944. Contemporary films taken by both sides show different points of view of the war. Sound effects are rather overpowering. Photographs, also from both sides, are revealing and some awake dormant feelings of 50 years ago. One which aroused old furies in Arthur, four years a POW and once in a *strafflager*, was of a self-satisfied-looking German Army officer in immaculate dress uniform, including leather gloves, testing the ropes around the necks of young members of the Resistance — boys and girls — who were about to be hanged from butchers' hooks. It will certainly remind later generations why we landed in Normandy.

Falaise, the Suisse Normande and Bagnoles-de-l'Orne

In August 1944, the small market town of **Falaise** set in a rocky ravine of the river Ante, known before mainly as the birthplace of William the Conqueror, hit the world's headlines. The Germans were making their last stand in Normandy, trying to hold the town while they regrouped a little to the south at Chambois. The British were driving south-east. The Americans were driving eastwards to the south of Argentan. The Free French were making for Argentan. The Canadians were coming down the road from Caen with Polish units. The battle for Falaise was fought street by street. Even the historic 13th-century Talbot tower of the castle where William was born became a German gun position and was shelled. The Canadians took Falaise on 17 August.

Falaise was almost a total ruin, but it has been neatly and spaciously rebuilt. It is prosperous and is a good touring centre for the Suisse Normande. It looks superb floodlit on a summer's night, the remains of its great castle standing guard high on a rock, the round Talbot tower, 35 metres high, fully restored.

This is the castle where Arlette the tanner's daughter came to Robert, the 17-year-old son and heir of the Duke of Normandy, and later gave birth to William the Bastard who became the Conqueror. The great keep with its soaring buttresses has six Romanesque arched windows at the top. William's son, Henry I of England, strengthened it and Henry II made it impregnable in its day. He and Queen Eleanor of Aquitaine set up court here and it was Eleanor's romantic idea in 1159 to send for troubadours from all over Europe to join a pageant called the Court of Love. Henry later imprisoned her for sleeping with a troubadour. Henry V strengthened the 13th-century tower, which has walls 4 metres thick, and named it after his General Talbot.

The inside is still interesting, with a fine chimney and original 12th-century windows in the Great Hall and a dungeon where Arthur, nephew of King John, and rightful heir to the English throne, was imprisoned by his uncle.

In St. Poix chapel is a memorial list of 315 of William's most important companions at the Battle of Hastings, so you can see if your English or Irish ancestors 'came over with the Conqueror'.

Northward from Falaise on the N158 Caen road are two old châteaux: 16th-century Aubigny, which has a church with statues of the lords of Aubigny in their contemporary clothes; and Assy (on the D91 right), a truly elegant 18th-century manor with a portico of Corinthian columns, reached by a fine avenue.

The D511 westward from Falaise leads into the most beautiful part of Normandy. From **Thury-Harcourt** right through the Suisse Normande to Domfront and Bagnoles-de-l'Orne is a countryside of woods, rivers, rocky ravines and lush valleys which are a delight to explorers in cars or on foot. Thury-Harcourt deserves to be a tourist centre, for every road leading from it is attractive and it is the gateway to the Suisse Normande, which is hardly like Switzerland but is beautiful and in places rocky and rugged.

Thury took the name 'Harcourt' around 1700 from the old Norman family whose castle lies in ruins by the Orne river, burned down in the 1944 fighting. Its park and gardens still run for 4km along the river, bordered by lovely trees and flowering shrubs. A charming 18th-century pavilion remains.

Take the D6 out of Thury, then quickly get onto the D212. This skirts the Boucle du Hom, a steep-banked loop of the river. From Le Hom the D212 northwards is attractive to within 12km of Caen. The D6 west past Mont d'Ancre is very attractive all the way to Aunay-sur-Odon.

For a lovely short circuit, follow the little D166 south on the left bank of the Orne, turn right to Culey-le-Patry and Campandré-Valcongrain, then right again to join the D6 back to Thury.

The D562 is delightful all the way to **Clécy**, the nicest place to stay for exploring the Suisse Normande. The little town itself sits on top of a hill, and has many old Norman houses. There is a superb model railway museum with tracks, scenery, stations and houses forming a replica of a route from here to Flanders.

On the way down to the river Orne is Manoir de Placy, a 16th-century manor house which is now a museum of old farming machinery, furniture and Bayeux porcelain. The river is lovely here. In summer it is lined on one bank with cafés and restaurants where you can sit at outside tables, and with a few seasonal tourist shops selling souvenirs, but not enough to spoil the river scene. There is a canoeing school, with shallow rapids and a little island to take shelter, and there is good fishing. The most pleasant spot is across the river bridge. Here is a beautiful old water mill, clad with roses and creeper; Moulin du Vey has been turned into one of our favourite peaceful hotels in France. You can sit on the terrace above a lawn running down to a balustrade on the river bank and drink an aperitif while in the restaurant behind you excellent dishes are being prepared. At night the sound of the river falling over the shallow rapids lulls you to sleep.

Moulin de Vey, by the Orne river at Clécy, is now a delightful hotel

63

All around are wonderful walks and drives among hills and woodland. One walk follows the long-distance footpath GR36 from Le Vey church to Le Pain de Sucre, from where you can see far over the Orne river. Another signposted Croix de la Faverie starts between the post office and the church (about an hour's round trip). There are fine views of the river passing under La Lande viaduct and the cliffs Roches des Parcs.

A lovely route from Clécy follows the D168 south-east past Croix de la Faverie to join the D23. Turn right through St. Christophe, which has a nice Logis with a rear terrace over the river, to Pont d'Ouilly. Cross over the D511 onto the D167 until you hit the D18. Go a few metres left along it then right onto a tiny road, which winds until crossing the river Orne and goes on to Roche d'Oëtre, a glorious beauty spot. This rock is in a magnificent setting, dominating the sinuous, wild Rouvre Gorges with a steep escarpment. You can see it from the belvedere of a café and nearby viewing table — the nearest scene to the mountains of Switzerland in the Suisse Normande.

Continue on the D301, then take the D21 left and the D239 right at Ménil-Hermei. The river itself goes through a series of gorges called Gorges de St. Aubert, which can be reached on foot. This is where Calvados ends and Orne begins. The hamlet of Rabodanges has a 17th-century château. Then comes the Rabodanges dam where the Orne becomes a reservoir lake stretching almost to Putanges-Pont-Écrepin, charming little twin towns connected by a modern bridge replacing the medieval bridge blown up in 1944. At the reservoir lake a few kilometres away you can bathe, windsurf, water-ski, picnic or eat and drink at the waterside restaurant. The Thursday market has been held for 400 years.

South-west of Clécy, the D962 forks left off the D562 to **Flers** in Orne. An industrial town which replaced iron works with cotton mills in the 1860s it now has electromechanical equipment factories and has little character. But it has a 16th-century château with towers reflected in the moat and pool and a pleasant shady park. A rather unusual building with a classical façade, it now contains the Town Hall and a museum. This has a mixture of subjects, including 17th–19th-century paintings, ceramics by Jean Cocteau, interesting works by the Norman painter and caricaturist Charles Léandre, and various souvenirs of Bocage history. Two small rooms are devoted to the local people deported to Germany as slave labour by the Nazis and to the British 11th Armoured Division which freed Flers on 16 August 1944.

The D962 continues to **Domfront**, which is spread along a crest of rock above the 70-metre gorge of the Varenne river — a spectacular site and also an obvious place for a fortress. The warlike and difficult Bellême family (the Montgomerys) built a castle here in 1011 but behaved so badly to the local people that they petitioned William the Conqueror's third son Henry Beauclerc for protection. So when he became King Henry I of England, Domfront became English. Henry II of England and his wife Eleanor of Aquitaine held court here with poets and troubadours.

In 1594 the Catholic armies of Catherine de Medicis besieged the castle, held by the Protestant Gabriel de Montgomery. He held the castle with only

150 men, but wounds, starvation and sickness forced him to surrender on condition that all lives were saved. Catherine promptly broke her promise and executed him.

Of this massive castle, high on a rock, there remain two huge sections of the keep and many of the rampart towers. Henri IV had it dismantled before any other bellicose baron could use it to cause trouble. Now it stands above orchards of apples and pears, its remains surrounded by flower gardens, with old half-timbered houses below in narrow streets leading to a beautiful little Romanesque church beside the river bank. In the museum at the town hall are more paintings and drawings by Léandre.

The D908 eastward goes through the narrow but most attractive Andaines Forest of oak, beech and silver pine. There are beautiful walks and drives on small forest roads. Bear right in the middle of the forest onto a beautiful road, the D335, and you come to Tessé-la-Madeleine, almost, though not quite, part of Bagnoles-de-l'Orne. One kilometre south on the D335 is Château de Couterne, a brick and granite building of the 16th and 18th centuries reflected in its lake.

Bagnoles has always been fashionable as a spa. Now it is more popular, but even heavy summer traffic does not spoil its elegance. The white casino reflected in its lake beside beautifully kept gardens, its racecourse alongside and its superbly groomed parks, which are given more space than the roads and buildings, give it a splendid look of the well-being and good breeding of slower, more settled days.

The spa is in a park just below the lake which is formed by the river Vée, a tributary of the Mayenne. It is used to treat circulation troubles and phlebitis, to prevent varicose veins and to reduce obesity. The story of its discovery is traditional in Europe. The knight Hugues de Tessé's favourite charger Rapide grew old and sick. Instead of killing him, the knight let him loose in the forest. He returned cured and frisky. The knight followed his hoof-prints and found the spring, which helped him as well. In medieval times, people would brave robbers and wolves to reach the springs.

There is a very good view of Bagnoles from Roc au Chien, a rocky spur reached by steps on the way to Tessé-la-Madeleine. The Town Hall here looks like a Renaissance château but it was built in 1850 for a rich lady.

Bagnoles is inevitably blessed with many hotels and restaurants. A particularly attractive hotel is in a manor house, Manoir du Lys, in Andaines forest on the way to Juvigny.

Ouistreham to Deauville, Honfleur and Inland

Merville-Franceville, on the opposite side of the Orne estuary from Ouistreham, was home to four German batteries during the Second World War. On D-Day the 13th Lancashire Battalion arrived by parachute, knocked them out and captured them. There is a little museum in one of the German bunkers to show you how it happened. And the swift action was

very fortunate for the delightful *belle-époque* seaside resort of **Cabourg** 6km eastwards which was the first coastal town in Calvados coming from Manche to get through the war unscathed. So it still has a delightful flavour of the Second Empire, of elegance and chic. True, some of its *fin-de-siècle* mansions along the promenade above its wide beach of golden sand look rather sadly neglected and have been divided into holiday flats, but the wide avenues still fan out from the hub of the town, the Grand Hotel and casino, linked by geometric semi-circular avenues, and many of these are still lined with attractive houses shaded by the trees of their old gardens. The very centre, Jardins du Casino, and shopping streets southward are very crowded in mid-summer now that the motorway from Paris and Rouen to Caen passes so near, but they were crowded when the writer Marcel Proust stayed in the Grand Hotel.

Though they call it the Pullman Grand these day only the name has changed. A superb, truly grand white building with blue-grey Norman roof, it has a main entrance opposite the bright flower gardens and another straight onto the promenade above the beach. To enter it is like going back in time, not only in atmosphere and décor but in its old-style service, its calm and comfort. There is a touch of Paris and Deauville in the fashionable clothes of many of the guests, too.

Cabourg's traditional trotting races are held on about 20 evenings from May–October.

The casino in the elegant spa of Bagnoles-le-l'Orne stands beside the lake

Dives-sur-Mer across the Dives river is double the size of Cabourg and semi-industrial, with a copper-alloy works. But it is still a working fishing port and has a new yachting marina.

Dives was the port where William's invasion fleet of 695 ships assembled in September 1066, to take aboard 12,000 knights and foot-soldiers. Followed by more than 2,000 other boats and ships it sailed to St. Valery-sur-Somme to pick up reinforcements, then to England.

The great timber roof of Dives's 15th–16th-century market still exists. The historic 16th-century Hostellerie de Guillaume le Conquérant has been partly rebuilt and turned into flats but still has a restaurant.

Painters and the Normandy Coast

The Normandy coast was first made popular by the British in the early 19th century. They came to bathe, and their seascape painters followed — Turner, John Cotman, the water colourist of the Norwich school, and especially Richard Parkes Bonington, who might have made a bigger impact had he not died at the age of 26. Bonington went to live in Calais, and he excelled in light effects and the use of sky in his landscapes. He loved the coasts of Normandy and northern France and passed on his enthusiasm and some of his techniques to his French friends Delacroix and Isabey, who become habitués of the coast. More French artists came, including Gustave Courbet, the exponent of Realism, who loved to paint landscapes and nudes, and had a great liking for Trouville. He introduced his American friend Whistler to the coast. Étretat's spectacular cliffs were painted by Courbet, Manet, the Swiss Felix Valloton and Matisse.

In 1844 the Honfleur-born landscape painter Eugène Boudin set up a bookshop and picture gallery in Le Havre, exhibiting his own paintings. Isabey saw them and they became friends. Boudin encouraged young Claude Monet to go to art school in Paris and virtually took over his art education.

It was Isabey who first took to drinking cider and eating in the Ferme St.-Siméon at Honfleur. He drew other artists there — Diaz, Daubigny, Courbet and Corot, whose clearly lit landscape paintings broke away from stereotypes and affected the work of younger artists. Monet found lodgings in the centre of Honfleur in 1864 and a group met often at the Ferme. Centred around Boudin, they included Monet, Courbet, Corot, Sisley, Pissarro and Cézanne. The Impressionist movement was born, seeking to produce a spontaneous impression of a scene or an object rather than a detailed, considered picture.

The name came from a painting by Monet. By 1866 he was so

destitute that he left Honfleur to take refuge in his parents' summer house at Ste. Adresse just outside Le Havre. In 1872 he painted a picture of the port of Le Havre which he called 'Impression Sunrise' (now in the Musée Marmottan in Paris). The artists got together to show their works in Paris in 1874 and the critics were not very impressed. 'The Impressionists' was a derogatory comment by a critic. They held eight exhibitions between 1874 and 1886, then the group dissolved. Monet stuck most strictly to the Impressionist tradition, keeping an intense belief in the changing effects of light, right up to his years at Giverny and his death in 1926. One of the lesser-known Impressionists, Daubigny, a member of the Barbizon school, had a great impact on the others through his devotion to the fleeting aspect of nature. He had a studio boat travelling the rivers of France. Raoul Dufy, born in Le Havre, later painted the social life of the Norman coast — race meetings, beach scenes and fashionable resorts such as Deauville and later the Riviera.

Dieppe became a fashionable centre for artists in the 1880s, when it was a snob resort. The studio of the local painter, important critic and writer of books on art, Jacques-Emile Blanche, who died in 1942, became the centre for many artists — Renoir, Monet, Whistler, the aging Pissarro, whose painting of Dieppe's St. Jacques Church is one of his greatest, and Degas, who introduced his English friend James Sickert.

The next resort on the Côte Fleurie, as the coast from Cabourg to Deauville is called, is Houlgate which has a splendid stretch of fine sands, sheltered by attractive wooded hills. The promenade continues to the foot of the cliffs, Falaise des Vaches Noires, at the east end of the resort, and from the top of these are wide panoramic views.

The beach at **Villers-sur-Mer** ex-tends from Falaise des Vaches Noires to Blonville-sur-Mer, about 5km, with a 2km promenade. Villers is little known outside France but is a very pleasant bathing resort with invigorating air and good sports facilities, backed by attractive woodland countryside. It has a casino, but is only 7km from Deauville, and French visitors use it as a cheaper base for enjoying Deauville's nightlife. It has six small hotels and several pensions.

Blonville-sur-Mer and Bénerville are really quieter extensions of Deauville sands. In Blonville's chapel are some modern frescoes of scenes from the Bible by Jean-Denis Maillart.

On the D513 to Deauville is one of Deauville's two famous racecourses, Clairefontaine, where racing is on the flat and over jumps. The other course called La Touques is in the south of the town just off the D513 where it becomes avenue de la République. **Deauville** existed originally for horse-racing and for its casino. Its season, which begins in July, ends with the Grand Prix race and the polo Gold Cup on the last Sunday in August. Until quite recent times nobody in France of any importance, pretensions or ambitions would have failed to be in Deauville in season nor would they have been seen dead in the place the rest of the year. Times have changed with modern transport and with other distractions. A lot of the important people or the very rich simply go for the day or one night for the Grand Prix, or for the international yearling sales in August.

During the season the magazine photographers take pictures of the 'best people' walking Les Planches, the wooden board promenade above the beach, or eating in Ciro's, the open-air promenade restaurant.

Deauville was converted from a fishing hamlet into a fashionable resort by the owner of Maxim's in Paris. He started a casino there, moving it across the river from the fishing village of Trouville because the Trouville people put up his rent.

Trouville is still a fishing village. Once it was for the servants of the rich staying at Deauville or the Paris middle classes. But it too has its Planches promenade and its Napoleon III Flamboyant casino. It is growing in popularity again as a holiday resort, and getting livelier, though it does not have the nightly balls, galas and regattas of Deauville in season. Like Deauville it has superb sands, a fine swimming pool and good sports facilities — plus the bustle and colour of the fishing harbour, and Norman-style fish market. The aquarium has sea and freshwater fish.

The Impressionist painters were fascinated by the light, sea, sky and sands of Trouville, Honfleur and Dieppe. In the Musée Montebello are works by Boudin, Jongkind, Dufy and Mozin.

The D513 becomes boulevard Aristide-Briand in Trouville. Bear left at the far end, turn left again and you reach La Corniche. At the cross of Bon Secours you can enjoy the superb view over the beaches of Trouville, Deauville and right along the Côte Fleurie.

At the end of the descent, turn back onto the D513 (boulevard Briand) and keep on towards Honfleur. This is La Corniche Normande, a lovely drive, but busy in midsummer. Nineteen kilometres long, it passes magnificent scenery and seascapes, with views through the orchards and other trees of the Seine estuary. Alas, you will also see the Seine's petroleum installations.

Inland from Pennedepie, between Trouville and Honfleur, is a very pleasant drive on the D62 and D279 for about 8km to the Forest of St. Gatien. It passes through Barneville, which has an 18th-century château in a lovely park. It also has a charming country inn with good cooking — Auberge de la Source, a good base for exploring Deauville, Trouville and Honfleur.

Return to Pennedepie to take the beautiful Côte de Grâce into **Honfleur**. From the Cross in Honfleur you can see the Le Havre roadstead and Tancarville Bridge. The little 17th-century chapel of Notre-Dame-de-Grâce, very attractive among its tall trees, has been a place of pilgrimage for seamen for centuries. It replaced an 11th-century sanctuary where seamen and explorers prayed before sailing to America on voyages of discovery or colonisation. On Whit

Ships have sailed from the harbour of Honfleur for 600 years, carrying explorers, corsairs, fishermen and yachtsmen

Sunday and Monday Honfleur holds a Seamen's Festival. On Sunday is the Blessing of the Sea. On Monday morning seamen and children carry models of ships to the sea and mass is said in front of de Grâce chapel because it is far too small to contain the crowds which assemble.

Honfleur is a most attractive little port, photogenic, full of atmosphere, but by no means a quiet hideout. Though yachtsmen dote on it and artists have painted it since before Impressionism was founded here, it remains a bustling, working port, very crowded in summer.

It rivalled Dieppe in the 16th–17th centuries, when it was home port to explorers and corsairs. In 1608 Samuel de Champlain sailed from here to found Quebec and his first 4,000 colonists were nearly all Normans and Percherons.

Louis XIV had the inner harbour (Vieux Bassin) built in 1668 to supply France's American colonies. It was only replaced as Honfleur's commercial dock 100 years ago. Now it is used by fishermen and yachtsmen and lures tourists and painters. The tall thin buildings around it mostly have bars, restaurants, antique shops, and art galleries on their lower floors.

The English occupied Honfleur during the Hundred Years War and when they left in 1468 it was poor and almost ruined. The people were so glad to see them go that they could not wait for stonemasons, most of whom were busy rebuilding much of France, to build a church as a thanks offering to God. So local shipwrights built a massive temporary church of oak from the Forest of Touques. You can see it in the cobbled market square, place Ste. Catherine, still in use, with its group of 17 angels still playing 17 different musical instruments on the panels of the organ gallery, and its separate weatherboard belfry still defying the salt blown in from the sea.

A local artist, Eugène Boudin, gathered together a group of artists to drink cider at a local farm, Ferme St.-Siméon. They founded the Impressionist movement. The farm is still there — a lovely 17th-century Norman building — only it is a Relais et Châteaux hotel now, superb but very, very expensive indeed. You can't just drop in for a glass of cider and a chat on modern art.

Honfleur's museum is named after Boudin. It has some of his paintings and pastels, and those of his friends, including Isabey, Monet, Huet and Jongkind, and a room devoted to Dufy and contemporary painters.

The spectacular 'Pont de Normandie', the bridge finished in 1995 joining the dock area of Le Havre to a road 4km east of Honfleur, is very useful to visitors using the Portsmouth–Le Havre ferry of P & O. As you cross it, look straight ahead to see the beauty of the bridge; the shore line at Le Havre is littered with huge oil tanks and factory chimneys. The route upriver across Tancarville bridge remains more attractive and generally more useful.

Pont l'Évêque, 12km inland from Deauville, has been a cheese centre since the 13th century, though the best is made at farms in the surrounding villages. From there, south of the A13, there is some charming countryside. The D579 is attractive, but the D48 which winds more or less parallel to it is even nicer. The river Touques runs between them. Attractive little roads criss-cross each other eastwards and south to Lisieux. Coquainvilliers on the D48 has a famous calvados distillery (Moulin de la Foulonnerie) where you can see cider being distilled into calvados, then taste it.

Lisieux, in an attractive setting in the Touques valley, is the commercial and industrial centre of the Pays d'Auge. Its tourism centres around the story of Ste. Thérèse de Lisieux. She was born in Alençon in 1873 of a very religious family, and moved to Lisieux

The enchanting fortified manor of St. Germain-de-Livet near Lisieux

when her mother died. Her sister became a nun in the local Carmelite convent, and she decided to follow. She was only 9 years old. At 14 she was refused entry into the convent so went on a pilgrimage to Rome and asked the Pope, who gave her permission to enter. At 15 she was a nun. She died of tuberculosis when she was 24 and might have been forgotten had she not left behind a life story (*The Story of a Soul*), which caused quite an impact. She was canonised in 1925, since when the cult has grown. Her body was removed from the cemetery to the Carmelite chapel where it is enshrined in a glass casket containing her effigy. The chapel was obviously too small to receive the increasing flow of pilgrims. So in 1929 a basilica dedicated to her was started on a hillside just outside the town. Building was halted by the Second World War, when Lisieux was heavily bombed by the Allies, but the building was finished in 1954. It is a huge, very high church in neo-Byzantine style and quite frankly seems far too ostentatious as a tribute to a simple, blameless little Christian girl. Mosaics and windows tell the story of her life. In the tourist season a little train will take you from here to the Carmelite chapel and to her home, Les Buissonets — a museum showing her toys and her communion robe. A *son et lumière* of her life is shown from early June to the end of September (9.30 pm). On the Sunday nearest to 15 July the Basilica of Ste. Thérèse is consecrated and on the last Sunday is the Festival of Ste. Thérèse, when her shrine is carried in procession. One wonders what the devout little nun would have made of it all.

The former cathedral, now the church of St. Pierre, is a gem. A beautiful Norman-Gothic building, it was consecrated in 1060 and finished in the 13th century. The lantern tower was built in the 15th century when the Flamboyant lady chapel was rebuilt. The 12th-century south doorway, flanked by huge buttresses, is called the Door of Paradise.

St. Germain de Livet château, 6km south of Lisieux, just off the D579, is an enchanting manor house of the 15th–16th centuries, reflected in a moat. Built in Renaissance style round a courtyard with an arcaded gallery, it is in a chequered pattern of green-varnished brick and sandstone, with a huge tower with pepperpot roof. But at one end is a timber-framed Norman house. Inside there are beautiful fireplaces and furniture, a 16th-century fresco of battle scenes and some unusual paintings.

The D579 continues to the cheese town of **Livarot**, where you can watch Livarot, Camembert and Pont l'Évêque cheeses being made and taste them in the little Conservatoire des Techniques Fromagères, 16 rue Lévesque (daily except Monday March–November) (see Chapter 3). Several producers around the town sell their cheese on the spot.

Orbec, south-east of Lisieux, is a little town of character in one of the pleasantest valleys in the Auge, 5km from the source of the Orbiquet river (down the attractive D130A southwards). Its Grande Rue has old wooden gabled houses with pleasant gardens and courtyards.

Argentan to Sées and Alençon

From the little cheese-marketing town of Vimoutiers on the borders of Calvados and Orne, the attractive little D26 road runs alongside the river Vie into Orne. It meets the D14 at Exmes, ancient capital of the whole Argentan region, now a hamlet of 341 people and an archaeological site. Fork right before you reach it onto the D305, cross the D14 and you are at Pin-au-Haras, one of the loveliest studs in the world, designed in 1715 by Jules Hardouin-Mansart, Louis XIV's architect, who designed much of Versailles, and Le Nôtre, who laid out Versailles' magnificent gardens. The setting of woodlands with lovely rides, and paddocks and meadows, is almost perfect.

The stud was set up by Louis XIV's minister, Colbert, as part of his master plan to make France strong again, and to improve the breed of French horses for war as much as peace. But the plan failed, Colbert died embittered, and the stud was closed during the Revolution. It reopened later in the 19th century. Now it breeds English thoroughbreds, Anglo-Arabs and French trotters for racing and show-jumping and the lovable Percherons (once the great French farm horses, now almost obsolete) for carriages and show. It runs a school, too, for grooms, smiths and any trade relating to horses and horse-racing except bookmaking. Guided visits take three-quarters of an hour, and the best time to go is between mid-July and mid-February when all the stallions are there. The very best time to see them is when they go out and return from their morning rides. On Thursday afternoons, from June–end of September, grooms in uniform bring out the horses to walk and trot in the courtyard. You can even pet the stallions. On the first and last Sundays of September and the second Sunday of October jumping, dressage and carriage-driving competitions are held. It is a superb scene.

The N26 southward is beautiful until Nonant-le-Pin. Westward it touches the Forest of Gouffern to **Argentan**, a small, peaceful but historic little town, mostly on the right bank of the Orne river. It was very badly damaged in the final battle for Normandy in 1944 and has been almost entirely rebuilt. So it has lost much of its old character. It still has the remains of a 14th-century castle built originally for Henry II of England by English workers. The 15th–17th-century St. Germain flamboyant church with a lantern tower has been restored — in fact, mostly rebuilt. So has St. Martin's church, which is Gothic-Renaisssance.

Argentan once vied with Alençon as a centre of lace-making. In 1874 by chance the original designs were found and now 'Point d'Argentan' lace can be seen 2km south at the Benedictine abbey where the nuns still make it. There is a display of old and new lace (afternoon visits except Sundays).

The superb nave of St. Pierre Cathedral, Lisieux, with strong pillars supporting wide arches

The N158 south from Argentan leads to St. Christophe-le-Jajolet where a curious pilgrimage takes place outside the 1899 chapel on the last Sunday in July and the first Sunday in October. St. Christopher is,

The delightful Château d'O seems to rise magically from its lake

of course, patron saint of travellers and therefore of motorists. So on these days motorists drive their cars past his statue near the church to be blessed. In the church you can see him blessing the occupants of a car and an aircraft.

Another 6km along the N158 at Mortrée a lane left leads to one of the most charming châteaux in France, Chateau d'O. It is a true 'fairy-tale' castle reached through a 15th-century gateway — a romantic vision of decorated turrets and steeply pitched roofs reflected in the waters of a lake-like moat where swans float by. You reach it by a narrow bridge, so it seems to be built on an island. Just strolling in the grounds is a joy.

The d'O family were powerful from medieval times and had a grim fortress here which was destroyed in the Hundred Years War. At the end of it, Jean d'O, with the lucrative job of Chamberlain to Charles VII, started to rebuild it. Charles Robert d'O continued the building but it was his grandson Robert, who is said to have lived in a lifestyle equal to the King's, who finished the superb château, which had progressed from Gothic to distinctly Renaissance, increasing its charm. But he overspent, and his family, his servants and some creditors stripped the château of its beautiful furniture and all his belongings as he lay dying with the doctors at his bedside. They did it thoroughly so that even the room where he died was bare.

The property was seized by his creditors, changed hands over the centuries, and lost all its lands, including superb forests. It has been magnificently restored and refurnished since 1973 by Mme Jacques de Lacretelle who uncovered many treasures, including the large drawing-room decoration of Apollo and the nine muses and imitation marblework. The long gallery is superb.

The D26 south from O takes you into Écouves Forest, 14,985 hectares of magnificent beech, oak, pine and spruce. Rising above the trees to 417 metres is a granite crest, Signal d'Écouves, highest point in western France with Mont des Avaloirs just outside Normandy. There are many pleasant walks and drives through the forest.

This is a superb area in which to stay a few days and explore. For instance, if you turn onto the N158 from Chateau d'O you reach the charming little town of **Sées**, where there are so many old buildings that motor cars seem to be an anachronism. You can see for miles the two spires of St. Latrium cathedral, 60 metres high. The cathedral was built between the 12th and the 14th centuries to replace an earlier one destroyed by Norse marauders. It was already subsiding in the 16th century and to prevent further trouble, the main porch was buttressed. It seems to have worked. St. Latrium is still there even if the main doorway looks somewhat crumbling. There are some fine 13th-century stained glass windows in the transept and a 14th-century statue of Notre-Dame-de-Sées facing the altar. Sées has an ancient bishopric and has many religious buildings grouped round the cathedral. The two most interesting are not open to the public. The old Abbey of St. Martin is a children's home, the old Bishop's Palace (*Ancien Évêché*) is a school. Notre-Dame-de-la-Place has a Renaissance organ loft.

The capital of Orne, **Alençon**, is an elegant, lively town. It was the seat for centuries of the powerful Dukes of Alençon, and their turreted fortress standing at the edge of a park in the town centre is now a prison.

Lace-making started in Henry IV's reign. Then in 1665, seeing the lords and ladies of Louis XIV's court spending a fortune on lace from Venice, Colbert brought in some Venetian lacemakers and set up a state-run school of lacemaking, École Dentellière, as part of his economy drive. Imports were banned. By the end of the century Point d'Alençon was established among the greatest lace of the world. The school still exists in rue Pont Neuf by the Sarthe river and in its museum, from the beginning of April until the end of September you can see how lace is made, as well as some beautiful examples of Alençon lace, old and modern, including a magnificent veil worn by Marie Antoinette. There is more fine lace in the Municipal Museum set up in the old Jesuit College to bring together all the exhibits from the 15th-century Maison d'Ozé and the Fine Arts Museum formerly housed in the elegantly curved 18th-century Hôtel de Ville. The new museum has many early religious works, and is strong in Dutch, Italian and French works from the 17th–19th centuries.

Opposite the Préfecture, which is a fine 17th-century former military headquarters, is a chapel dedicated to Ste. Thérèse de Lisieux (see page 73). It adjoins the house where she was born in 1873.

South-west are the Mancelles Alps, hardly alpine but attractive gorse-, and broom- and heather-covered granite hills above the winding Sarthe river. South-east is the very attractive Perseigne Forest

Lace has been made in Alençon and Argentan since the 17th century, but little is made now

The ancient buildings and streets of Alençon happily survived the fighting in 1944

which is in the Sarthe Département. But the D311 road from Alençon running through it crosses back over the twisting Orne boundary at Mamers, becomes the D955 and leads to Bellême and its forest, both well inside Orne. **Bellême** stands on the top of a 225-metre spur overlooking the forest and the beautiful Perche countryside. It is still slightly medieval with a formidable 13th-century city gate, La Porche, flanked by two towers. Rue Ville-Close, built over the ruins of the old citadel, is lined with classical 17th–18th-century houses. No. 24 (the old governor's house) and No. 26 (the elegant Hôtel de Bansard des Bois) are alongside a pond which was once part of the castle moat.

The Bellême Forest to the north is beautiful, its 2,400 hectares covered mostly by tall old oaks. The attractive D938 out of town passes the pleasant Herse lagoon. From La Perrière on the western edge of the forest there are panoramas of the countryside to the Écouves and Perseigne forests on fine days.

The D938 road from Bellême to **Mortagne-au-Perche** is attractive in stretches. The market town of Mortagne stands on a hill above a green valley with splendid views, especially from the Jardin Publique. It is the home of the Percheron horse and the countryside around is famous for horse-breeding. Once a fortified town, it is now a pleasant little place with lively shopping streets and a good Saturday market. All that remains of the fortifications is Porte St. Denis, a 15th-century arch topped by a two-storey 16th-century building. Alongside is Notre-Dame church, built between 1494 and 1535 with a massive façade tower and enlarged in the 19th century. Its Flamboyant and Renaissance styles do not quite blend. The woodwork on the choir stalls, pulpit and altar panels is superb. It came from the now-ruined Valdieu abbey in the forest. Mortagne is the capital of *Boudin*, the black pudding, and here the Brotherhood of Pudding Tasters holds its international championships (see Chapter 3).

The D8 eastward through the forest of Reno Valdieu is a beautiful road passing clumps of fine old oak and beech trees. The long-distance footpath GR22 goes through the forest and there are several forest roads. Northwards, 8km past Autheuil and across the N12 is Tourouvre, where the Perche Forest begins. It's a great forest for walkers, with old forest rides radiating from Carrefour de l'Étoile and pleasant pools. D8 is an attractive road all the way through Valdieu Forest to Longny-au-Perche, running alongside Longny Forest which is dotted with little lakes joined by streams.

North on the D918 through the Perche Forest an attractive road branches off left at Randonnai and after passing lakes and the river Avre, reaches the Abbaye de la Trappe, isolated in the forest. Founded in 1140, it was here that the severe Trappist reforms took place in the 17th century which led to the Cistercian rules of perpetual silence (except in prayer), abstinence from flesh, fish and wine, and hard manual labour. There is an audio-visual presentation of the monks' life.

The D918 continues to **L'Aigle** on the river Risle, a town with a tradition of iron and steel which now makes such steel items as needles, pins and staples. It has a big Tuesday market. Its church of St. Martin is a strange mixture of styles and centuries with a small 12th-century tower, an elaborate 15th-century Flamboyant square tower with statues, charming modern statues in niches by Belmondo and modern windows by Max Ingrand.

The 17th-century château, possibly designed by Jules Hardouin Mansart, was used for the Revolutionary tribunals. It is now the Town Hall. The château is very pleasant but converting much of the gardens into a big car park has not improved it. In an out-building is a small but unusual museum of June 1944, where you can see wax figures of wartime leaders, including Churchill, De Gaulle, Roosevelt and Stalin and hear their recorded voices — useful to film and TV directors and actors.

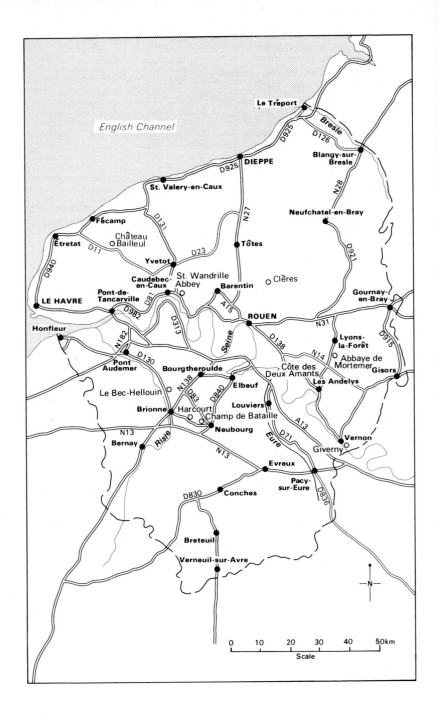

English Channel

Le Tréport

Bresle

D925

D126

DIEPPE

Blangy-sur-
Bresle

N28

St. Valery-en-Caux

D131

N27

Neufchatel-en-Bray

Fécamp

Château
Bailleul

Tôtes

Etretat

D11

D23

Yvetot

D921

D940

Clères

Caudebec-
en-Caux

St. Wandrille
Abbey

Barentin

Pont-de-
Tancarville

D81

Gournay-
en-Bray

LE HAVRE

A15

ROUEN

N31

D915

Honfleur

D982

D313

Seine

D138

Lyons-
la-Forêt

N182

N14

Abbaye de
Mortemer

Pont
Audemer

D130

Bourgtheroulde

Côte des
Deux Amants

Gisors

Les Andelys

Le Bec-Hellouin

N138

D83

D840

Elbeuf

Brionne

Harcourt

Louviers

Champ de Bataille

Neubourg

Eure

A13

Vernon

Bernay

Riste

N13

Giverny

N13

Evreux

D71

Pacy-
sur-Eure

D830

Conches

D836

Breteuil

N

Verneuil-sur-Avre

0   10   20   30   40   50km

Scale

6. Eure and Seine

Eure, Lisieux to Evreux

The boundaries of the Eure Département wind and twist eccentrically, especially to the west where it meets the Département of Orne. In the east it does follow the Eure river itself round the forest of Dreux, but at Bueil wanders over it eastward to cross the Seine at Vernon, takes in the Pays Vexin to Gisors and the Lyons Forest, then comes back over the Seine at Pont-de-l'Arche where the A13 motorway crosses. It cuts along the south bank of the Seine, missing the loops like Brotonne Regional Park and passes the Tancarville Bridge to reach the Seine estuary by the mouth of the Risle river, 6km from the Calvados border near Honfleur.

When you cross the Tancarville Bridge from north to south you are in Marais Vernier — drained marshlands. The drainage project was started by Henri IV, who brought in Dutchmen to build Digue des Hollandais (Dutchmen's Dike). Not until 1847 did local landowners complete the drainage to farm the land. Later the drainage system was abandoned until 1950. Since then miles of canals have been dug to drain the water into a lake, Grande Mare, which is now the centre of a reserve for wild flowers and for Camargue horses from the south of France and Scottish bulls. The village of Ste. Opportune-la-Mare has a little museum of apples and cider.

Pont-Audemer, down the N182, is a delightful former port on a network of little waterways which form the river Risle. Half-timbered and stone-faced houses with wrought iron balconies, which fortunately survived the 1944 shelling, overhang the water like a smaller Bruges. Especially superb is the Auberge du Vieux Puits, a gorgeous half-timbered 17th-century inn in a flower garden. Inside among old furniture, beams and engravings are served superb traditional dishes, many of them Norman. Huge fires burn on colder days. Flaubert called it 'Hotel de la Croix d'Or' in *Madame Bovary*.

Little bridges cross the waterways. But Pont-Audemer is no sleepy decaying old town. Once known for its tanneries, it now makes paper and electronic equipment. It has a most pleasant atmosphere. Its Monday and Friday markets stretch right down the main street and are very lively. St. Ouen's church, started in the 11th century, enlarged in the 16th, has fine Renaissance stained-glass windows and striking modern windows in reds and greens by Max Ingrand. Two alabaster relief panels, one of St. George, were brought from England in the 15th century.

The D130 which follows the river Risle goes to **Corneville-sur-Risle**, which became a national joke around 1900 because of a funny operetta by Robert Planquette, who also wrote the light opera of *Paul Jones*. The unfortunate Marquis de la Roche-Thulon had promised Corneville church a carillon of twelve bells, but when they arrived he could not pay for them. They were bought by the innkeeper, who put them in his inn instead of in the church. They are still there, are still played and the inn is called Les Cloches de Corneville.

Montfort-sur-Risle is pretty, with willows overhanging the river and the very pleasant rolling Montfort forest reaching its streets. But if you cross over the river on a small bridge after Corneville the little D39 route on the left bank is even more attractive. You must cross back at Pont Authou to the D130 to reach Bec-Hellouin, the abbey where Norman and English history were made (see Box).

Just upstream on the opposite bank a lovely little road, the D38 from Authou, goes through the Livet valley to Livet-sur-Authou, with a photogenic castle, church and park, and to Launay Château, which you cannot visit but which you can see through the main gate at the end of an avenue of beeches — a Regency building with beautiful wing-pavilions in formal gardens. Continue onto the D137 which reaches Cormeilles, a small town in charming country on the Calvados borders, with ruins of a 12th-century abbey.

Brionne, 6km south of Bec-Hellouin, was an important medieval strong point for commanding the Risle valley. It is built on a series of little islands as the river Risle divides into several streams. Now industrial and commercial, it is nevertheless very pleasant and a popular tourist centre for exploring the valley and attractive surrounding country. Of the old fortifications which William the Conqueror besieged, the early 12th-century Donjon remains — a typical square Norman keep. There is a museum, Maison de Normandie, in a typical old Norman house, showing Norman craftsmanship, with products for sale.

The D137 south-east from Brionne passes **Harcourt**, which has a castle which belonged to the great Harcourt family. It was built by a companion of Richard the Lionheart, Robert d'Harcourt, in the 12th century and strengthened in the 14th century. The family lost it in the Revolution. In 1828 the Académie d'Agriculture took it over. Louis Gervais Delamere, the forestry pioneer, planted a superb forested park with trees from many countries, many of which have now reached great heights. The curtain wall of the castle now only half surrounds it, but it still has its towers. Inside, the grand 17th-century staircase, old kitchen and Louis XIV furnished rooms are worth seeing.

Small roads left lead to another château, the huge beautiful 17th-century mansion Champ de Bataille, in a deer park behind sturdy ornate walls. It was built in pale stone and rose-coloured brick by the Harcourt family between 1680 and 1701, taken by the State during the Revolution and returned to the family after the Second World War in compensation for the

The 17th-century Auberge du Vieux Puits serves old Norman dishes

Bec-Hellouin Abbey

Bec-Hellouin Abbey was founded by a knight named Herluin who, in 1034 retired from fighting, changed his war-horse for a donkey, and set up a little cloister. Eight years later an Italian clerk named Lanfranc, who had been teaching in Avranches, joined him. The number of monks grew and the abbey was built.

When young Duke William was besieging the Duke of Burgundy in nearby Brionne (1047–50), Lanfranc befriended him and became his adviser. It was Lanfranc who persuaded the Pope to lift William's excommunication, and William made him Prior to his new abbey of St. Stephen's at Caen, built as a penance. After the conquest of England, William made Lanfranc Archbishop of Canterbury and virtual ruler of England while he was away fighting the French in Normandy.

Bec became the most respected seat of Christian learning in Europe. Its abbot was another Italian scholar, Anselm, who succeeded Lanfranc at Canterbury and is buried next to him in Canterbury Cathedral. It was he who started the struggle for power in England between Church and Crown which ended in the murder of Thomas à Becket. Becket's patron, Theobold, a Bec monk, became Archbishop of Canterbury in 1139.

Bec deteriorated until the 17th century, when it accepted the Maurist reform of zealous Benedictines who were trying to put discipline back into the order. Bec became famous again as a seat of learning. Closed in the Revolution, its buildings, even its church, were pillaged and destroyed. The monks did not return until 1948. Now the beautifully restored silver-grey tower of St. Nicolas, built originally in 1467, peers again over the trees and a new abbey has been built in the vaulted hall of the Maurist refectory. The new church is long and light and contains an 11th-century sarcophagus with the remains of Herluin. Gardens, lawns and a traditional fishpond are carefully tended by white-robed monks (closed Tuesdays).

At the entrance in the Abbatiale is a collection of cars from 1920 onwards, all in running order.

loss by wartime bombing of Château Thury. Two low, long identical wings (85 metres long), joined by balustrades, face each other across a huge courtyard. A magnificent gate opens onto the park.

The house is full of treasures and objets d'art, and the wood panelling is excellent. Equestrian events are held in the château grounds.

Just below Brionne the D130 meets the great N13 road, and 5km to the west, the N138 takes you to **Bernay**, a typical little Norman town on the Charentonne, a tributary of the Risle. It grew around an abbey founded by

William the Conqueror's grandmother, Judith de Bretagne, in 1013 and a century later was the 'capital' of wandering troubadours. Bernay's original abbey-church by the Town Hall is regarded as pure Romanesque. It was started in the 11th century by Guillaume de Volpiano. Shamefully neglected for centuries, the church has now been well restored.

Ste. Croix church (14th–15th centuries) has relics from the old Bec-Hellouin abbey, including tombstones of Bec abbots. The Notre-Dame-de-la-Couture basilica has a 16th-century statue of the Virgin which draws crowds of pilgrims on Whit Monday.

Take the pretty D33 down the river valley to Broglie in Pays d'Ouche. It's pronounced 'Bro-y'. The name came from princes of a Piedmont family who took it over in 1716 and changed its name from Chambrais to their own. They altered the medieval château, and the family still own it. They have taken a very active part in the life of France over the years, and the family includes an 18th-century general, two prime ministers, a writer and a Nobel Prize winner.

The D33 continues attractively down the river valley to the D819 where you can turn left to Glos, then take the D54 left to Rugles, a metal-working town on the edge of the Breteuil Forest. An attractive road, the D141, goes through the forest to the market town of Breteuil, delightfully enfolded by an arm of the river Iton, which almost surrounds it and forms a little lake bordered by public gardens. The inside of the church has a beautiful arcaded nave with pillars dating back to William the Conqueror's reign.

Southward is **Verneuil-sur-Avre** which grew from a fortified city built in the 12th century by Henry I of England as part of the Avre defences of Normandy against the French. A diverted arm of the Iton river still laps the old town walls. The massive blank 12th-century Grise tower of red brick survives from the castle. The church of Ste. Madeleine has an ornately magnificent Flamboyant tower which totally dwarfs the rest of the building. It is made up of three tiers capped by an octagonal lantern. The 24 statues which decorate it are splendid, the long windows of the 15th–16th centuries strangely delicate.

Notre-Dame, originally in red stone and Romanesque, has been much altered through centuries. It has a host of statues by local carvers, including a beautiful 13th-century Virgin by the pulpit. Many old houses have survived in the town, including wooden ones.

North from Breteuil it is worth taking the attractive little D23 through the forests of Breteuil and Conches. Turn right at the D830 to **Conches**, a delightful little town on a spur, almost surrounded by a small river, the Rouloir, protected from heavy traffic by a ring road and well worth visiting. Its narrow streets are rich in medieval timbered buildings. In the gardens is a stone wild boar. The forest is rich in game and so in autumn are the butchers' shops and restaurant tables.

Ste. Foy, an elegant Gothic 15th–16th-century building, stands on the site of an 11th-century church. A local warrior, Roger de Tosney, on his way back from fighting the Moors in Spain, returned to his home town (then called

Evreux Cathedral has been repaired or partly rebuilt several times since the 12th century

Douves) through Conques in south-west France to pray at the shrine of a child saint called Foy. He stole the child's remains, renamed his town Conches and built a shrine to house the saint's relics. They are now under the modern high altar of the rebuilt church, which has absolutely superb 16th-century stained glass and a fine modern tapestry.

The D140 north-west from Conches goes to the magnificent château of Beaumesnil. It was started in 1633 and took seven years to build. You can walk round the park (except in August) to see its beautifully ornamented baroque façade reflected in the water of the broad moat. The gardens were laid out by Le Nôtre.

The little D25 runs north-east through the Beaumont Forest to Beaumont-le-Roger, and the D31 east takes you to the cathedral town of **Evreux** on the river Iton, surrounded by rich fertile plains — the administrative capital of Eure Département and the main agricultural market for the region. Obviously accustomed through the ages to rebuilding, the people of Evreux made a very good job of restoring their town after the Second World War, planning attractive settings for historic treasures, such as the last of the ancient ramparts, the old Bishopric, the great cathedral and the 15th-century belltower. At the foot of the Gallo-Roman ramparts are gardens and a walk. The river Iton, almost a refuse dump by 1945, has been cleared, channelled between walls of old stone and walks made along it. The shopping area is pleasant, there are wide modern avenues and around the Bishopric little bridges crossing streams of the Iton river.

The restored cathedral is quite remarkable. Partial destruction through the centuries has left a superb mixture of styles from the 12th to the 17th centuries. All that is left of the original church are the arches in the nave. The Renaissance façade is spectacular. The interior is high and cool with wonderful stained glass which was hidden away for safe keeping in the Second World War. The great rose window of paradise in the south transept is beautiful and the 15th-century windows in the lady chapel showing historical scenes are interesting. Wood carvings and ironworks are all worth seeing.

A lovely view from the river Iton of the cathedral at Evreux, a blend of styles

A path from the cathedral banked by lawns leads to the 15th-century partly fortified former Bishop's Palace. The museum inside is devoted mostly to Gallo-Roman times. The 15th-century belltower is truly elegant. Its tall slender stonework capped by a spire, rising from a path beside the river, was once part of a city gate, and its tocsin bell still rings out the hours.

The former Benedictine abbey-church of St. Taurin, the first Bishop of Evreux, is 14th–15th-century and has a lovely Romanesque blind arcade and three fine 15th-century windows. Its real treasure is a chiselled and enamelled silver reliquary containing St. Taurin's bones, presented in the 13th century by Louis IX (St. Louis). It is a miniature model of a chapel, showing the saint himself with his crozier.

The N13 continues through Evreux eastward to the river Eure at **Pacy-sur-Eure**. Its St. Aubin church has some fine statues. The scenery around here is splendid along the D836 both ways and the smaller D71 northward. As the Seine is only 12km to the east, it makes a good base for exploring.

South from Pacy the D836 passes attractive scenery almost all the way to Ivry-la-Bataille, named after the battle in 1590 when Henri IV defeated the Catholic League troops under the Duke of Mayenne. The half-timbered house where Henri stayed is still there and 7km north-west is an obelisk memorial to him put up on the orders of Napoleon in 1804.

From Pacy to Louviers take the D836 to Chambray. Cross the river onto the D71, which is attractive nearly all the way. **Louviers** is being overrun by big roads, by industry and traffic. The A13 motorway almost passes through

---

A Hazardous Place to Live

Through history, living in Evreux has been hazardous. It has been constantly fought over, destroyed and rebuilt. The Romans built it first, then the Gauls enlarged it, and it prospered until the Vandals sacked it in the 5th century. In the 9th century the Norsemen destroyed the fortified town.

The count of Evreux joined the French against the Normans and William the Conqueror's son Henry I of England destroyed it in 1119. Then in 1193 King John of England betrayed his ally King Philippe-Auguste of France and Philippe burned Evreux down in reprisal. In 1356 Jean the Good, King of France, besieged the forces of the rival house of Navarre and set fire to the town again. Then in 1379 the Emperor Charles V, fighting the French, besieged it and starved the people. It was damaged again and again by Normans, English and French. Its own Huguenots took it in 1590. In 1940 the Germans bombed it so heavily that its centre burned for a week. In June 1944 the Germans held out for a while here and the Allies bombed and wiped out the railway and area around the station.

The rebuilding has been intelligent and pleasing.

it and the new road system is horrendous in places. But it has several arms of the Eure passing through, and it is skirted by the pleasant Louviers forest. It retains some well-preserved half-timbered houses and a splendid Flamboyant church. The south porch has some superbly intricate stonework, and the 16th- century stained glass in the nave blends unusually well with bright modern glass. There are many artistic treasures in the church. The remains of the Franciscan convent of 1646 are beside an arm of the Eure river.

A museum of stage and screen alongside the Town Hall is intended to become more international. Called the Musée des Décors de Théâtre, d'Opéra et de Cinéma it is devoted to the scenery designed by Georges Wakhevitch, who lived at Tosny near Louviers and died in 1984. He designed sets for some of the greatest plays, operas and films, ever produced (including sets for Peter Brook, Sir Laurence Olivier and Jean Cocteau). More than 150 models show sets, scenery, actors and costumes and there are many drawings for sets. There are audio-visual shows with musical background in English, French, German and Japanese. He created scenery for 300 plays, 140 films and 200 operas, so you might well recognise some of the scenes.

To see Louviers but sleep in peace, stay at Les Saisons chalet hotel in the little village of Vironvay to the east. The food is good.

Le Havre to Rouen

Le Havre was built in 1517 on the orders of François I, because Harfleur had silted up, and its development changed the story of the Seine and the history of France.

The town's prosperity was assured when it became the main port for supplying England's rebellious colonists in America in the War of Independence. Last century it became not only the main commercial port for America, but important as a passenger port. One of the earliest transatlantic steamers, the *Washington*, sailed from 1864 between Le Havre and New York.

Although such a busy commercial and naval centre, Le Havre was, until the Second World War, a town of old houses, little streets and blind alleys dating back to its original chessboard plan. It was interesting and quaint, with delightful bistros.

During the war it suffered 146 air raids. Nearly 5,000 of its citizens were killed, nearly 10,000 houses destroyed totally and another 10,000 badly damaged. Even after the Battle of Normandy was won and Paris liberated, the Germans still held Le Havre. The siege began on 2 September 1944. From 5–13 September Allied air raids were almost ceaseless. Before they gave up on 13 September the Germans blew up all the port installations which had survived. It was Europe's most damaged port. Even by the standards of other terribly bombed cities such as Hamburg and Coventry, Le Havre was flattened. It was a chilling sight. Though the British and Americans helped to clear up the mess, it took two years. Rebuilding began in 1946.

Le Havre has become a monument in concrete, planned by Auguste Perret, who believed that 'concrete is beautiful'. It is now the second-biggest port in France after Marseilles. The new town was planned right through from the posh cliffside suburb of Ste. Adresse to the historic port of Harfleur which is now just part of Le Havre's industrial zone. Some call it a remarkable example of successful town planning. Others find it cold and soulless. It was built in the fifties, when vast 'living units' were in fashion. These are broken up by tall tower blocks. The same principle was applied to public buildings. The huge square, place de l'Hôtel-de-Ville, is dominated by Perret's Town Hall, all of 108 metres long with a 72-metre high, 17-storey plain concrete tower. The gardens below humanise it a little.

Perret himself also designed the huge church of St. Joseph, with a bare tower 109 metres tall, like a massive rocket. It is topped by an octagonal bell-tower and simply does not look French. One could see it in Stalinist Moscow or 1930s New York. The stained glass completely transforms the church from inside — 12,000 pieces of glass set into concrete-framed panes, with gold the predominant colour, produce a glowing light in daytime. The high lantern is supported by four great square pillars, like towers. It is warmly awesome.

Henri Colbosc's church of 1964 behind the Town Hall is very different, with an interesting belltower. Quite different and very much lower is the new cultural centre in place Gambetta, by the Brazilian architect Oscar Niemeyer. Under flattened bowl-shaped roofs are a concert hall, theatre and conference centre.

On the seafront by the outer harbour is the Musée des Beaux Arts, built of glass, aluminium and steel with a roof of glass with aluminium slats. It is cleverly designed to filter daylight or artificial light into different galleries on various levels which are reached by gangways. It is functional and performs

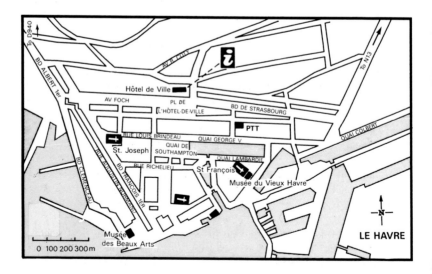

its function very well. Its extensive collection of paintings extends from the 16th century to the present. Inevitably, it is strongest in Impressionist works with a fine collection of drawings, paintings and gouaches by the Honfleur artist who lived and sold his work in Le Havre, Eugène Boudin. There are 300 of his works. Four paintings by Monet include the splendid 'Towers of Westminster' and 'Falaise à Varengeville'.

Seventy works by Raoul Dufy, born here in 1877, are from his wife's collection. Other notable paintings are by Courbet, Renoir, and Pissarro.

The Musée du Vieux Havre is in a 17th-century timber-framed house which miraculously escaped war damage. It is alongside Bassin de la Barre and deals with Le Havre's history. The models of boats are interesting.

Avenue Foch, which runs from place Hôtel-de-Ville to the sea at Porte Océane has shady trees, statues and shops as pricey and as good as in Paris. The most delicately attractive modern architectural work is the 'Pont de Normandie', the 1995 bridge, 856 metres long, from Le Havre docks to near Harfleur, built to resist winds up to 300km an hour.

Poor Harfleur has not quite been swallowed by industrial France. It still has its famous St. Martin's church with an 83-metre steeple — a landmark since the 15th century. Henry V landed here in 1415 in the campaign which reached its climax with victory at Agincourt.

Ste. Adresse was once a separate town and still has its mansions surrounded by gardens up the steep slopes of Cap de la Hève. From the grassy terrace of its ancient fort you can see over Le Havre across the Seine estuary to Honfleur. Ste. Adresse is the holiday resort area and has some very good restaurants serving fine fresh fish — Beau Séjour, Nice-Havrais and Yves Page.

We shall take the right bank of the Seine to Rouen and return on the left bank. You pass under the end of the Tancarville Bridge to the little industrial town of **Lillebonne**, once a Roman port and military base called Juliobona. At the castle William the Conqueror talked the barons of Normandy into going with him to invade England. The castle was rebuilt in the 12th–13th centuries, but there isn't much left except a round tower which you can climb. You can see the layout of a 2nd-century Roman amphitheatre which could hold 10,000 people. Down by the river are Port-Jérôme's oil refineries. Take the D81 to the Seine at Norville and follow it along the river to Villequier and Caudebec-en-Caux, a very pleasant road. Château Etelan at Norville is a Gothic-Flamboyant house which was once a fort. It is used now for concerts and exhibitions. Its chapel has 16th-century murals and wood carvings.

Villequier is in a lovely position at the foot of a wooded hill and it is a great pity that it is remembered for a tragedy. Early last century a family called Vacquerie, boat-builders from Le Havre, had a house there. The writer Victor Hugo used to love staying in the village. His daughter Léopoldine married young Charles Vacquerie in 1843. Six months later they were drowned in the river, caught by the Seine bore, the high tide which has now been tamed by engineering works. Hugo expressed his sorrow in one of his best poems, 'Contemplations'. You can see the tomb of the young couple next to Hugo's wife Adèle's grave beside the old church, a statue to Victor Hugo on the

Caudebec road, and a Victor Hugo museum in the old Vacquerie house. The church has a stained glass window of a naval battle.

Villequier is a charming place on a nice day, when you can walk along the quays or sit beside the river and eat in or outside one of the two simple inns.

Between Villequier and **Caudebec-en-Caux** are pleasant views of the Seine. Caudebec was a delightful, picturesque town of old houses and riverside promenades until 1940, when it was burned down by the Germans. It was pleasantly rebuilt, and still has a wonderful Flamboyant church which Henri IV described as 'the most beautiful chapel in my kingdom'. It has a pleasant atmosphere, too, and a lively Saturday market held in place du Marché since 1390. The Brotonne bridge over the Seine, completed in 1977, 1,280 metres long and suspended 50 metres over the water, has altered the river view considerably. But it has taken away much of the noisy, heavy commercial traffic which pounded along by the river night and day, and is beautiful in its own right. There are excellent river views from the terrace behind the Town Hall at the end of the quay.

Past the Town Hall is the Musée de la Marine de la Seine, a museum devoted entirely to the history of Seine navigation, with some interesting wooden boats. There are three very old houses, including a fine example of 13th-century architecture called Maison des Templiers, with a little museum of local history.

The church of Notre-Dame was built when the English occupied the town in the 15th century. A stained-glass window over the north door came from England, a gift of the last English garrison commander around 1440. Other glass is 16th century with an outstanding St. Peter beside the crucified Christ above the high altar. Large statues, which came mostly from the old abbey of Jumièges, have been well cleaned and returned to their original colours. The church is famed especially for its great organ with 2,300 pipes and splendid loft, built during the reign of François I.

Above the D982 in rue St. Clair is the spiky-towered 19th-century Manoir de Rétival, in a park overlooking the river. Beautifully furnished in antiques, it is now a peaceful hotel.

Along the D982 after you have gone under the Brotonne bridge, a little road left leads to St. Wandrille Abbey (see Box, p 96). There's another old abbey, Jumièges, within the next loop of the Seine. Take the D143 right off the D982. The abbey is partly in ruins but still beautiful, with the ruins of the abbey-church particularly impressive. The nave, rising to 27 metres, remains with twin towers of 43 metres.

The abbey was built in the 10th century by Duke William Longsword of Normandy on the ruins of one founded in the 7th century and destroyed by Norse raiders — the Duke's ancestors. The new one was Benedictine and was a centre of scholarship as well as providing almshouses. It was consecrated in 1067 in the presence of William the Conqueror. It suffered in the Hundred Years War and was down to 12 monks

The modern Brotonne bridge over the Seine rises 50 metres above the river

The Seine

Until recently the Seine was the most important route in France — highway to Paris, highway to the sea.

Even in the Bronze Age, around 2500BC, when rivers were often the only routes through dense forests, the traders gathered on the banks of the Seine. Their boats sailed to Cornwall to bring back tin from the mines. On the Seine it was alloyed with copper to make bronze. The Romans built the first great road beside the Seine all the way from Troyes to Harfleur, then the major port.

The Norsemen, experts at penetrating rivers under sail and oar, used the Seine each year to loot churches and monasteries, pillage and destroy towns and villages, and rape and massacre any people they did not take as slaves. For two centuries, from the 9th to the 11th, they arrived each spring, went back with their loot and their prisoners before winter. They were brilliant navigators, good horsemen and tough fighters. No local lords could stop them. The monks fled from their abbeys, and the peasants abandoned their lands and houses to find protection around the castles of the lords.

Then in 911 the Norsemen settled under Rollo and the former pirates built the well-run state of Normandy within a century. The Seine had again become the commercial route and remained so. Napoleon said that 'Le Havre, Rouen and Paris are a single town of which the Seine is the main street'. For centuries it was a barrier, too. There was no bridge across it between Le Havre and Rouen until the great Tancarville road bridge was built in 1959. Communication between the two banks was by little ferries (*bacs*). Tancarville Bridge had a great effect on France's economy, opening up a link between Le Havre and western France. It helped to take commercial loads off the Seine and put them on the new motorways. The opening of the great Brotonne suspension bridge in 1977 from Caudebec-en-Caux continued the process of road links taking over from river links.

Since 1848 the banks of the Seine have been stabilised and work has been done to allow large ships to go upriver. Before then sailing boats took four days to get to Rouen — if they had luck with the weather. Many sank, especially between Villequier and Quillebeuf. The cutting of the Tancarville Canal for 15½ miles in 1887 allowed river barges to reach Le Havre without going through the Seine estuary. The cutting of an estuary channel between dikes from the Risle estuary and Honfleur to control the silting of the estuary between 1948 and 1960, has allowed much bigger boats to go up the Seine to Rouen.

The Seine valley, especially just upstream from Le Havre and around Rouen, has developed industrially in recent times, from cotton mills and cement works to fertilisers and electronics. New power stations have been built recently. But the biggest boom has been in petrol refining and allied industries, to which the huge tanks by the estuary bear witness. Four great pipelines with a total length of 1,186km pump petrol, diesel and domestic heating oil to Paris.

Though in ruins since the French Revolution, the ghostly abbey of Jumièges is still impressive

when it was suppressed during the Revolution and its buildings sold for building stone. The lantern tower was blown up. The 17th-century Abbot's Lodge survived and was preserved by a new owner in 1853. It now belongs to the Historic Monuments department. Some of its treasures are preserved in the village church nearby, built in the 11th century and enlarged in the 16th.

A *bac* (car ferry) crosses the Seine from Port-Jumièges nearby. Follow the attractive D65 across the loop of the Seine to the river bank and alongside the river to Duclair. This is fruit country and in blossom time it is worth taking the smaller D25 which follows the whole southern part of the river loop. A 'Route des Fruits' is marked and stalls sell fruit in season.

At Duclair you can sit on a bench or outside a bar and watch the boats go by on the river, though lorries making for the river ferry can spoil the peace. Duclair is one of two places where the famous Rouen ducklings are bred — a cross between wild and domestic ducks. The other place is Yvetot.

From Duclair you could cross the next river loop direct to Rouen, but it is a lot more fun to follow the little roads between the river and the forest of Roumare, a pleasant forest of oaks, beeches and hornbeams, with footpaths and drives.

The D982 from Duclair is very pleasant to St. Martin-de-Boscherville, where the abbey-church of St. George, founded in 1080 by William the Conqueror's tutor, was saved in the Revolution by becoming the parish church. You can hire horses to ride in the forest at Le Génetey, 1km to the south.

Sahurs, on the bottom of the loop, has a 16th-century chapel belonging to a manor house. From Sahurs you can see the ruins of Robert le Diable's castle on a cliff, with the charming village of La Bouille below it. There is a car ferry across.

St. Wandrille Abbey

The abbey of St. Wandrille was founded in AD 649 by Count Wandrille. At their wedding feast, he and his bride announced that their love was too beautiful to be sullied. He started a monastery and she went into a convent. He was such a fine figure of a man that he was called 'God's True Athlete'. His abbey, called La Fontenelle, became famous and produced so many saints that it was called 'the Valley of the Saints'. This meant nothing to the marauding Norsemen, who destroyed the abbey, church and school. The Norman dukes rebuilt it and by the 13th century it had a great Gothic church. It became wealthy and flourished until the Revolution, when the monks were thrown out and the buildings left to decay.

In the middle of the 19th century, the English Marquis of Stacpool bought it and turned it into a house. He helped to preserve the 14th-century cloisters and the delightful Flamboyant lavabo with a laughing jester warning against drunkenness.

In 1894 the Benedictines returned but were expelled from France under the anti-clerical laws of 1901. Then Maurice Maeterlinck, the Belgian author of *Life of the Bee* and a playwright, lived there. In 1931 the monks returned. They restored the Norman refectory, cloisters and 17th-century chapter house. In 1966 they acquired a 15th-century tithe barn, 48 metres long, and moved it 50km, stone by stone and timber by timber, re-erected it and made it into a church. A fine new organ provides accompaniment to the Gregorian Chant, which can be heard at mass each morning and afternoon vespers.

Just before you reach the road into Rouen, beside a papermill at Croisset, is the riverside Pavillon Flaubert where the novelist wrote many of his works and died suddenly in 1880.

Rouen's industry is mostly on the left bank of the Seine and continues on the riverside for many kilometres as far as Moulineaux, where the charming church is from the 13th century with 13th-century windows. Over the motorway is the beech forest of Londe. Here on a wooded cliff are the remains of the castle of Robert le Diable (the Devil), father of William the Conqueror. He was also known as Robert the Magnificent! The château was destroyed in 1204 by King John of England, rebuilt by Philippe-Auguste of France, then knocked down by the people of Rouen themselves in the 15th century to stop the English taking it. There is a superb view over the Seine from the towers. In the old dungeon is a waxwork museum of the Norsemen who marauded this far up-river, and in the courtyard a full-scale model of a Viking boat.

At La Bouille you have left Rouen and its suburbs. The people of Rouen used to say, 'He who has not seen La Bouille has not seen anything'. Monet, the painter, loved it. And it is still charming. Under a steep wooded hill, it has a pretty little square, old church, picturesque old waterfront, little old shops and several good restaurants.

La Bouille could still be living in Monet's days but for the summer tourists and the big modern Seine barges which sometimes stop to shop for bread and wine. The drive along the D93 and D64 roads between the Seine and the forest of Mauny is very pleasant and leads to the ferry to Duclair, but if you are keeping to the left bank you then have to come back 11km to Yville-sur-Seine, so it might be better to take the D93 then the shorter, equally pleasant D265 across the loop.

In the next loop of the Seine is the lovely Brotonne Forest. All the roads through it pass through beautiful scenery, from the big D313/913, which joins the A13 motorway to the Brotonne Bridge, to the little D40 running through the middle. Forest roads, walks and drives among thick glades of beeches, oaks and pines are so seductive that you feel like forgetting your journey and just strolling and resting among them for days. There are a few hamlets. **La Haye-de-Routot** at the south end has a population of under 200 people but pulls crowds of tourists in season, especially on the night of 16–17 July when a tower of wood 15 metres tall capped by a cross is lit and people pluck flaming brands from it. The ceremony is a tribute to the patron saint of the village, St. Clair, to ask his protection for their houses against fire. You can see

The Seine-side village of La Bouille, loved by Monet, still lures artists

bread cooked in the centuries-old way in wood ovens in La Haye and sabots made by hand. But its pride is two yew trees, hundreds of years old, 16 and 14 metres round. One contains a chapel, the other an oratory.

At La Mailleraye-sur-Seine is a 16th-century church and a castle chapel of 1589 with Renaissance stalls and statues.

Vatteville, on the D65, has a 17th-century mill and fine old glass in its church. Vatteville was a port in the 16th century. The road from Vatteville round the west side of the loop soon becomes very attractive. It is fruit country and Vieux-Port is a lovely hamlet on the river with thatched cottages among orchards.

Rouen to Vernon

Rouen is a bewildering place these days — a big inland port, a huge industrial city, very modern with ugly concrete flyovers and junctions, and road systems which fool any visitor. But on the right bank is the beautiful, historic old town, much rebuilt after terrible damage in 1939–45, and one of the great treasures of France.

We are, perhaps, lucky to have any of the old Rouen left. It is so important as a port, the fifth biggest in France, that some people suggested that a

completely new city should be planned, just leaving a few of the old buildings which were not too badly damaged.

The plan agreed was to restore the old city as far as possible, to move the left-bank factories to the outskirts and build a modern residential area near the river. The residential area is mostly unattractive, however, and the factories should have been moved further out.

The old city is a joy, but you must explore it on foot. Parts are for pedestrians only, others are a maze of narrow streets. Start at the place du Vieux-Marché, where St. Joan was burned in 1431. It is surrounded by beautiful 16th–18th-century houses, many of them timber-framed. But not all is old. There is a 20-metre high concrete cross on the spot where Joan of Arc was burned, called La Croix de Réhabilitation. The new church of Ste. Jeanne-d'Arc by Louis

The Pavillon du Gros Horloge in Rouen has a carved arch across the street. On each side is a huge clock with a single arm

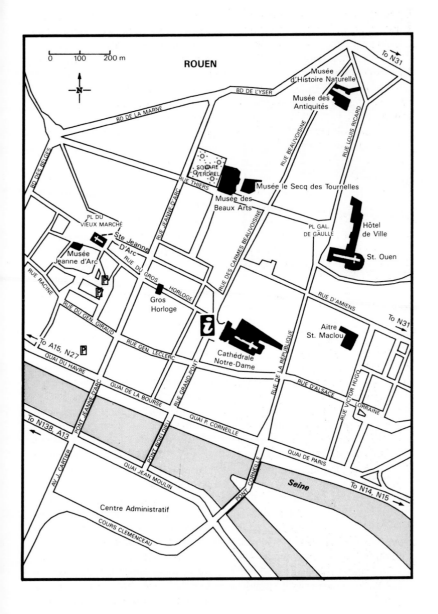

Rouen Cathedral is a Gothic master-piece. The charming Flamboyant staircase inside was built in 1480

Arretche, finished in 1979, may look slightly out of place here but is a fine daring piece of modern design. Its grey slate and bright copper deliberately symbolise the ash and flames of her death. The lovely 16th-century stained-glass windows from the bombed church of St. Vincent have been brilliantly integrated into the modern building.

Rue du Gros-Horloge, the busy shopping street of half-timbered old buildings east from the square, contains one of Rouen's two greatest treasures and leads to the other.

The wonderful Renaissance clock with golden faces on each side which spans the street on a bridge is a masterpiece. The clock is single-handed and gives the phases of the moon as well as the hour. The arch is decorated with sculptures of the Good Shepherd and his flock. A 14th-century belfry stands next to it, still ringing its bell nightly at 9 p.m. as if the medieval curfew had never been lifted. You can climb the spiral staircase for a fascinating vista of the city, port and countryside beyond.

At the end of the street is the other treasure, the beautiful Notre-Dame Cathedral, begun in the 12th century, reconstructed in the 13th century after a fire with financial aid from King John of England, and restored over the last 30 years after terrible war damage in 1940 and 1944, which left it in danger of complete collapse. It has been reinforced with stainless steel.

It is a true masterpiece of French Gothic — vast, airy, 137 metres long and oriented towards Jerusalem and the rising sun. Its façades are a mass of pinnacles, statues and openwork, flanked by two very different towers, the 12th-century St. Romanus tower in early Gothic style and the ornate Tour de Beurre (Butter Tower) built from 1485 to 1506, paid for by dispensations sold to those who did not want to fast (go without butter) in Lent. The Tour de Beurre now has a carillon of 56 bells. The great cast-iron spire, which can be seen for miles, was not begun until 1825. The main finishing touches were put to the cathedral in the 15th and 16th centuries. Happily all the fine stained-glass windows except one were removed for safekeeping in 1939.

The sumptuous west face was the one painted several times by Monet in different lights. It is superbly

The old centre of Rouen has been superbly restored after damage in the Second World War

Joan of Arc

It was the Burgundians who captured Joan of Arc at Compiègne and a French Bishop of Beauvais, Cauchon, who persuaded them to sell her to the English for 10,000 gold ducats.

She was tried for heresy and sorcery. Bishop Pierre Cauchon promised her a fair trial. The first session opened on 21 February 1431, before an ecclesiastical court.

Joan's defence, against tricky legal and religious questioning, amazed lawyers and churchmen. But she had little chance, for the French as much as the English and Burgundians, wanted her dead. She had become an embarrassment, even to her beloved Dauphin, to whom she had given the courage to become King Charles VII, and more so to the Church and the military commanders.

She was found guilty, and on 24 May tied to a scaffold in St. Ouen's cemetery and given a chance to recant. In panic, she did so and was sentenced to prison for life. Cauchon told the angry English, 'We will get her yet.'

She had promised that she would no longer wear men's clothes, but her guards took away the women's clothes she had been given. To relieve herself she put on the men's clothes and went outside. She was judged to have broken her promise. She was burned at the stake in Rouen's old market place on 30 May.

For political reasons, Charles VII declared the trial irregular in 1456. It took the Catholic Church longer to admit its mistake. In 1904 she was declared 'Venerable', in 1908 'Blessed' and she was canonised in 1920, to be made the patron saint of France.

Her stubbornness in not listening to military advice was her downfall. But she had rallied Frenchmen when their morale had collapsed and the Dauphin and his advisers were skulking in the Loire and he was being called 'King of Bourges'. And she had ended English rule in France for ever.

carved and quite breathtaking. Two of its doors are 12th-century, its centre door from the 16th. Here too are priceless 13th-century stained-glass windows.

The interior is a blend of different styles. The early Gothic nave is simple. The lantern tower rising to 51 metres on groups of up to 27 columns is brave and bold. The 13th-century choir is beautiful but simple with high, pointed arches supported by pillars with huge round capitals. The altar is modern, of Aosta marble with an 18th-century Christ by Claude Clodion, a rococo sculptor. The two angels on either side came from the destroyed church of St. Vincent.

Perhaps the most moving part of the cathedral to most visitors is the chapel of St. Joan of Arc, with modern stained glass by Max Ingrand. And the most impressive are the ornate early Renaissance tombs in the lady chapel of the Cardinals of Amboise — Georges d'Amboise, Minister to Louis XII and Archbishop of Rouen, and his nephew. The ambulatory chapels have recumbent figures of Rollo, founder of Normandy, Richard the Lionheart (Richard I of England), Henry Plantagenet, second son of Henry II of England, and William Longsword, Duke of Normandy and son of Rollo. The Renaissance building facing the west door, once the Treasury, is now the Tourist Office.

Rouen has been called both 'the city of spires and belltowers' and 'the city of museums'. Both are true and you would need many days to explore its churches and museums.

St. Maclou church, 15th-century flamboyant Gothic, is behind the cathedral. It is much restored after bombing. The Maclou Cloister (Aître St. Maclou) was a medieval cemetery and has carvings of gravediggers' tools and a Danse Macabre. It is now the School of Fine Arts.

Another superb church which needed much restoration was the former abbey-church of St. Ouen, largest of the legion of Rouen churches, and one of the finest Gothic churches in France, though the main façade was replaced by a dull one in 1845. Its chancel and nave together are 134 metres long. The 14th-century glass is splendid, the choir grill is a masterpiece of art in iron.

The huge Fine Arts Museum (Musée des Beaux Arts) in place Verdrel has some superb paintings (including works by Gérard David, Rubens, Renoir and Velázquez). A room is given to the Rouen painter Théodore Géricault, a founder of Romanticism in art, known for his powerful, spontaneous brushwork. Inevitably there is one of Monet's many paintings of Rouen Cathedral, but more impressive is his 'Rue Montorgueil Decked Out With Flags' — a riotous display of colour. Very interesting are the portraits by Jacques-Emile Blanche (1861–1942), including those of Cocteau, Stravinsky and Mauriac.

Additional interesting sights and museums in Rouen are listed in the Practical Information section.

Rouen's industry and suburbs fill much of the loop of the Seine and stretch for several kilometres from the left bank. The Rouvray Forest to the south is right on Rouen's doorstep but a portion is a military camp and it has a car-racing circuit to the south, next to Roches d'Orival, a rock escarpment with excellent views over the river and countryside. The path to them is steep and can be difficult and slippery when wet. Curious rocks overhang the road from Oissel to Orival.

You can see the Seine shipping and Rouen itself from the belvedere at Bonsecours on the edge of the right-bank suburbs. Mostly the right bank is more attractive than the left, but except for little stretches the attractive route does not really begin until Côte des Deux Amants.

Take the N14 out of Rouen through Bonsecours and turn right on the D7 to Belbeuf, with an 18th-century castle in a pleasant park. Nearby are the bare St. Adrien Rocks with fine river views. The busy N15 leads to Les Authieux, where the Renaissance windows in the church are certainly

Overleaf: On the clifftop above Les Andelys on the Seine, Richard the Lionheart built a formidable castle

Loved and Unloved

Of its two great literary sons, Rouen is very proud of Pierre Corneille, the dramatist. It has only recently forgiven the novelist Gustave Flaubert for what he wrote about Rouen's bourgeois society.

If he had been able to get a law practice in Rouen, Corneille might not have written plays. His first play, *Mélite*, was first performed in Rouen in 1629, before Paris. *Le Cid* was the work which could have been his undoing. Richelieu had hired him as one of the 'five poets' to write to order, but he defied him and Richelieu tried to get *Le Cid* panned by Paris critics. Adverse criticism was swamped by public enthusiasm.

Corneille's family mansion, where he was born and where he came back to live from 1640 to 1662, is now a Corneille Museum, with much memorabilia, including his desk and library with first editions of his works. It is in rue de la Pie, off place du Vieux-Marché (open daily except Tuesday and Wednesday morning).

The school he attended, in the 17th-century Jesuit College, is now called Lycée Corneille. Flaubert was a pupil there, too. So were Guy de Maupassant (short story writer and novelist), Jean Corot (the landscape painter), and André Maurois (the novelist and biographer). The philosopher Alain taught there. Corneille's brother Thomas was a good dramatist, too.

Flaubert was born in Hôtel-Dieu in place de la Madeleine where his father was a surgeon. Though it is now called the Flaubert Museum, more of it is devoted to medicine than to the writer, with historic documents on medicine and instruments from his father's time (closed Sundays and Mondays).

Flaubert studied law in Paris but didn't like it. He became friendly with Victor Hugo and the poetess Louis Lolet, who was his mistress. His first great novel, *Madame Bovary*, became famous for the scandal it caused. It has long been regarded as one of the masterpieces of French literature. It is the story of a middle-class wife in Rouen who is desperately unhappily married and turns to vice. It was condemned as immoral and its author prosecuted (unsuccessfully). The uproar was caused not so much by its immorality as its scathing portrayal of Rouen's bourgeoisie.

Flaubert did most of his writing at Croisset in his mother's house. It is 9km west of Rouen by the D982 and the D51. One wing, now a museum, is all that is left (closed Thursday, Friday morning).

He was a friend of Maupassant's mother and encouraged Maupassant to take up writing professionally.

worth seeing. Take the D13 here to Ymare and turn right onto the pleasant D95 and D20 to avoid the riverside industry. At Pitres the D19 follows the river. This is a delightful area, with islands in the Seine and the attractive Côte des Deux Amants hill behind you. A little road leads to the top, from where there are magnificent views over the Seine valley. The hill is named after two lovers whose story was told by Marie de France in the 12th century. The story is that the King of Pitres didn't want to lose his daughter Caliste so he said that no man could marry her unless he could carry her at a run to the top of the hill. Her lover Raoul succeeded but dropped dead from exhaustion. Caliste died, too, and the lovers were buried where they fell.

The roads round the right bank (the D19, the D11 and the D313) are delightful all the way to Les Andelys and Vernon. **Les Andelys** is one of the most pleasant places on the Seine, not only for its great castle but also for its busy atmosphere. Grand Andely stands on a hill capped by the remains of Gaillard castle, one of the most renowned forts in France. Petit Andely is a hamlet on the Seine banks where the fishermen's harbour has been made into a marina.

The views from the castle ruins are absolutely magnificent, especially those along the Seine. You can reach it by driving up to its car park from where there is a good view, then climbing up a steepish path.

Richard the Lionheart, King of England and Duke of Normandy, built the castle in 1196 to bar the route to Rouen from the French forces of King Philippe-Auguste. It was completed in a year and you can see how strong it was from the 5-metre-thick walls of what remains of the keep. While Richard held it, the French did not dare to attack. But when he was succeeded by his weaker brother, King John, Philippe took it by a trick. A few Frenchmen got in through the latrines, let down the drawbridge and swarmed in. Rouen fell and France captured Normandy. The castle was demolished in 1603 by Henri IV in the Wars of Religion.

Two French queens were imprisoned here, accused of adultery — Blanche, wife of Charles IV, and Marguerite, wife of Louis X, who was strangled with her own hair because her husband wanted to remarry.

Grand Andely, lively and crowded in summer, was rebuilt after damage in 1940. The 13th–16th-century church of Notre-Dame has fine stained glass from the 16th century to modern times. Two pictures inside are by Quentin Varin, teacher of Nicolas Poussin who was born here in 1593. The Musée Nicolas Poussin in rue Ste. Clotilde contains a famous painting by him 'Coriolanus Moved by the Tears of his Mother'.

Petit Andely has a charming little square with a 12th-century Gothic church, St. Sauveur, and an 18th-century coaching inn, Chaîne d'Or, which looks out onto the old river tow-path, the river and an island with the derelict mansion of a millionaire. Walks along the Seine are pleasant. There is a Seine bridge at Les Andelys and 6km upstream at Courcelles there is a handsome suspension bridge.

The D313 runs between the Seine and the forests of Andelys and Vernon. You can get the best view of **Vernon**, which is over the river, from the bridge over the Seine. An ancient town founded by Rollo on the boundary of Normandy, it was rebuilt after the Second World War as a residential town with wide well-planned avenues and resort amenities to lure the people of Paris and Rouen for weekends. Alas it lost many old timbered houses, but a good one is left next to Notre-Dame church. The church was built in the 12th century but altered before the Renaissance. The 15th-century west front has a magnificent rose window with galleries on either side, and inside there are 17th-century tapestries.

There are attractive wooded isles in the Seine and just downstream of the modern bridge across the river at Vernonnet you can see the wooden piles of the old bridge. On the hillside above them are the remains of Château des Tourelles, a fortress built by Henry I of England in the 12th century to protect the bridge and stop an invasion by river into Normandy. On the opposite bank in Vernon itself is the much-restored keep (Tour des Archives) of a second fortress which Henry built.

Two kilometres along the D181 west of Vernon is Château de Bizy, an elegant manor in the style of an Italian palazza. Built in 1740, it was much altered in the 19th century, and has a very attractive courtyard and a lovely wooded park with waterfalls which was laid out in the 18th century by Garnier d'Isle. Inside, the rooms have lovely Regency woodwork and 18th-century tapestries, with Empire-style furniture and mementos of the three marshals of France who have owned it — Suchet, Masséna and Davout. There is a small collection of 19th-century carriages in the stables.

Five kilometres south-east over the river along the D5 is one of the most enjoyable and attractive sights in Normandy — the house and gardens of the painter Claude Monet at **Giverny**. Both have been beautifully restored. The garden has been replanted with the same types of flowers that were seen when he laid it out in 1883, including fascinating old roses. His beloved water gardens and lily ponds with a Japanese bridge are just as he painted them so often in every season and many different lights. It is a magical place. Try to stop in Vernon and arrive at Giverny before the main stream of visitors arrive and return when they have gone. Garden and house are open from the beginning of April to the end of October except Mondays (telephone for times of opening: 32.51.28.21). Monet lived here from 1883 until he died in 1926.

Downstream from Vernon over the Seine is **Gaillon**, where the Renaissance movement was launched in France by Cardinal Georges d'Amboise at the end of the 15th century. Returning from an expedition to Italy with Louis XII, he rebuilt Château de Gaillon in the Italian Renaissance style. He was Bishop of Rouen and it remained the Bishop's Palace. Alas, it was wrecked during the Revolution, used as a prison, then gradually torn down so that only a beautiful doorway flanked by two towers and a few ruins survive. Gaillon has some nice old wooden houses. The town is 2km from the bridge over the Seine to Courcelles on the road between Vernon and Les Andelys. A small road follows the left bank of the Seine to the bridge at Les Andelys.

The famous lily pond which Monet painted so often at his house in Giverny

Pont-de-l'Arche is by the river on the edge of the pine forest of Bord and gets its name from the first bridge built over the lower Seine before even Rouen had one. It is surprisingly pleasant considering how near it is to the industrial Seine. Nice walks and a little road cross the forest.

Le Havre, Dieppe, Le Tréport

Étretat, beloved by painters and writers, and very fashionable in the last century, is still a lively and elegant resort, popular with Parisians, some of whom have summer homes there. It is the first resort up the coast from Le Havre. Its spectacular setting between cliffs eroded into unusual shapes brought painters here when it was a fishing village more than 100 years ago. It was discovered by a writer and editor of *Figaro*, Alphonse Karr, in the 1830s. He publicised it in Paris and made it fashionable. Boudin, Monet, Courbet, Isabey, Delacroix, Degas and Matisse all came to paint the natural arches and needles cut in stone by the sea and the fashionable beach scene. One needle rock at sea stands 70 metres high. Writers liked Étretat, too, especially Flaubert, Gide, and Maupassant, who brought his family there.

You can reach Falaise d'Aval at the south end by climbing some steps from the promenade and walking along a path. The view is superb. At the north end a chapel with a slender spire, Notre-Dame-de-la-Garde, stands on another cliff, Falaise d'Amont. You can drive up or walk up the steps and path. There is a good view, but an even better one from the cliff-edge belvedere. Beside the church is a museum and monument to Nungesser and Coli, two French airmen lost in 1927 trying to fly the Atlantic.

Étretat wakes up in spring. The casino is open, thatched fishermen's huts sell fish on the beach, and the covered market is packed with people. The hotels reopen, and so do the glass-screened restaurants on the promenade. Cars arrive from Paris on Friday nights bringing families for the weekend. It is very much a living resort, recovered from its wartime role as a German fortress against invasion, though missing many lovely villas which the Germans knocked down in order to build concrete defences.

At Bénouville, the first coastal hamlet on the way to Fécamp, is an 18th-century château. A local story tells of the seigneur of the château during the Revolution who refused to run away. Hearing that local armed Republicans were coming to attack, he told his chef to prepare a superb meal and open a barrel of good cider. By the time the Revolutionaries had finished their feast, they were all friends.

Yport, a village resort protected by high white cliffs, has a big beach at low tide, and is good for rock-pool fishermen. Small fishing boats are winched up onto the sands, and in summer it is a watersports centre. In St. Martin's church are some unusual paintings of fifteen stations of the cross by a local painter Jef Friboulet. Maupassant stayed here and wrote *Une Vie*. Local people believe that the village was founded by Carthaginians.

At **Fécamp** along the attractive D211 or D940, Julius Caesar built his galleys for the invasion of England. Under William Longsword Fécamp was fortified and became the Norman capital. His son Duke Richard I, great-grandfather of William the Conqueror, built the abbey. Legend had it that an iron casket containing Christ's blood, taken from his wounds by Joseph of Arimathea, had been washed up here, hidden in the trunk of a fig tree. Fécamp became an important place of pilgrimage.

Cradled between two protective chalk cliffs, Fécamp has been a fishing port since the 6th century. Until 1970 a huge fleet of trawlers used to sail to Newfoundland to return with cod, which was smoked or dried in the town. Now only a handful of boats go out on one- to three-day trips, fishing off Cornwall or in the North Sea. Le Havre, Dieppe and Boulogne have taken the trade. But it is a pleasant town with a nice atmosphere.

The abbey had a great reputation for scholarship and was richly endowed. Nothing is left of the abbey itself — the last bits of it were incorporated into the Town Hall after the Revolution — but the 12th-century abbey-church of the Holy Trinity, one of the biggest in France, is there, with a Sanctuary of the Precious Blood behind the High Altar. Pilgrimages still take place on the Tuesday and Thursday after Trinity Sunday. The Renaissance façade does not quite go with the severe Norman Gothic interior. Most visitors come to Fécamp to see the Benedictine liqueur distillery (see Chapter 3, page 26).

The pretty D28 south-east of Fécamp winds inland to meet the D11. Turn left along the D11 and you reach Château Bailleul. It was built by Bertrand de Bailleul in the middle of the 16th century. It is rather an odd building. From the sides, the façades are fort-like and heavy, with almost no windows. The front has a Renaissance façade, elegant, balanced and beautiful. It is in a delightful park with lovely oaks, many statues, a 16th-century chapel and garden of aromatic plants. The furniture inside is excellent, with wonderful Renaissance pieces and Renaissance tapestry.

Once the Valmont valley road, the D150, from Fécamp was pretty, but heavy industrialisation has taken place, with factories and mineral mining. Valmont Abbey was built in 1169 by Nicolas d'Estouteville after a vow made in battle, when he had a narrow escape, and the Benedictine monks came from Hambye Abbey in Manche. It had to be rebuilt in the 14th century after a fire, and was much altered in the 17th century. Although a ruin, the abbey-church looks lovely in its grass setting and the Chapel of the Virgin, still intact, is a Renaissance gem. The nearby château of the Sires of Estouteville still has its original keep from the 11th century, flanked by a Louis XI wing and a Renaissance residence, the François I wing, where the owner lives. François used to be a guest here and great fêtes were held. Unfortunately in the Revolution an owner who wanted to prove how bourgeois he was to avoid trouble had a lot of the château knocked down, including the chapel, and altered the François wing.

The D79 coast road from Fécamp to Veulettes has good views or pretty country nearly all the way along. There are some little beaches.

There is a delightful drive inland through the Durdent valley to Yvetot. Take the D10 from Veulettes, then the D268, which is especially attractive, as far as its junction with the D131. This is typical Caux countryside, with farm-steads, many with old Norman half-timbered thatched houses and barns. They are protected by banks topped with trees, among big fields of wheat, flax and sugar beet, with copses and woods to break the monotony.

Cany-Barville is a pleasing little town among beech woods, with an 18th-century Mairie and market hall. At Barville, 2km to the south, is the beautiful Château de Cany, built in a delightful park on an island between two arms of the little Durdent river. An imposing 17th-century manor house, it has two square side towers with pointed roofs. The furnishings include family portraits, tapestries and lovely furniture.

Héricourt-en-Caux is a simple but charming little place, with picturesque river scenes, old watermills and an old French village atmosphere. One of the inns (Auberge de la Durdent) has the river running through its garden and a rivulet has been diverted so that through a glass panel in the dining-room floor you can see trout swimming. The little chapel of St. Riquier is 18th-century and on the edge of the village is the fountain of St. Mellon where until this century pilgrims brought sick children to bathe.

The D131 leads to the pleasant, busy little town of **Yvetot**. In 1940 the Germans took it, pillaged it and set it on fire with flame throwers. The town had to be completely rebuilt. Now it has one of the most interesting modern churches in Europe, St. Pierre. Designed by Yves Marchand, it is round, in concrete and glass, and it is the glass which makes it beautiful. A huge panel over the central doorway shows St. Peter standing against a huge fisherman's net which reaches to the top of the building. Rising from the side is a slender 45-metre belfry. Inside are the magnificent cylindrical walls of stained glass by Max Ingrand — possibly his greatest work. The colours are almost dazzling, and the changes of light through the day would surely have fascinated Monet. At the centre the Virgin and apostles can be seen round the crucified Christ. Other panels show French saints and religious leaders. Behind in the Virgin's Chapel are windows depicting episodes in her life.

At Allouville-Bellefosse, 8km south-west along the D34, is the oldest tree in France — an oak claimed to be 1,000 years old, certainly reported to be old already in the 13th century. In 1696 the local *curé* put two chapels in the hollow trunk, accessible by stairs and galleries. Its branches now have to be supported and an oak board roof protects it. Before the Revolution it had two massive neighbours — a beech and a pine but these were chopped down and burned. Some smart local man turned the oak's chapels into 'Temples of Reason' and they were spared.

Returning to the coast, the first little resort after Veulettes is **St. Valery-en-Caux**, between two high cliffs. Until 1940 it was a thriving port and fishing town, but it was wiped out in the war. The local people have rebuilt it with

The glass wall in dazzling colours, by Max Ingrand, in Yvetot's round church

great difficulty into a very pleasant resort, using the long harbour as a yachting centre. Fishing boats are actually increasing in number. It is one of the few resorts of this coast which does not fall asleep in winter. Even the casino opens all the year. It has a famous fish-shop started by Francis Beaufour, author of books about the sea and fishing boats. Facing the port is a beautiful Renaissance house called Maison Henri IV because he is supposed to have stayed there. The lofty modern chapel Notre-Dame-du-Bon-Port with a huge slate roof is highly original.

Veules-les-Roses, 8km along the coast, is another delightful little seaside resort hidden between high wooded cliffs. It became popular with theatrical people from Paris in 1830. La Veules river, which runs through the pretty little town alongside thatched half-timbered cottages, is only 1,100 metres long and said to be the smallest river in France. It has become a family resort, with a children's playground above the pebble beach and several restaurants offering cheaper meals.

The coast road leads to some pleasant village resorts. At Sotteville you must go down 250 stone steps to reach the beach. Quiberville, in a cove with a sand and gravel beach, is a little summer resort for families. Then it is lined with stalls selling shellfish, ice creams, hamburgers and souvenirs, with the fish often being sold direct from boats dragged up to the roadside.

Old grocers' shops have survived the supermarket invasion in little places like Veules-les-Roses

113

You climb up a cliff road with sea views to Ste. Marguerite-sur-Mer. There is a steep walk from the beach, but it is an attractive place with pine woods and rare plants. Its 12th-century Romanesque church with 16th-century Renaissance alterations has modern stained-glass windows by Max Ingrand, depicting the story of Ste. Marguerite herself.

Varengeville is only 3km away by a pretty road, or you can walk there past Ailly lighthouse and through Vastérival, where there is a beautiful gorge.

Varengeville is delightful and worth many hours for exploring. Gorges lead down to the sea and it is quite difficult to see its houses among the trees. The little church is near the cliff edge and had to be saved recently from collapsing into the sea. Though mostly 14th-century, it still has some original 12th-century features. There is a lovely modern window by Georges Braque, who worked with Picasso and had a great influence on other painters. He lived nearby and his grave is in the little churchyard with a tomb by his pupils in his style.

An avenue of beeches leads to a quite remarkable Renaissance manor house in the Florentine style with a beautiful dovecote. It was built for Jean Ango, the owner of a corsair fleet operating from Dieppe who became rich and powerful, then died destitute. Built in black and white stone around a quadrangle, it has raised arch galleries topped by a frieze with the monogram of François I, who often stayed there. Standing in the centre of the courtyard is the huge dovecote, like a round tower with an oriental dome. It housed 1,600 pairs of doves, which showed Ango's seigniorial importance for only lords were allowed dovecotes and the number of doves signified the size of their lands. Don't miss the floral park of Moutiers (open 15 March–15 November) and its Lutyens house (viewing by appointment, telephone 35.85.10.02).

Just south of St. Aubin-Gruche-sur-Scie and east of Offranville inland is Miromesnil, where the local guides say that Guy de Maupassant, the great writer, was born in 1850. Literary circles say that he was born in Fécamp but that his mother rushed him to Miromesnil to register his birth so that he should be born at a good address! There is a statue to him on the edge of the park. The chapel of the original château still stands. Windows range from 1583 to modern. Miromesnil is 16th-century and was once the house of the Marquis of Miromesnil, Minister to Louis XVI.

Henri IV had his headquarters in 1589 in the château at Arques, eastwards on the D54 and D56. It now lies in ruins at the foot of an impressive keep. The Flamboyant church, built in 1515, still stands.

At Martin-Église on the edge of the forest of Arques, the fine old 16th-century manor house is now a restaurant and hotel Manoir d'Archelles. The best way to see it is to stay — or at least eat, for the cooking is very good and much of it performed where you can see it.

On the coast before Dieppe is Pourville. It is now just a hamlet on a big beach which gets plenty of people in summer. It was virtually destroyed in 1942; on the clifftop is a museum with emphasis on the 1942 raid, with guns, tanks and armoured cars.

It was to **Dieppe** that the English first exported their passion for sea-

Jean Ango made a fortune in the 16th century running a corsair fleet attacking foreign ships. He hired Italian Renaissance craftsmen to build Manoir d'Ango at Varengeville, near Dieppe

bathing. The future Napoleon IIII's mother, Queen Hortense de Beauharnais of Holland, launched the sea-bathing fashion at Dieppe in 1813, and when the eccentric Duchess of Berry took up the fashion in 1824, Paris followed. Dieppe was called 'the doyenne of French beaches'. It is still a popular resort, especially for 'le Weekend'. But it is also essentially a Norman port, going about its own business, which ranges from fishing to making Alpine-Renault sports cars. It is this which makes it one of the most interesting places for British visitors. The shops, the bistros, the restaurants are aimed at the French more than the British tourists and are genuinely French.

British tourists are part of Dieppe's history, not a modern phenomenon. There was a regular boat service from Brighton in tthe 18th century and the Newhaven packet was running daily by the 1850s. Now the Newhaven–Dieppe Stena boats carry more than a million people each year, 80 per cent of them British.

A new Stena Sea Lynx Catamaran started in summer 1996 from Newhaven, taking about 2 hours compared with 4 hours for the boats. The ferry terminal, on quai Henri IV since our grandfathers' day and superbly convenient, just round the corner from the beach promenade and from Grand' Rue, the main shopping street, has been moved, alas, across the bridge from the town, with a circuitous route to the town centre for cars and a bus for foot passengers. Yachtsmen have stolen quai Henri IV. But it is still lined with small restaurants with very reasonable prices. Here they serve the 'catch of the day' — red mullet, sole, haddock, brill, shrimps, mussels,

Pirate Financier

Jean Ango's father, a ship builder and owner, tried to found colonies in the New World. Jean Junior, born in Dieppe in 1480, found a more lucrative trade for his ships. The Portuguese, English and Dutch called them pirate ships. In France they were corsairs, for Ango had letters of marque from King François I for his piracy. These gave him permission to seize Portuguese ships, which he did with enthusiasm — taking more than 300 in a few years. He did not hesitate to seize English merchantmen, too. His fleet varied between 20 and 30 ships and once blockaded Lisbon. The excuse was that the Portuguese were accused of seizing any ships seen off the coast of West Africa.

Ango became very rich from his loot and very powerful. He built himself a palace of wood in Dieppe and the beautiful Renaissance manor at Varengeville, for which he imported Italian builders and decorators. François made him his maritime counsellor and mayor of Dieppe. François was incredibly ostentatious and spent fortunes on fêtes and display, on women and on building castles. He was always broke. Ango lent him a lot of money and paid much of his ransom when he was captured by the Spanish. The king and queen stayed at his houses.

But Ango's sumptuous houses had made others jealous, including François' queen, and he fell from favour, lost his money and died in poverty at his manor in Varengeville in 1535. He was buried in a chapel which he had built in St. Jacques church in Dieppe.

langoustes, oysters and especially scallops (*coquilles St. Jacques*) in which Dieppe fishermen specialise. But the best fish restaurant is still Marmite Dieppoise in rue St. Jean. Dieppe is the fourth biggest fishing port in France. The fishermen live mostly across the bridge from the town in a traditional fishermen's village called Le Pollet — interesting and a good subject for photographers.

Quai Henri IV runs into Arcades de la Poissonerie where lines of restaurants have pavement terraces, crammed on fine days. Dieppe has a wonderful choice of low- and medium-priced restaurants.

Grand' Rue and its side roads have a superb choice of small, family-run shops, some with windows piled with fresh chickens, ducks, and cheeses. Next door you may find a posh boutique or a shop selling baby clothes.

The Saturday market is superb, spilling from Grand' Rue into rue St. Jacques and rue St. Jean, all packed with stalls offering farm fresh butter, pâté, cheeses, sausages of many shapes and sizes, mountains of local vegetables, barrows of fish,

Braque designed this window for the village church at Varengeville, where he was later buried

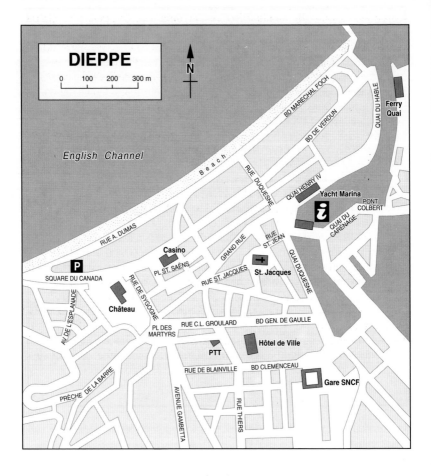

including great basket of oysters, mussels and scallops.

At the end of Grand' Rue is Café des Tribuneaux, still packed and chaotic as it was when Monet, Renoir, Gauguin, Pissarro, Whistler and many others used to sit there drinking and discussing art. Oscar Wilde, too, after he had finished his prison sentence, used to meet here his friend the Yellow Book artist, Aubrey Beardsley. Wilde lived at Berneval 10km east of Dieppe under the name of Melmoth and wrote *The Ballad of Reading Jail* there. Late last century there was a colony of 3,000 British expatriots. The Prince of Wales (later Edward VII) used to pop over to see his mistress the Duchess of Caracciola but the others ignored him!

Shelling by the Royal Navy altered the face of the long Promenade and its roads. A few of the *fin-de-siècle* hotels are left but the ornate old casino and its grand hotel, which were used as German headquarters, were knocked down. This is the casino where the beautiful Lady Blanche Hozier used to queue with sandwiches waiting for opening time. Her daughter Clementine became the wife of Winston Churchill. The new casino and the Présidence Hotel were built in the post-war 'box' era, but the hotel is very comfortable.

The Promenade has a large grass verge, and on the beach is a rebuilt swimming pool and beach restaurant. Parked cars along the promenade have rather spoiled the view in summer.

St. Jacques church is big enough to be a cathedral. Built in the 12th century but much 'restored', it has a 13th-century nave, a 15th-century tower, and 18th-century dome — a mixture of Flamboyant-Gothic and Renaissance styles. The line of Brazilian Indians on the frieze above the sacristy door commemorates Dieppe's explorers.

The castle survived the bombardments of 1694 and 1942. It really does dominate the town from its clifftop position at the end of the seafront. Built between 1435 and 1635 as defence against the English, it was the headquarters of Dieppe's governors.

The museum is known for its beautifully carved ivories — boxes, ships in bottles, and sculptures. Tusks were landed from Africa and India in the 16th–17th centuries and there were once 300 ivory carvers. Most of them fled to Holland or England when Protestantism was banned in France. The museum also has beautiful models of ships and maps and navigation equipment. They include a model of *La Dauphine* in which the Florentine chief navigator of François I sailed from Dieppe in 1524 and discovered the site of New York, which he called Angoulême Bay. There are also good pictures by Boudin, Renoir, Pissarro, Blanche, Dufy, Fantin-Latour, Courbet, and others.

From the 14th century, governors of Dieppe lived in the castle; now it houses a museum of ships and ivory

In square du Canada below the castle is a memorial to Dieppe's New World explorers of the 16th–18th centuries and a plaque to Canadians and Britons killed on the 1942 Raid.

Puys, 4km east of Dieppe, is now virtually a suburb, with the town's second beach, but it was a fashionable area discovered in 1868 by the writer George Sand.

Berneval-sur-Mer, 10km east of Dieppe, is a much-admired little seaside resort, a real village by the sea. In the Dieppe Raid the Canadian Commando which landed here was sadly decimated. More damage to the village happened in 1944 and it was almost rebuilt.

At Criel-sur-Mer turn left to Criel Plage and take the little coast road to Mesnil-Val, a pleasant old hamlet with a good clifftop sea view and a steep lane down to the beach. The hotel and restaurant in a 17th-century farmhouse, La Vieille Ferme, is delightful, with excellent cooking.

Le Tréport at the mouth of the Bresle river on the border of Normandy and Picardy, is a lovable old-fashioned resort and fishing port which fills with Parisians in summer and becomes very lively. Les Mers-les-Bains across the Bresle is technically in the Somme Département but is in fact the quieter half of Le Tréport.

Le Tréport's long wide shingle beach is backed by high cliffs with good views reached by a chairlift from the town. The action takes place round the harbour and quays where there are plenty of restaurants, shops and cafés, and a casino. They are very busy at summer weekends. Le Tréport became fashionable when Louis-Philippe was King (1830–48). His favourite palace was at Eu and as he stayed there quite a lot, fashionable Parisians followed. Queen Victoria, who liked him and his wife, used to stay with them at Eu and liked Le Tréport.

On the road to Eu, hidden away up a bank on the right-hand side but with a roadside sign, is an attractive hunting lodge of Louis-Philippe's son, the Prince of Joinville. It is now a peaceful hotel (Pavillon Joinville) in parkland with a restaurant in a building in which the Duke installed a model farm.

Eu can be quite sleepy in winter, very busy with traffic in summer. The castle, started by the notorious assassin Henri, Duke of Guise, in 1578 was not finished because he was murdered by Henry III for plotting to get the crown. Since then it has been altered and 'restored' often and is certainly not a masterpiece. But King Louis-Philippe loved it, and when he was forced to flee to exile in Surrey he left behind fine furniture, portraits, tapestries and glass which are still there. Viollet-le-Duc, who rebuilt Notre-Dame in Paris, redecorated it in the 1870s. Now it is the Town Hall.

The 12th–13th-century church of Eu is dedicated to an Irish saint, St. Laurent, Laurence O'Toole, Primate of Ireland, who died in Eu in 1181. His recumbent statue is in the crypt. The church is plastered with turrets and pinnacles, and the inside is huge. The church organ is historic, and was repaired in 1977.

Dieppe has been a destination for cross-Channel visitors since the 18th century

A little road from Eu passes south-east through the Eu forest with glades of huge beeches. It is criss-crossed by little roads with large patches of open country and a few hamlets. Though it is attractive it is not all forested.

The Seine to the Bresle

Gisors is on the eastern boundary of Normandy and was when the dukedom of Normandy started. The castle, whose ruins still dominate the town, has been there since the time of William Rufus, son of the Conqueror. He entrusted the design to Robert de Bellême, Earl of Shrewsbury.

The strong 11th-century keep which stands on a high artificial mound is now surrounded by the lawns and flowers of a public garden where the moat used to be. The surrounding wall with eight round and triangular towers was built by King Philippe Auguste at the end of the 12th century when King John of England lost the castle to him. The main entrance is guarded by the most massive of the towers, Tour du Prisonnier. Its name comes from unusual graffiti, carved by prisoners in a dark room which was once a cell. There are religious scenes, figures of saints, including St. George slaying the dragon, and names and dates from the 14th to the 16th centuries. One dated 1575 reads 'Mother of God remember me!'

Down in the town are medieval houses, a 17th-century wash-house on the river and the splendid church of St. Gervais et St. Protais, begun in the 12th century. Construction went on until the 16th century. In June 1940, it was so badly damaged that it was believed to be beyond repair. After a long process of devoted work it has been restored. As most of the building was done in the 15th–16th centuries, it combines Gothic and Renaissance. The delicately carved doorway flanked by a tower is in François I style with a cupola on top, and an unfinished tower is from Henry II's time.

The Normandy boundary almost follows the river Epte north to **Gournay-en-Bray**, but the attractive D915 criss-crosses it. Beauvais is to the east.

Bray makes most of the soft (crème) cheese produced in France, Gournay being the centre of the industry. A local farmer's wife learned in 1850 from a Swiss cowherd how to make a soft cheese by mixing fresh cream with curds. Petit-Suisse was born.

West from the D915 and the border the delightful Lyons beech forest begins. It has thinned somewhat past Bosquentin but thickens within a few kilometres and stretches to a total of 30km west covering 100 square kilometres. It is a real paradise for people who want to wander by car or on foot. There are so many small beautiful roads that you don't need a plan. Any road will do.

The trees reach incredible proportions and heights. Just off the N31 west of Gournay is Hêtre de la Bunodière, a beech 42 metres high. It gets a mention on the yellow Michelin map. Hêtre à Dieu (God's beech) between Menesqueville and Abbaye de Mortemer is 300 years old. So is Le Gros Chêne, an oak 3km south of Lyons-la-Forêt.

Beauvais Cathedral

Though it is in Oise, Beauvais is only 30km from Gournay-en-Bray and its cathedral of St. Pierre well repays a detour.

Somehow this magnificent Gothic building, the highest cathedral in France, survived the German bombing of 1940 which wiped out the rest of the town.

The strange thing is that it was never completed. Its choir is the highest in the world and absolutely magnificent. This part was begun in 1247 but it was too daring, with its height and its glass, and threatened to collapse in 1284. It was only saved by new support piers. The windows were made of slender panels of stained glass, much of which has survived.

In the 16th century, builders once again tried too hard. They built a tower with a 161-metre spire, which collapsed in 1573, destroying the tower and seriously damaging the transept and its Flamboyant façades. Beauvais was unable to afford the rebuilding *and* a new nave, so the nave was never built. The result was called by an irreverent modern architect 'the finest Gothic greenhouse'. In fact, it is light and attractive with superb stained glass from the 13th and 15th centuries and a modern rose window by Ingrand. The famous ornate astronomical clock, built last century, has various figures performing at each hour, with the Last Judgement at noon.

Almost next door is the Galerie Nationale de la Tapisserie, where you can see how tapestries are worked, and some delightful examples. Beauvais was a great centre for weaving wool and silk tapestries until 1939, when the looms were evacuated to Arbusson for safety. They are now at the Gobelins in Paris.

It was the hunting forest of the Dukes of Normandy, was used by guerillas fighting the English in the Hundred Years War and was an RAF dropping zone for British agents and supplies for the Resistance in the Second World War.

Lyons-la-Forêt, an old foresters' village in the centre, has grown into a pretty little town, still peaceful except in very high summer at weekends when tourists come. The old timbered woodsmen's houses have been restored and colour-washed, which may not be authentic but is pretty. The 15th-century church has a wooden belfry. The 18th-century covered market made of forest oaks takes up much of the square and there are old inns, including two with good rather pricey restaurants — Le Grand Cerf and the justly renowned La Licorne, here since 1768.

Hidden deep in the forest 4km south of Lyons is the 12th-century Abbaye de Mortemer. It was originally Benedictine but the Cistercian Order took it over and held it until it was closed in the Revolution. The remains are just north of the hamlet of Lisors and are part of a farm. A little train takes you on

a tour in guided groups. The tour includes the conventual building, rebuilt in the 17th century, with a museum of monastic life and the monks' fishing lake (open afternoons from Easter to mid-September; Sunday afternoon the rest of the year).

Among French and English kings who stayed in the abbey was Henry I of England. He ate a hearty supper of lampreys (little eels) and died next day of a surfeit of them. Lampreys have a poisonous black thread which you must remove. Perhaps the French monks didn't!

Two kilometres along the D715 north-east is Source Ste. Catherine, with an oratory where young girls still come to pray for a husband. There are several interesting little churches, including those at Lisors and Menesqueville in the south, La Feuillie in the north, and Beauficel-en-Lyons in the east. At Fleury-la-Forêt, north-east of Lyons, the very Norman 17th-century château is now open on Saturdays and Sundays. It has delightful furnishings, with a superb old kitchen.

Vascoeuil at the north-west edge of the forest, where the Andelle and Crevon rivers meet, has a restored feudal château (14th, 15th and 16th centuries) in which there is now an international culture centre. It is called Michelet House after Jules Michelet, who lived here when he was writing his Histoire de France. In the grounds half-timbered old Norman thatched cottages have been reconstructed.

Along the N31 road to Rouen is

The old covered market in Lyons-la-Forêt, a tranquil town in the heart of the forest

125

Château Martainville. Built between 1485 and 1510 it has been made into a most interesting folk museum of Upper Normandy with exhibits from everyday life from the 15th to the 19th centuries — furniture, pottery, glassware, pewter, copper pans (closed Tuesdays).

The D12 north-west from Vascoeuil leading to Ry is a pretty road. **Ry** was the model for Flaubert's 'Yonville l'Abbaye' in *Madame Bovary*. Emma Bovary was based on Delphine Couturier, the doctor's wife who died in 1848. The doctor's house is now a chemist's shop. A Gallery Bovary has been opened in an old cider factory with 300 automata of scenes from *Madame Bovary*. Shops in the book are still recognisable in the town. The 12th-century church has a lantern tower and charming Renaissance porch.

Further along the road at Blainville the ruins of a medieval château were discovered in 1968 and have been unearthed. The attractive church in a chequered pattern of sandstone and flint was founded in 1488 by Jean d'Estouteville, one of whose distinguished Norman family defended Mont-St. Michel against the English.

North from the forest on the D921 is **Forges-les-Eaux**. Once an iron centre with furnaces fed with charcoal from the Bois de l'Epinay alongside. Now it is a pleasant but unexciting spa town. Eight curative mineral waters can be drunk in a *buvette* at the entrance to the spa park. Outside the park are a 17th-century façade which was once part of a convent at Gisors and another of a hunting lodge belonging to Louis XV, formerly standing near Versailles. There is also a casino. In the park is a grotto built for Louis XIII and his minister Cardinal Richelieu to take the waters, and massive bronzes of them. A pool formed by the Andelle river is in a beautiful setting.

Aumale to the north-east is just in Normandy — a dairy centre on the river Bresle among the famous Bray pastureland which stretches way past Neufchâtel and down to Gournay. A Count of Aumale was a brother-in-law of William the Conqueror and fought at Hastings in 1066. His descendants became the Albemarle family. The church of St. Pierre et St. Paul, Gothic with Renaissance touches and 16th-century glass, was restored recently from war damage in 1940.

West along the N29 is **Neufchâtel-en-Bray**, celebrated for its cheese — soft, white, with an AOC (*Appellation d'Origine Contrôlée*) guaranteeing that it comes only from the local area. Most is still made on farms and packed in straw in various shapes — square, brick, even heart-shaped but most often cylinder (known as Bondon de Neufchâtel).

A civic centre has been built in Neufchâtel with a good small round theatre of red brick, set among green lawns. Eleven km north-west at Croixdalle off the D56 the Germans launched the first flying bombs against England.

North from Aumale and Neufchâtel is the forest of Eu, jealously preserved by the old dukes of Normandy so that any peasant found hunting in it paid with his life. It was still a royal hunting reserve in the middle of the last century, used by Louis-Philippe and particularly by his third son, the Prince of Joinville, whose hunting-lodge Pavillon de Joinville between Eu and Le Tréport is now an hotel.

The forest spreads from Eu itself south-east alongside the Bresle river, frontier of Normandy and Picardy, to Blangy-sur-Bresle, where it becomes a bit thin on trees in places until reaching Basse Forêt d'Eu, 10km north-west of Aumale. It belongs now to the Forestry Administration, who have laid many forest drives and paths. To enjoy its tall beeches and great oaks, you must walk.

Blangy-sur-Bresle has had a varied life. The war left it badly damaged. In 1940 the British 51st Highland Infantry Division and French 31st Cavalry, who still had horses, were told by General Weygand, French Commander-in-Chief, to hold the line of the river Bresle at all costs against the German *Blitzkrieg* tanks. They did, for three days. But the Germans had already outflanked them and reached the Seine at Rouen. So the belated order from Weygand to retreat across the Seine was too late. They tried to hold the line of the river Arques to the river Béthune, but heard that the Germans had reached the coast at Veulettes, much further south. They fought their way back to St. Valery-en-Caux. Graves of more than 2,000 British are scattered from Blangy to St. Valery.

After the War, Blangy was rebuilt. It was never beautiful but had some charm as a very French little working market town. But the boom in road transport smothered it and even its attractive little inns became shabby as lorries and cars pounded through en route to Rouen, Amiens and Paris. Now at least it has a sort of ring road, and is beginning to breathe again. Most French guides do not condescend to mention it, despite its important position at the junction of several main roads. But it has one hotel-restaurant which is not shabby — the Hôtel de Ville, with eight bedrooms, nice meals, and despite its name not a mayor or bureaucrat in sight!

You can see the inside of the Château at Mesnières-en-Bray only on Saturday and Sunday afternoons from Easter to the end of September, but it is a superb building from outside. You will find it on the D1, 6km north-west of Neufchâtel. Renaissance and with a strong Italian influence, it was built in the 15th century around a square, but the gallery which closed the square was demolished in the 18th century.

Four kilometres along the D1, the delightful D12 to the right goes into Hellet forest and left into the beautiful Forest of Eawy, with a multitude of dirt drives and surfaced roads to explore. It is another beech forest, 6,475 hectares, with majestic trees. The Varenne river, rich in trout, borders its west side and the Béthune its north-east side to Arques-la-Bataille.

The D12 runs down to St. Saëns, a pleasant little town.

A wonderful route returning from the Seine, the Loire or the Dordogne to Dieppe is the drive through the forest of Lyons, up the attractive D46, D41 to Buchy, then the D41 and D38 to St. Saëns and through the Eawy forest on little roads. It takes time but is a superb journey. And from Dieppe, coast roads will take you to Boulogne or Calais.

Clères – A Good Day Out

Clères, 20km north of Rouen, has something in common with Beaulieu in Hampshire. But although its old car museum is not quite in the class of the British National Museum its castle is much older, and it is a very good place for a family to spend the day.

The castle, started in the 14th century, but partly built in the 16th, is a typical Norman fairy-tale manor. It was largely rebuilt last century but some old parts remain and in the town are 15th–16th-century half-timbered houses and an old timber-covered market place.

The castle stands in the middle of a wildlife park, mostly for birds, started in 1920. Peacocks, flamingos, storks and cranes roam the grounds with oriental ducks and geese and more than 450 species of waterfowl. There are indoor and outdoor aviaries of rare birds, deer, antelope and kangaroos. On an island in the lake are Indo-Chinese gibbon monkeys.

The huge Musée des Automobiles de Normandie opposite the market has a good collection of veteran and vintage cars, modern racing cars, a steam fire engine of 1876, military vehicles of the Second World War and pre-1900 bicycles. The zoo is open mid-March–end September (tel. 35.33.23.08). The auto exhibition is open all year (35.33.23.02). The surrounding countryside and roads are very attractive.

Part Two
Somme, Picardy, Pas de Calais

7. The Somme Valley

The Somme Estuary and Valley to Amiens

Few foreigners have even heard of the little family resorts between the river Bresle at Le Tréport and the estuary of the Somme. Yet one of them is called Brighton-les-Pins. French families are loyal to them, especially families from Abbeville which is only 30–40km away, and they can get horribly crammed with summer traffic.

Ault, the first resort over the Normandy border stretches along a dip in the coast to a terrace with views to Le Tréport, then climbs to the cliffs of Onival, beyond which is Hable d'Ault, once a bay, now a marshy area with lagoons and little waterways. Cayeux-sur-Mer has a 160-metre breakwater-promenade above a sand beach which stretches to Brighton-les-Pins. The climate is 'bracing' — that is, windy. It is caravan country. You can visit Brighton's lighthouse (1 April–30 September daily).

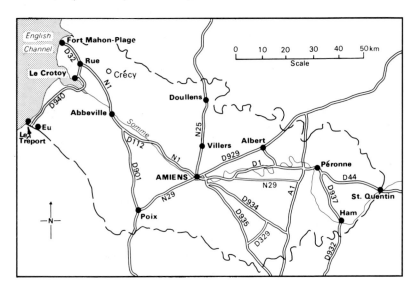

A road with good sea views alongside a beach of pebbles, then dunes, takes you to Le Hourdel, a little fishing port used by knowledgeable yachtsmen. Many of its houses are built in the old Picardy style. Turn inland onto the D3, which leads attractively to Cape Hornu, a wild spot with fine land, sea and coast views. Alongside is **St. Valery-sur-Somme**, an important port in its day, and still a delightful fishing port, at the sea end of the Somme canal, the canalised river which runs for 18km to Abbeville. St. Valery faces the equally attractive fishing port of Le Crotoy across the bay. Even in recent times the bay of Somme has silted up. During the First World War the British used St. Valery as a base to bring in men and materials on quite a scale. Now there is a channel through for coasters, fishing boats and yachts but much of the bay has become salt marshes where herbs and grass grow, wonderful *pré-salé* pasture for feeding sheep and lambs. The town is divided into two. Ville Basse has a 2km promenade along the sea wall, from which you have views of the bay, and of Le Crotoy. It is pleasantly shaded with trees and flowers and backed by villas with gardens and a sheltered beach below. But you may find bathing means a long walk. The sea goes out for miles. Below the sailors' memorial, Calvaire des Marins, just inland, are charming fishermen's cottages.

Ville Haute still has some old fortifications with two old gates — Porte de Nevers, 14th–16th centuries, and Porte Guillaume, between two splendid towers. The Chapelle des Marins at Porte Guillaume is also called Chapelle de St. Valery. Nearby is the 17th-century abbey château from the former Abbey of St. Valery.

William the Conqueror's fleet sheltered in St. Valery on the way to invade England, waiting for the right weather.

The D940 from Eu just by-passes St. Valery and sweeps over the canalised Somme to Noyelles-sur-Mer. Just east is a very surprising cemetery of 850 Chinese, buried here in 1918. They had come from various British cities as part of the British army's labour force, and were dockers at St. Valery. They died sadly in an epidemic.

The road skirts the great salt-marsh pastures to Le Crotoy, a delightful if not pretty fishing port. On the marshes the noise of the sheep and seabirds can be almost alarming.

There is another way of going from St. Valery to Le Crotoy — by an old steam railway. It runs on Saturdays and Sundays for 17km via Noyelles from 3 July to 12 Sept. The fishing boats at Le Crotoy line a wooden pier.

Le Crotoy is a bathing resort and yachting centre beloved for over 60 years by British and French. A plaque shows where there was once a château pulled down in 1674. Here Joan of Arc was imprisoned by the Bourguignons. She was finally handed over to the English and taken via St. Valery to Rouen and death.

Jules Verne lived in Le Crotoy from 1865 to 1870 and here he wrote *Twenty Thousand Leagues Under the Sea*.

The road continues to **Rue**, a port in the Middle Ages, then a peaceful little town, a centre for fishing and hunting. Now it is being developed a little as a dormitory town for Abbeville. Chapelle du St. Esprit is a highly decorated 15th–16th-century church, the refuge of one of three crucifixes said to have been discovered near Golgotha in Jerusalem and brought back by a crusader in 1101. The chapel has a strong massive belfry. Alas, apart from services, it is open only in July and August.

Legend says that the people of Abbeville stole the crucifix, but when they tried to take it away in a cart, the horses refused to move, proving that it belonged in Rue. In rue Soufflets there are unusual 14th–15th-century houses.

Great sand-dunes separate Le Crotoy from Fort-Mahon-Plage, which has its own vast beach of fine sand. Apart from the beach there is little excitement about it but it is lively with French families on holiday in summer.

A tiny road leads to St. Quentin-en-Tourmont where there is an ornithological park. The dunes are superb for studying migratory birds at the right seasons but they have been disastrous at times for poor little St. Quentin, burying churches and houses through the centuries.

Eastward from Rue is the Forest of Crécy — the same Crécy where the great battle was fought in 1346 and 'the flower of French chivalry perished', destroyed by the archers and yeomen of England. The army of Edward III of England, who had arrived in France claiming the French throne by heredity, was attacked near Crécy-en-Ponthieu by Philippe VI of France and his ally and brother King Jean of Bohemia who was blind but took to the field. The English used archers like a mass bombardment, throwing up a constant barrage which fell among the French and decimated them. Then they fought with swords and axes. The French lost between 20,000 and 30,000 men, including 1,300 knights. Jean of Bohemia, who had himself strapped to his horse, was killed. To this day, in his honour, the Prince of Wales has his black shield and plumes on his coat of arms. A cross stands where he fell (on the D56). A flagstaff at Moulin Edouard III marks the spot of a long-since-gone mill from which Edward watched and directed the battle.

The forest is delightful. Its 4,300 hectares of oak and beech are crossed each way by old carriageways and paths made by order of Louis XI and now carefully marked and sign-posted with picnic spots in peaceful places. The biggest road from Crécy village south-west to Lamotte-Buleux (the D111) is very pretty. It leaves the forest at Forêt-l'Abbaye.

Abbeville's importance as an industrial and commercial centre grows and traffic grows with it, despite heroic efforts to make passing traffic miss the centre. Until 20 May 1940, it was still a medieval town, with the high towers of the church of St. Vulfran standing above its old houses. The French army, in retreat from the German tank divisions, tried to make a stand here. German Stuka dive-bombers destroyed 2,000 houses, killed hundreds of people and set light to the whole town.

It was rebuilt as a modern town and is just developing its new personality. St. Vulfran abbey-church (started in 1488), in place

Wars have failed to destroy the 13th-century Amiens Cathedral, the largest in France and a Gothic jewel

Hôtel-de-Ville, has been restored. The central doorway of the Flamboyant west front contains a lion rampant with the French royal arms, to commemorate the marriage in 1514 of the beautiful young Mary Tudor of England and Louis XII, who was 52. North of the place is the Musée Boucher-de-Perthes, named after the 19th-century archaeologist who made important prehistoric finds in the Somme valley. It contains an archaeological section, paintings and 3,000 engravings.

Château de Bagatelle, at the edge of town on the Paris road, is a ravishing 18th-century manor house in red brick and white stone, set in a lovely park and gardens. It was built by a Dutch manufacturer by instalments, with as much as 15 years between finishing the ground floor and starting the next. Tastefully furnished, it has delicate wood panelling (open afternoons Easter–October, all day July, August, shut Tuesdays).

Nine kilometres north-east of Abbeville by the D925, is **St. Riquier**, which has a remarkable abbey-church, largely 15th–16th-century Flamboyant Gothic, with a nave 96 metres long. The square flamboyant tower is lavishly carved and thick with statues. Inside is a beautiful wooden Christ and some impressive 16th-century wall paintings. St. Riquier is an appealing little town. At the Abbeville road entrance is a little house with a gable in the shape of Napoleon's hat, built by a soldier of his *Grande Armée.*

The D112 road along the right bank of the Somme south-east from Abbeville is quite the most attractive route to Amiens. Start on the D901 to Pont-Rémy, then stay on the right bank. Pont-Rémy's castle, on an island in the Somme, dates from the 15th century but was rebuilt in 1837 in what the French rather sarcastically call 'Gothic-Troubadour'.

Long is a pretty village on the right bank with a bridge over the Somme to Le Catelet and a series of lagoons. Long's attractive and elegant château (Louis XV) is in red brick and white stone.

The D112 meets the N1 at Flixecourt but after 4km at Yzeux you can take the right fork on the N235 and cross the Somme later to Picquigny, a pleasant little place below the substantial ruins of a castle. A strong wall still surrounds the keep of the castle. There is a pavilion named after Madame de Sévigné, whose letters have become part of French literature and history. She wrote to her daughter from Louis XIV's court about court life and state personalities and events. Sometimes bitchy, often witty, always outspoken and courageous, she revealed the inner history of her times in great detail.

Dreadfully battered in both world wars, **Amiens**, capital of Picardy, has been reborn as a modern and thriving manufacturing town, especially known for the famous velvet made here since the time of Louis XIV, but now also for electronics and gastronomic specialities such as chocolates (*tuiles en chocolat*), macaroons, Picardy pancakes (*ficelle picarde*, stuffed with ham or mushrooms, cheese and cream) and duck pâté in pastry (*pâté de canard en croûte*).

The towers of its cathedral, the biggest and probably the most perfect in France, still stand proudly over the modern buildings which emerged from the rubble. In the First World War the cathedral was hit by nine shells but escaped

The magnificent west façade of Amiens was completed around 1236

almost intact. Miraculously, it also survived the terrible destruction of the Second World War.

It was built on the site of a Romanesque cathedral burned down in 1218, and was finished in 1238. The façade and the towers took another 200 years. Last century, some 'restoration' was carried out by Viollet-le-Duc who restored Notre-Dame in Paris. Its west façade is particularly impressive, with two towers of uneven heights, a great rose window, three doorways with high arches and rich decoration of statues of apostles, prophets and kings. The spire of the 16th century blends beautifully with the rest of the superb building. The nave is 145 metres long, the longest in France, and spacious. Beautiful stained glass lights the interior. A hundred and twenty-six slim pillars support the vaulted roof, lit by high windows. The 110 Flamboyant choir-stalls are a masterpiece of early 16th-century carving in oak, with over 3,000 scenes, some from the Bible, some from everyday life and some satirical. The carved screen in the ambulatory is ornately magnificent.

In strong contrast to the cathedral is the rather ponderous modern concrete Tour Perret in place Alphonse Fiquet, by the same Auguste Perret, colleague of Corbusier, who rebuilt most of Le Havre. The tower is 104 metres high with 26 storeys. There is a fine view from the top. Perret also designed the new railway station.

The Musée de Picardie has some interesting exhibits. On the ground floor are rooms containing Egyptian, Greek and Roman antiquities and prehistoric finds. The first floor has remarkable paintings of the Puy Notre-Dame d'Amiens, a fraternity who held competitions in poetry and painting in the cathedral annually from the 14th to the 18th century and presented the best painting annually as a cathedral altar-piece. There are also works of mostly 18th-century painters and sculptors, as well as some moderns.

Alas, the *hortillonnages*, the market on water, is dying out. For centuries punts piled high with vegetables were poled to market from the market gardens along the criss-cross network of irrigation canals. You could hire a boat and buy from the stalls along the waterside. Modern housewives prefer the speed and efficiency of the supermarkets. But there are fruit and flower stalls in the tourist season and at some weekends, and you can explore the waterways by hired boat (from Café de l'Île aux Fagots).

135

Caves and Commanders

Just west of the N25 which runs north from Amiens, at Naours, is a remarkable underground city, used as a refuge by local people from invading Barbarians from the third century onwards and later from Norsemen. It was used again during the Wars of Religion and then in the Thirty Years War as a French refuge from the English. It was rediscovered in 1887 by the local *abbé*.

The caves, called *muches*, are laid out as a town to shelter 3,000 people. They have 2km of streets, 300 rooms, a curious chapel with three naves, stables, cowsheds, storerooms, and wells.

The German General Rommel used the caves in the Second World War as underground shelter and headquarters. Some rooms now contain a museum of old trades of Picardy — potter, blacksmith, weaver, etc. The old village of Naours above has fine old Picardy houses. Open daily. It's cold down there.

Doullens, further up the N25, is at the junction of the Authie and Grouches rivers. Here in the Town Hall on 26 March 1918 British and French commanders met in crisis talks. The huge German offensive towards the coast had led to fierce disagreement on tactics between the Allies, made worse by a dual command. Lord Milner and Generals Haig and Wilson represented Britain. Poncaire, Clemenceau, Foch and Pétain represented France. The debate was not friendly. But suddenly Haig, the British Commander, said in a soft and conciliating voice, 'If General Foch would consent to give me his advice, I shall be very happy to listen.' So Foch was made Commander-in-Chief and with one command the Allies won. You can visit the room where they met.

A pretty road, the D8, runs down the valley of the river Selle south from Amiens to Conty and beyond, and the parallel bigger road back to Amiens (the D210) is almost as nice, but does not follow the river. Another charming road from Conty goes westward to Poix-de-Picardie, rebuilt after its destruction in 1940. This country of lush valleys, lined with pastures and poplars, is little known to outsiders, especially tourists hurrying down the D901 from Amiens cathedral to Beauvais cathedral.

The Somme Valley between Amiens and St. Quentin

East from Amiens the town of **Corbie**, between the Somme and Ancre river, was once of such importance that the abbot of its abbey was automatically a count and could mint his own money. The abbey was founded in 657 by Ste. Bathilde, wife of the Frankish King Clovis III, and was later under the direction of St. Adalard, cousin of the King of the Franks and Emperor of the West, the Emperor Charlemagne. You can still see the ancient monumental doorway of the abbey in the huge place République. The rest was knocked down in the Revolution except for the church of St. Pierre, built between 1502 and 1740, and the *Collégiale* church of St. Etienne, built in the 11th–13th centuries. St. Pierre lost its choir and transept in 1815, pulled down because the ruin had become dangerous. The remainder, however, is restored.

Cross the Somme on the D1 and 2km along the D23 on the left is a memorial and cemetery for the Australians killed in the Battle of Amiens in 1918. The Aussies had a fierce fight with the Germans for the hills of Villers-Bretonneux to the south, which they won, but not without the loss of 10,000 men.

From Corbie, the little D233 running into the D42E is an attractive route following the right bank of the Somme to Cerisy and Chipilly, then wandering just north past a series of little lagoons to Bray-sur-Somme. This little town on the Somme canal is an important fishing centre, with good fishing in the Somme river, the canal and the neighbouring lagoons. Down the D329 south of Bray, just over the Somme from Froissy, a little train runs down the valley to Dompierre-Becquincourt. The journey takes 1½ hours, and it runs mostly on Sunday afternoons from Easter to the end of September. It also seems to run on Wednesday and Saturday afternoons from mid-July to the end of August, but do check.

North from Bray the D329 leads to **Albert**, a town on the river Ancre. It was called Ancre before 1619 when Charles d'Albert, Duke of Luynes, was given it by Louis XIII, so he gave it his name. It had to be rebuilt after the First World War.

The Germans established themselves in Autumn 1914 in strong positions on chalk ridges above the town. Not until July 1916 did the British 4th Army begin an attack, after an artillery bombardment of furious intensity. The Battle of the Somme had begun. For every 100 yards gained, thousands of men died. The French gained ground around the Somme itself. Then the British 5th Army joined in. The Germans were swept east and the French reached the gates of Péronne. The Germans retreated to their strong Hindenburg line. Poor Albert's troubles were not over. In their offensive of March 1918, with a force outnumbering the British 2 to 1, the Germans retook it, claiming 90,000 prisoners and 1,300 guns captured. But their attack on the slopes west of Albert failed and what was left of the town was in British hands by 22 August.

There is a marked tour of the battlefields and cemeteries (25km) called Circuit des Souvenirs (Route of Memories) but not many people go these days. The few survivors of the battle are in their 90s, and the children of the dead have others to mourn down in Normandy. Those who do go are much younger — interested in history and almost unbelieving of the slaughter and damage of the First World War. Beside the D151 north of Albert on a hilltop at Thiepval stands the huge monument designed by Sir Edwin Lutyens, dedicated to 73,367 British dead. On the D73 is the Belfast Tower, memorial to the dead of the Ulster Regiment. West beyond the D50 between Beaumont-

Hamel and Auchonvillers is the most evocative memorial of all — the Memorial Park to the Canadian Newfoundland Regiment. Beneath the statue of a caribou, the trenches have been left as they were, with a black stump of a tree marking the German lines — so close. Of course, grass covers the battlefield now, not mud, and the barbed wire had to go. The sheep which are there to crop the grass got caught in the wire, just as wounded and dying men did in those ghastly days nearly 80 years ago. You can glimpse something of what it must have been like if you can imagine the ghastly noise and the fear.

Back at Bray-sur-Somme, a little road east leads to Suzanne, where festivals are held in the château. Just past the village is the hamlet of Vaux and a sharp right almost at Maricourt takes you to Belvédère de Vaux. From a platform by the roadside there are splendid views over the lagoons among tall grass where they are joined by the Somme canal. In the distance is the silhouette of Péronne.

You can reach Péronne either by returning to the Somme and crossing it at Éclusier, a fisherman's delight, then turning left along the Somme on little roads, or by going north from the Belvedere to Maricourt, taking the D938 right past Curlu and over the A1 motorway, a pleasant road most of the way. It passes Cléry-sur-Somme, a hamlet with a little zoo, alongside more and bigger lagoons.

Péronne is at the meeting place of the Somme and Cologne rivers, near to the branching of the Canal du Nord, and it has lagoons rich in fish. It is a great town for fishermen and the local specialities are eel pâté and smoked eels. There is a commercial port on the Canal du Nord which doubles now as a pleasure-boat port. This canal runs north all the way to the east of Cambrai to join the Canal de la Sensée into Douai, where it joins the Canal de la Deûle to Lille and into the river Lys. Southward, it joins the Canal de Somme through Péronne and further south one arm of the system makes a loop to St. Quentin and joins other canals and rivers which go in several directions; the other arm joins the Oise and Aisne rivers at Compiègne. There are many possibilities for boating.

Péronne was occupied by the Germans in the First World War and was almost totally destroyed in the Battle of the Somme, not for the first time. It was besieged and bombarded for 13 days by the Prussians in 1870.

Battered by wars, Péronne keeps some reminders of its turbulent days. In one of the four massive towers of the 13th-century château, Louis XI of France was held prisoner by Charles le Téméraire, Charles the Bold, Duke of Burgundy. In 1465 Charles took the town because Louis had sent agents to stir up the city of Liège to revolt against him. They agreed to meet at Péronne castle. Louis walked into the trap. When he arrived, Charles imprisoned him and forced him into a humiliating treaty in which he had to help with the punishment of Liège. Louis had the last word. He stirred up the Flemish towns and Swiss republics against Charles. The Swiss defeated Charles twice and killed him in 1477.

Charles III of France, who made peace with the Norsemen and persuaded Rollo to settle in Normandy instead of raiding and pillaging every spring, was twice imprisoned in an earlier castle by the local count and died here of star-vation in 929. The present château was taken by the Duke of Wellington in 1815 in his advance on Paris. The building is enclosed by a colossal 17th-century brick bastion. Only the Porte de Bretagne remains of the old town wall, but it still has its drawbridge and outer defences.

In the Town Hall, which has a Renaissance façade, there is a collection of antique coins. As well as fishing, it is now a centre for watersports.

Just past Roye (22km south of Péronne) on the N17 is the majestic restored Louis XIV Château de Tilloloy in brick and stone.

Ham, 16km south-east of Péronne, on the canalised Somme, is an ancient fortified town, rebuilt after being damaged in 1917. Its castle, damaged by the Germans in 1917, was built in the 13th–15th centuries with 11-metre-thick walls. From the beginning it was used as a state prison. Prisoners ranged from pirates to ministers of deposed kings, notably some of the ministers of Charles X, who was kicked out by the citizens of Paris in 1830. The best-known prisoner was Louis Napoleon, later the Emperor Napoleon III.

Napoleon III

Louis Napoleon was imprisoned in Ham château after he had landed at Boulogne in August 1840 to try to take over Fance. He spent six years here, writing Bonapartist propaganda, editing a dictionary of conversation and making love to his jailer's daughter!

He had been sentenced to perpetual imprisonment. But in 1846 he escaped, dressed as a workman named Badinguet. A pipe in his mouth, a plank on his shoulder, he passed the guard-post and made his way to England. Two years later he was back in France, supported by the working people, at whom he had successfully aimed his propa-ganda. He was elected Deputy for Paris, took his seat in the Assembly on 13 June 1848, resigned two days later and left France. He was recalled by his constituents in September and won the election for the presidency of France.

With military help, he dissolved the constitution, and put down a popular rebellion with imprisonment, deportation and a great deal of blood. France seemed to give in, for he was re-elected for 10 years by 7 million voters.

In 1870 he found a pretext to declare war on Prussia, but he never got across the Rhine. His corrupt army was completely defeated, France suffered appallingly for his arrogance, and he was banished in March 1871. He and his Empress Eugénie lived peacefully in Chislehurst, Kent, where he still has a memorial on Chislehurst Common, put up by the local people. His son Louis escaped to England, went to the Gunnery Academy at Woolwich and was killed fighting as a British officer in the Zulu Wars of 1879.

At Offoy, 6km north-west of Ham, is an attractive park of 35 hectares, nearly half of it lagoons. It is called Domaine des Îles and has a little zoo (open 1 March–30 October).

St. Quentin, 25km from Péronne, is a big industrial town which has switched most of its production from textiles to chemicals and metalworks. The St. Quentin canal links it through the northern waterway system to the industrial cities of Belgium and northern Germany. The canalised river Somme has left a big lagoon along which a beach has been made and you can hire boats. It is very pleasant and cleverly arranged.

Although occupied by the Germans for four years in the First World War and very near the front line, it has kept some of its ancient buildings. The enormous basilica of St. Quentin was built between the 12th and the 15th centuries. Its nave is nearly 35 metres high and its solid massive belfry can be seen for miles. It is a formidable Gothic building rather than beautiful, though the south porch is superb. The lovely but sombre glass dates from 1230. The 4th-century tomb of St. Quentin is in the crypt.

The Town Hall, begun in the 14th century, has a highly ornate Flamboyant façade from 1509. The pretty belltower was added in the 17th century. Inside the Town Hall is a lovely Renaissance chimney-piece.

The Musée Antoine-Lécuyer is devoted mostly to works of the great 18th-century pastel painter Maurice Quentin de la Tour, who was born and died here. He painted portraits of well-known people in a vivacious way. He had a great talent for catching the liveliness and spontaneity of the people he painted. He himself was eccentric but very popular in the town and in Paris. He was, it is said, abrupt to the point of rudeness with his aristocratic clients but delightful to fellow artists. (Museum shut Sunday mornings and Tuesdays.) The Musée d'Entomologie (11 rue des Canonniers) has one of the world's biggest collections of butterflies and insects, with 600,000 specimens.

Despite its industry and traffic, St. Quentin is a pleasant, lively place. Its leading hotel, the Grand in rue Dachery, is a shining example of how a dated old hotel can be made beautiful and comfortable inside without knocking it down. Its restaurant, Le Président, is also one of the best in northern France.

At the village of Bohy, near to Bellicourt (14km north of St. Quentin) is a First World War US memorial and cemetery.

The exuberantly Flamboyant 14th-century Town Hall in St. Quentin gained its belltower 300 years later

141

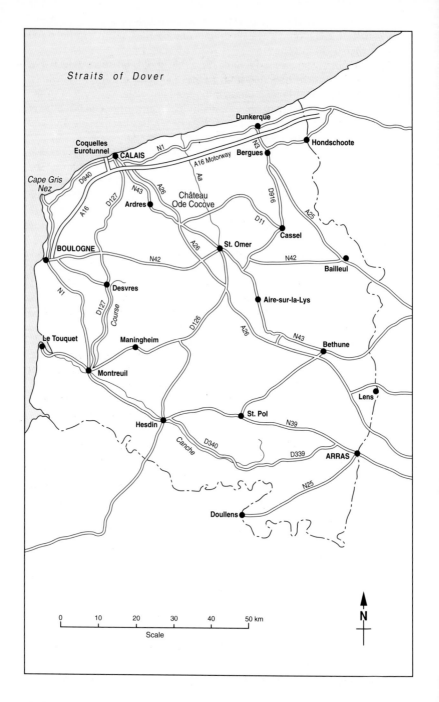

8. Boulogne, Calais, Dunkerque

Montreuil and Le Touquet

Montreuil is one of the most delightful towns in northern France. It spreads down a high hill from the remains of a medieval castle and still has narrow medieval streets and buildings, with little squares and little individual shops and cafés. But it is a living town, not just a tourist showpiece. Down in the big square at the bottom of the hill a Saturday morning market is held to which people come to shop from all round the area.

From Montreuil castle French knights rode out in 1415 to fight England's Henry V at Agincourt. Inside is a formidable list of those who were killed. Now you can walk under trees round its 700-year-old ramparts and see for miles across the countryside, even to Le Touquet's lighthouse.

Montreuil was by the sea in the Middle Ages, joined to the coast by an estuary channel, but the sea receded. It still calls itself Montreuil-sur-Mer.

Next to the castle is a more modern 'château' — a charming house in pretty gardens built by an Englishman early in the century. Now it is a charming hotel called Château de Montreuil and owned by one of France's very best young chefs, Christian Germain. The narrow streets beyond lead to place Gambetta with the church of St. Saulve. This has been constantly remodelled since it was built in the 11th century, so it is something of a mixture. Its magnificent nave is mostly Flamboyant. Inside are statues, 18th-century paintings and the treasures of the Abbey of St. Austreberthe, including a 7th-century wooden cross with splendid silverwork.

Across the square next to the hospital is the Chapelle de l'Hôtel Dieu, 15th-century, in Flamboyant style but much rebuilt. It contains wonderful chapel furnishings, with lovely panelling and a baroque altar with gilding and mirrors.

Round the corner from this square is the little place Darnetal, with a fountain. On the corner is one of Montreuil's institutions, Restaurant Darnetal. Here the chef-patron serves classical dishes at reasonable prices in a cosy bar-restaurant with interesting ornaments.

By the big market square stands a memorial to General Douglas Haig,

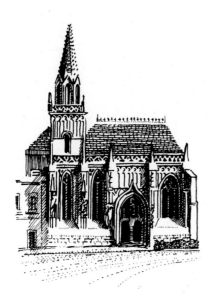

The Flamboyant Gothic chapel in Monteuil was built in the 15th century as the chapel for the hospital (Hôtel-Dieu)

British Commander in the First World War. He had his headquarters 5km south-east at Château de Beaurepaire from 1916 to 1919, and Montreuil itself was the main garrison town. Napoleon's Marshal Ney had his headquarters here in 1804 when he was preparing for the invasion of England that never happened and Napoleon visited it often from his own headquarters in Boulogne. In the Second World War the Germans, awaiting an Allied invasion, had their headquarters for the defence of this coast in the château which is now the hotel.

When Montreuil was a port its sailors had a long-running feud with Rye in Sussex, then also by the sea. They raided each other's towns, looted, including treasures from houses and churches, and captured women. Montreuil seems to have had the best of the private war. Between times, they were smuggling from both ports.

The N1 by-passes Montreuil. It has several pleasant old-fashioned hotels, including the France where the writer Lawrence Sterne started his Sentimental Journey in 1760, and is a good touring centre, with some charming drives down the valleys of small rivers through lush and wooded countryside.

The valley of the river Course along the D127 to Desvres is especially attractive. Begin along the D150 north from Montreuil, through Neuville to **Estrée**, on the Course river. This is a true little French village with an inn, farms with old-fashioned farmyards, old cottages and a cemetery of ornate tombs. The river Course, still rich in trout, divides Estrée from Estréelles, with a combined war memorial on the bridge. That is seemingly the only thing these villages of under 300 people share. They have a different mayor, schools, churches, saints' days and fêtes. They fell out in the Wars of Religion in the 16th century, when Estrées was Catholic and Estréelles was Protestant, and they have hardly forgiven each other. Montcavrel, 3km along the D150, is worth a detour. It is very pretty, with a Flamboyant village church, a 12th-century castle with a tower and moat, and the tiny river Brimoise running through. The village inn serves cheap meals.

The D127 from Estréelles is

Christian Germain, chef-proprietor of Château de Monteuil hotel, has worked for the Roux brothers in Britain

becoming a little more popular with Britons seeking a prettier route than the N1. They drive through Boulogne forest to pick up the D127 at Desvres. People from Boulogne have built a few attractive bungalows, too, but it is not crowded and is quite delightful. Drift slowly along it, pulling off to little unspoilt villages like Recques-sur-Course, where Ney held a great reception in the château for Napoleon and his family, at Beussent's trout farm, where you can fish, buy, or just look, and the little hamlet of Engoudsent. Enquin, Parenty and Bezinghem are all worth a few hundred metres diversion, while Inxent, on the road, has an old village church and an old village auberge which serves the best meals on this route, but also the priciest — although that does not make them expensive. Elizabeth David praised Auberge d'Inxent back in 1960 in her book *French Provincial Cooking*.

Hucqueliers is only a few kilometres from the D127 and the equally attractive but wider and more hurried D126. Hucqueliers is in the valley of the river Aa, which is not as attractive as the Course but very pleasant between Wicquinghem and Fauquembergues on the D148 and the D129. It is a jolly village with shops and little restaurants and an inn where local people — from farmers to football team — meet and eat.

The D126 is especially attractive as far as Maninghem, and is a very good route from Montreuil to St. Omer or the charming old town of Aire-sur-la-Lys.

The Canche valley south-east from Montreuil is followed by two roads, both pretty — the main N39 which carries a lot of traffic and the little D113 along the right bank which becomes a little less attractive at Beaurainville but does pass alongside the very pleasant Hesdin Forest into Hesdin itself. You could cross over the Canche at Beaurainville and take the N39.

Hesdin is an historic little town, and its Thursday market days are delightful. Its market square is overlooked by a Town Hall which was once the palace of Marie of Hungary, the sister of the Hapsburg Emperor Charles V. Hesdin was on the frontier of Charles's great empire, which included the Austro-Hungarian Empire, Spain and the Netherlands, and was fortified to guard the river crossing. Marie's ballroom is now a theatre. You can visit the Town Hall. It has an absolutely superb ornate gatehouse. Inside is a room of 17th-century tapestries, and the ballroom. There are good views from the top of the 1876 belfry. The 16th-century Gothic church has an interesting Renaissance doorway. Among narrow lanes and little stone bridges over streams you might get a feeling of *déjà vu*. Hesdin was used for shooting the TV series of Simenon's 'Maigret'.

Hesdin Forest has several drives and footpaths. The D928 takes you very near to Azincourt, which we call Agincourt. In 1415 Henry V and his exhausted English army, weak with sickness, defeated a French Force nearly twice its size here, partly because the French commander Constable d'Albret drew up his men crowded together on a narrow plain between two woods but mostly because of the English longbowmen from villages where archery was the main sport of yeomen. Ten thousand Frenchmen were killed, including hundreds of knights from noble families. The commemorative chapel of the battle was destroyed in the Revolution and now a simple cross marks the historic spot in peaceful farmland. The D123 south from Azincourt back to Hesdin passes through Auchy-lès-Hesdin, where the old abbatial church of St. Georges has a plaque with a list of French nobles killed at the battle and buried here.

The Canche runs alongside the D340 after Hesdin. You cannot often see the river but there are some delightful *Villages Fleuries*. At Fillièvres, opposite a pretty millpond bordered by flowers, is a watermill converted into an auberge, Vieux Moulin, with good family cooking. Boubers-sur-Canche further along is bigger and has a tree-shaded square with a café-restaurant dominated by a large old village church. The gardens and houses are so ablaze with flowers in season that it has been the best of France's floral villages.

For a pleasant if circuitous route south from Montreuil to avoid the congested N1, take the little D139 to Maintenay, then drive along the delightful valley of the river Authie. Technically, the river is just in the Département of Somme as far as Le Ponchel.

Start along the Authie's north bank on the D119 from Maintenay, then take a narrow lane marked Vieux Moulin and cross the river over a tiny bridge by a mill-café. Over the river the roughish road climbs a hillside to join the D192, where you turn left along the river's south bank to the Abbaye de Valloires, a 12th-century Cistercian abbey, altered in 1700 after a fire, now a children's school. The abbey and church are open 1 March–early November.

Argoules, 2km along the river, is a charming leafy village with old cottages and houses among lime trees around a manor, a little 16th-century church and a simple village inn where you can eat interesting meals and stay in simple rooms (Auberge du Gros Tilleul).

Downstream beyond the N1 the Authie passes Nampont-St. Martin where there is a golf course with its clubhouse in a 15th–16th-century fortified house. The river runs into the sea in a bay between Berck-Plage in Pas-de-Calais Département and Fort-Mahon-Plage in Somme. The Authie is rich in trout.

The direct route to Le Touquet from Montreuil is by quite a pleasant road, the N39, but it can be busy. More pleasant is to take the D917 alongside Montreuil's market square, signposted to Berck, then take a little road right on the edge of Montreuil, the D139, signposted to La Madelaine. Here it is worth taking a slight detour down to the river. Alongside it is Auberge La Grenouillère, a simple little old inn with a well-deserved Michelin star. The D139 continues through attractive country (though there can be floods in winter) to meet the D143. Turn right into Le Touquet through La Forêt, the old forest where the rich built villas in the 1920s or earlier and where the rich still live.

The other way into Le Touquet is through Étaples, the fishing port and market town over the river Canche, called by Tommies recuperating from wounds in the First World War 'Eatapples'. Because of one-way systems, you come into Étaples along the river and if you go straight into Le Touquet over the bridge, you miss a lot.

Unless it is rush hour, do turn right into the market square. It is chaotic and fun — even the local supermarket and certainly the old local inn, the Lion d'Argent, where the wounded Tommies used to drink. The atmosphere is the same, but the meals have improved greatly in the last few years.

The other place not to miss is further along the quay from the bridge. Here the boats land their fish and sell it in a little modern market. Above is an excellent fish restaurant, Aux Pêcheurs d'Étaples, with views from picture windows across the estuary to Le Touquet.

Le Touquet Forest

Le Touquet Forest and dunes were part of a hunting estate until 1876, when the founder of the great French newspaper *Figaro*, M. de Villemessant, had an idea when hunting to turn it into a resort. But it was the British who built it up.

In 1903 a British company called Le Touquet Syndicat Ltd bought most of the area still called La Forêt and built pricey villas for the rich and famous from London.

In the 1920s it was a weekending spot for London's smart set. Many stage and film stars had villas there. Noël Coward and his friends owned villas there until they moved to St. Tropez. The casino was one of the world's top gambling establishments and was owned by Monsieur André of the even smarter casino at Deauville. P.G. Wodehouse, the novelist who invented Bertie Wooster, was living here in 1940 when taken away to internment by the Nazis.

Even in the 1950s a few British millionaires still had villas in the Forest, including the flamboyant Sir Bernard Docker, boss of Daimler cars, and his ex-showgirl wife Nora. They also had one of the world's biggest private yachts and a gold-plated Rolls-Royce. Reminders of the British are still there in the names of the houses — Byways, Anchorage, Lone Pine, even Mandalay.

Until very recently there was a definite class division between La Forêt, with its casino, the plush and fashionable Westminster Hotel and the even plusher Hotel Hermitage (now flats) and its riding stables, and La Plage, where ordinary French and British families spent their holidays. Almost everything shut in October to reopen in spring, including the villas. But recently little blocks of apartments have replaced the pretty but decaying baroque villas which lined the promenade road, and although they do not look anything like so charming, they are warm enough for their owners to spend weekends there at any time of year or even live there if they work in Boulogne. And some of those rich villa owners in the Forest are coming to live in them on retirement. With many winter shows, conferences and exhibitions in the Palais de l'Europe, Le Touquet is never quite dead.

Le Touquet is still called 'Paris-Plage' and it is mostly Parisians who arrive each summer weekend. And Parisian industrialists, stockbrokers and lawyers own a good half of the expensive villas in the forest. The rest are owned by Belgians or industrialists from Lille. The town still has chic and style. Most shops are branches of shops from Paris, and most shut down when the season finishes.

Le Touquet really does provide for many holiday interests. For children there are miles of sands, dunes to climb, mussels and cockles to collect in the estuary, gentle karting on the promenade, four-wheel 'bikes' to pedal around, and horses to ride in the forest.

For sportsmen there are sailing, windsurfing, show-jumping and horse-racing at the very pleasant Hippodrome, tennis whatever the weather on international championship outdoor courts or indoor courts with natural light, and golf on an international championship course. There is sandsailing, too.

There's sunbathing very publicly below the promenade or more privately in the sand dunes, swimming in the sea or the huge pool on the beach, good shopping, lovely forest or coastal walks, a casino and the huge Palais de l'Europe with a lot of shows and exhibitions, sophisticated night-clubs and teenage-oriented discos. The cheaper hotels are a little disappointing. The 'best people' still stay at the Westminster which once more has a restaurant. Restaurants come in all types, sizes and price ranges.

There's a good market — Thursdays, Saturdays, and Mondays in summer. Le Touquet is successful proof that the old-fashioned seaside holiday is not dead in northern France.

When Le Touquet was founded at the end of the last century, Parisians built villas along the seafront for le weekend

149

Just after Merlimont, south of Le Touquet, is a manor house with a camp-site and a children's 24-hectare fun park, Bagatelle, to which Parisians come even for a day's outing. You pay an entrance fee for yourself and the children and for this they can join in almost any of the attractions from the Big Wheel to pedalos on the lake. A few special attractions cost extra.

Berck-Plage is a mixture of family beach resort and treatment spa for people with bone diseases, mostly children. It is not very attractive, having too many scruffy bars and slot-machine 'amusements'. It is lively in season. What Berck does have is a magnificent 12km sand beach, all the way to the Canche estuary, so it doesn't get crowded, even on the sunniest days.

Boulogne and Hinterland to St. Omer

Julius Caesar sailed from Bononia — now called **Boulogne** — to invade England in 55 BC. Napoleon waited impatiently with his *Grande Armée* in 1802–5 while 2,000 flat-bottomed boats were built to invade England and even raised the massive Colonne de la Grande Armée in anticipation of his coming success, but Nelson put an end to that plan at Trafalgar. Hitler's forces waited there to invade England in 1940, building barges, and Hitler himself toured the coast and looked at Dover cliffs from Cap Gris-Nez to the north as Napoleon had done. But the RAF put an end to *that* plan.

Then the British invaded Boulogne — several million of them each year. The number of Britons roaming the streets and mangling the French language in shops did detract a little from the French atmosphere of Boulogne, even in Haute Ville, the old walled town up the hill. Then the ferry company P & O switched all their ferries to Calais, mainly because the A26 motorway, running right down to Burgundy, and the A16 to Belgium, both ended at the bigger port. Suddenly, without warning, just before the 'Chunnel' opened, Stena Ferry Line moved their boats to Calais, too. Boulogne was devastated. Its big new ferry terminal was deserted, its little restaurants were empty, many shops had to shut. Even its Prisunic depart-ment store closed. Hoverspeed's hovercraft brought in a few British week-enders and day trippers. But Boulogne was becoming mainly a fishing port again — one of Europe's biggest, supplying Paris and other cities, but still leaving a good choice in the quayside market, open until mid-day except on Sundays. The stalls sell sole, lemon sole (*limande*), coley (*lieu noir*), red mullet, eels and shellfish, especially mussels (*moules*), for which Boulogne is famous.

Then the A16 motorway was extended from Calais to Boulogne (32km) and Hoverspeed added bigger Seacat (catamarans) to their hoverservice. Many British motorists using Calais now make for Boulogne. It is still a very good place to shop, with a wealth of small shops selling fashion and cheaper clothes, bakers, charcuteries, cake and chocolate shops, mostly in rue Faidherbe and Grande Rue or adjoining roads. One of the most famous shops in France is Phillippe Olivier's cheese shop in rue Thiers. He buys the cheeses

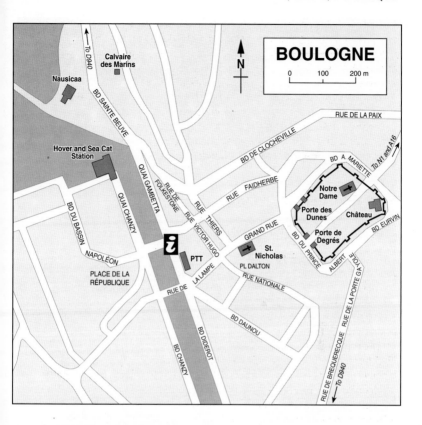

from farmers and dairies all over France, then matures them in caves under the shop at exact temperatures and humidity. The choice is bewildering. Top restaurants from Paris to London and New York boast 'Cheeses by Philippe Olivier'. Famous with restaurants and with wine-loving Britons is Le Chais, a big wine cellar with splendid value in the range of wines from French vins de table to such great wines as premier cru Margaux and Meursault. It is best reached by driving up boulevard Daunou from boulevard Diderot, and turning sharp left by the railway bridge into rue Deux Ponts.

Opposite St Nicolas church in place Dalton off Grande Rue an enjoyable and useful food market is held on Wednesdays and Saturdays spreading up Grande Rue. In place Dalton is an institution of Boulogne, Alfred's old bistro, famous for its shellfish platter until recently jam-packed and noisy lunchtime and evenings. Now Alfred has retired, and it is quieter in evenings. His son says: 'We not only miss the English — the French don't eat in restaurants so often.' Another Boulogne institution is Bar Hamiot opposite the fish quay. The Hamiot family has gone but from around 6am until very late at night a stream of locals and British visitors drop in for coffee, beer or wine with a croissant, sandwich, plate of mussels or oysters, or a steak with *frites*.

151

Boulogne has its gourmet restaurants, too. Tony Lestienne's La Matelote serves the best dishes of Boulogne fish. 5km south at Pont de Briques is a delightful inn La Rivière. Jean and Dominique Martin deserve their Michelin star for the most pleasant meals at reasonable prices.

Boulogne's biggest attraction is Nausicaa, a superb aquarium which replaced the historic casino. It has the most imaginative display of live fish in Europe — worth crossing the Channel to see.

If you walk up rue Faidherbe to Haute Ville, turn right at the old town walls along the boulevard to

The fascinating old walled town of Boulogne miraculously survived over 400 RAF raids in 1940

Porte des Degrés, a gate which was kept shut from the siege by Henry VIII of England in 1544 until 1895 and is now open only to pedestrians. Mount the ramparts and walk along gravel paths between rose beds to the castle and on to Porte des Dunes.

Haute Ville has survived by a near-miracle. When Hitler's barges were massing to invade England, the RAF bombed the port 487 times, wiping out the lower town almost completely, yet missing Haute Ville. The castle (13th-century) was built on Roman foundations and strengthened so successfully by Vauban, Louis XIV's great military architect, that in 1940 Hitler's Second Panzer Division failed to take it. When France surrendered, the Boulogne garrison marched out with flying colours.

The cathedral of Notre-Dame still stands proudly dominating Boulogne, though different architectural critics have taken very different views of it. Its glory is the superb Italian dome decorated by Vatican craftsmen. The cathedral was built between 1827 and 1866 to replace one destroyed during the Revolution. It has been called 'a synthesis of the Pantheon in Rome, Les Invalides in Paris, and Wren's St. Paul's Cathedral in London'. It has also been called 'massively domed and ill-proportioned'. It is built on sites of other churches dating back to AD 636, when legend says that a statue of the Virgin, standing in an open boat, was pushed ashore by angels.

For political reasons, to help his claim to Boulogne against the Dukes of Burgundy who held the port, Louis XI pronounced the statue 'a true Madonna' in 1477. Pilgrims arrived from round Europe, making Boulogne rich. Fourteen French kings, five English kings, and many nobles, murderers and evil-doers prayed here for absolution from their sins.

Crab seller in Boulogne's famous quay-side fish market

Various statues were burned or stolen through the centuries. The present one, by a local artist

Paul Graf, was made in 1924 in 12th-century style and weighs 12,020 kg. Each August it is carried in procession, followed by fishermen, farmers and girls in traditional head-dresses.

The 11th-century cathedral crypt, an underground labyrinth of 14 rooms with painted pillars, was discovered about 100 years ago. Here Edward II of England married Isabelle, daughter of Philippe IV of France in 1308.

The centre of Haute Ville has a 13th-century grey stone belfry tower, an 18th-century town hall and an 18th-century house, Hôtel Desandrouins, called rather imperiously Imperial Palace because Napoleon stayed there while awaiting his 'invasion'.

Boulogne was one of the earliest beach resorts in France — discovered by the English very soon after Dieppe. Beach bathing started in 1789 and in the 19th century lured colonies of Britons to live in Boulogne. Napoleon III returned, and so did such fashionable people as the eccentric and flighty Duchess of Berry. Parisians built elegant houses and Boulogne became the fashionable resort. Between the two world wars, Le Touquet took over and Hardelot drew the golfing visitors. Then in the Second World War all those elegant 19th-century Boulogne houses were bombed and

Hardelot Plage

Hardelot Plage, between Le Touquet and Boulogne, was developed by Sir John Whitney around 1900 as a rival to Le Touquet. Along its huge sand beach and in the forest behind, he built villas with little turrets and balconies. The pseudo-Gothic castle became the clubhouse for his golf-course. The sands became international headquarters for sand-yacht racing. A Monsieur Blériot built a villa and practised flying along the beach — although to cross the Channel he moved to a beach nearer Calais and Kent. The English arrived and laid a cricket pitch, and King George V and Queen Mary spent two holidays there. Then in the Second World War the Germans flattened almost everything to build blochhouses of the West Wall against Allied invasion. By 1945 there were only six damaged houses and 54 blochhouses left. Little was built until the 1960s. Then Francis and José Lesur, whose family had helped to build the original Hardelot, took over. They built beachside apartments and villas, set up a sailing club, schools for sailing, wind-surfing, sand-yachting and for wind-surfing on land, a thrilling new sport. Then they built a second international golf-course and Hôtel du Parc, a comfortable modern hotel with superb swimming pool and indoor tennis in a park. It was opened in 1992 by Prince Edward — following in his great-grandparents' footsteps. Young, active Parisians bought weekend flats and villas. Now the English nip over for golf and water-sports. Some buy villas for retirement, too.

concrete took over. Boulogne is now a very likeable, busy port and tourist town.

Le Portel, almost part of Boulogne to the south, is an old fishing village which became the beach for the families of Boulogne. Its sand beach has rocks and rock pools and behind is a promenade facing an islet fort (l'Heurt) built by Napoleon in 1804.

High above the north end of Boulogne is the spectacular Calvaire des Marins — a memorial to sailors who died at sea.

You can reach Napoleon's Grande Armée column by taking a track to the left off the N1 3km north of Boulogne. Begun in 1804 under Napoleon's orders it was finally finished by King Louis-Philippe in 1840. Made from local Marquise marble, it is 53 metres high and 4 metres in diameter. Napoleon, of course, stands on top. A staircase with 263 steps takes you to a platform where there are splendid views, sometimes to the English coast, and over the countryside. On the coast northwards towards Calais is Wimereux, with a beach of shingle, sand, low-tide rock pools and seaweed, loved by children.

The D940 to Cap Gris-Nez is pleasant with high dunes between Wimereux and Ambleteuse. Cap Gris-Nez itself is pleasant on a sunny day with gentle winds. It *can* be very windy, wet and unpleasant indeed. Channel swimmers usually aim for it.

The attractive D191 inland crosses the N1 and A26 near Marquise, then continues through Hardinghen and Hermelinghen into lovely rolling country around charming farming hamlets with little cottages and churches. It is a peaceful world which people hurrying south have no idea exists. Nor have most French people.

North from Hermelinghen is the Guines Forest. East and south are pretty little roads through more farming land, to the forest of Tournehem, west of St. Omer.

Another delightful area is south-east of Boulogne along the D341 through the dense Forest of Boulogne, where there are fine walks and picnic spots. The road leads to Desvres, where they have made pottery since the 18th century using old designs from Delft, Moustiers, Nevers and Rouen.

To the south is the delightful D127 along the river Course. To the north is Desvres Forest with some lovely drives, particularly if you take the D253 to Bournonville, then turn west to the pretty village of Crémarest. From here take the D238 back to the D341 through the forest again to Boulogne.

The N42 east from Boulogne to St. Omer is not a pretty road but there is some pleasant scenery and deviations. After cutting through the Boulogne Forest turn left for a kilometre to Le Wast, a charming village with an interesting little church and a manor house hotel specialising in fish (Château des Tourelles).

The D252 back to the N42 passes Château Colembert, a huge 18th-century manor and a beautiful church reconstructed in the 18th century. Another very interesting church is at Surques, just north of the N42 from Escoeuilles. It is fortified with a big rectangular tower (1619).

Lumbres has a cement works and a paper mill but its square is pleasant, and it has attractive walks along the right bank of the river Aa and trout fishing. Above all, it has a mill on the Aa called Moulin de Mombreux which is a delightful hotel with superb cooking by Jean-Marc Gaudry. Take the little D208 into St. Omer through Wisques, a pleasant hillside village. Behind high walls is the Benedictine abbey of St. Paul, a mixture of 15th-century and 1953 architecture. To hear the daily Gregorian chant you must get to mass at 9.45 am.

St. Omer is one of the most underestimated towns in North France. It still has an air of 18th-century elegance. The merchants' houses 300 years old, the ancient shops and cafés in the cobbled Grande Place tilting all ways, and the waterways all make up a scene which lures photographers and artists. The market on Saturdays in Grande Place is one of the most important in the North.

The huge 12th-century basilica of Notre-Dame, containing many statues, sculptured tombs and a 16th-century complicated astronomical clock, stands overlooking the beautiful public gardens among ramparts at the west end of the town.

In a very elegant house of 1766 on rue Carnot is the Musée Sandelin. It contains good Flemish, Dutch and French paintings. Well worth seeing is the porcelain collection of 700 pieces, including a lot from Delft and a collection of pipes, for which St. Omer was once renowned. The star of the museum is a 12th-century masterpiece in gold and enamel — the Cross of St. Bertin by a Meuse Valley goldsmith Godenfroid de Huy. (Museum closed Mondays, Tuesdays.)

St. Omer is at the meeting of the Aa and Neuffosse rivers and has 300km of waterways (watergangs) excellent for canoeists and fishermen (pike, perch, bream, eels). Flat-bottomed punts move along them piled with the produce of the famous market gardens which stretch to the forest of Rihoult-Clairmarais. The gardens produce superb vegetables, especially cauliflower. From the Clairmarais road (the D209) passenger boats will take you in season on canal trips long and short.

Nineteen kilometres southward you find the likeable, rather chaotic old town of **Aire-sur-la-Lys**. It's a well-preserved market town with interesting little shops, many old houses in its 18th-century square, a 15th-century church and a 16th-century Town Hall with a superb Renaissance balcony. Château de la Redoute was once a fort built by d'Artagnan of the Three Musketeers. Now it is a fine manor house in a beautiful park with a trout lake, converted into an hotel-restaurant called Les Trois Mousquetaires. It is family-run in the old-fashioned way of French hotels.

From Aire there is a charming route south-west to Montreuil. You take the D157 west which runs beside the river Lys past Delettes where it becomes very attractive, running into the scenic D126 with a lovely stretch past Maninghem.

Calais, Dunkerque and Hinterlands

Calais is a much-maligned town. It has interesting shops, quite a lot of atmosphere and a good beach. English for centuries, then the bolt-hole of English émigrés, it seemed to be ignored by Paris. It built up its own industries, including textiles, and its port handles many imports and exports. The recent building of two motorways right into town has attracted ferries which traditionally used Boulogne; and a new network of modern roads, with flyovers, double tracks, and new suburbs with big apartment blocks have changed the face of the historic old port. Calais is determined to compensate for the loss of traffic using the tunnel to cross from England. But the visitors who stay even a few hours still find a very pleasant old town. Near to the port are still shops and restaurants aimed at tourists but used also by local people. The centre is place d'Armes, where the rebuilt 13th-century watch-tower is the only remnant of the medieval square destroyed in the Second World War. Among comfortable hotels is the Meurice (about £65 per room per night) — direct descendant of the inn built by the Calais post master to offer comfortable sleeping and eating accommodation to stage coach passengers en route from London to Paris. The descendant of the last in the chain is the Meurice in rue de Rivoli, Paris — four-star luxury (about

Rodin's sculptures outside Calais Town Hall commemorate the 14th-century townsmen who saved their town

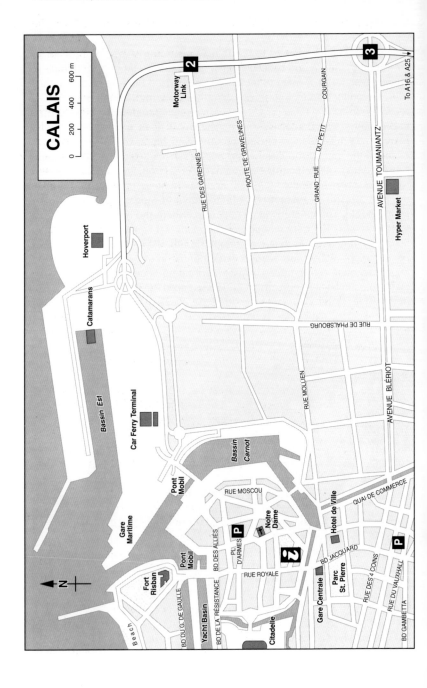

£400 per room per night) and Michelin star for cuisine. Up the hill past the railway station are the local shops, place Crèvecoeur where a market is held on Thursday and Saturday mornings (good for butter, cheese, vegetables and fish), and the Town Hall, which has been rebuilt in 15th-century Flemish style.

Outside the Town Hall is Rodin's evocative statue of the Burghers of Calais — a tribute to the six local dignitaries who offered their lives to Edward III of England after an eight-month's siege if he would spare the other townsfolk. Edward was persuaded by his Flemish queen, Philippa of Hainault, to spare all of them. The English ruled Calais for much of the time between 1347 and 1558. Henry VIII in particular used it as a headquarters for looting and sacking the North. Calais was finally freed from the English in 1558 by François, Duc de Guise. Left over from the English rule is the church of Notre-Dame, built in English perpendicular style.

Last century, many Britons hid in Calais from creditors as they did in Boulogne. As 'Emma Lyons', Nelson's Lady Hamilton came in 1815 to die in poverty and misery at No. 27 rue Française. Beau Brummel, arbiter of fashion and manners, uncrowned king of Bath and Tunbridge Wells, fled here in 1816 to avoid his creditors and the wrath of the Prince Regent, a former friend. He stayed for 15 years under his first names of George Bryan.

At the end of a mole in the harbour by the maritime station is a memorial to the British — the Green Jackets (the Rifle Brigade) who made the last stand on an island in the harbour to try to save Calais from the Nazis in 1940 and there is a simple little wartime museum in a bunker used by the German navy as headquarters in 1940–4.

The sand beach, popular with local people and backed now by flats, stretches to Blériot-Plage, from where Louis Blériot took off in his little monoplane in 1909 to be the first man to cross the Channel in a heavier-than-air machine. Backed by the old D940 coast road, the sand beach continues for 13.5km to Cap Blanc-Nez. At Sangatte, the next village, the French dug in 1877 the experimental beginnings of a tunnel under the Channel but the British would not collaborate: army generals painted a picture of French armies pouring through it to invade England! Now the new Euro tunnel emerges nearby, close to the village of Coquelles, the N1 and the A16 roads. The tunnel information centre is like a hillside glasshouse, with a viewing tower with 360° panoramic views of the area, an audio-visual show of the digging and completion (45 minutes), and a remarkable shopping, eating and climbing centre called Cité de l'Europe, probably the world's biggest hypermarket. Three minutes drive away at Coquelles is a new Copthorne hotel (tel 21.46.60.60 Fax 21.85.76.76).

On Cap Blanc-Nez is a memorial to forgotten heroes of the First World War — the French and British sailors of the Dover Patrol, whose little boats swept the Channel for German mines and submarines, night and day from 1914–18.

Halfway between Cap Blanc-Nez and Cap Gris-Nez is the little beach resort of **Wissant**, a favourite haunt of the British middle classes from the late 18th century until 1939, now popular with British school parties, campers

Aeronauts

The old walls of Boulogne's Haute Ville have 17 towers. In the western corner is Gayette tower with a plaque to Pilatre de Rozier, the first human to fly over Paris, in a Montgolfier balloon in 1783. Two years later he tried to cross the Channel from this tower with his partner Romain. At 580 metres their balloon collapsed. They are buried in nearby Wimille churchyard.

In the hilly Guines forest, north-east of Boulogne and south of Calais, is a column on a remote hillside to the men who made the first Channel crossing 129 years before Blériot's first plane crossing — the French Colonel Blanchard and the American Dr. Jeffries.

and windsurfers. It has magnificent white sands. In fact, the English who came here first called it White Sand and the French turned that into 'Wissant'. The little old church has an effigy of the martyred Ste. Wilgeforte, daughter of a king of Portugal. If a woman prays to her, the saint will untangle her from an inconvenient marriage or liaison!

This winding, climbing and falling coast road is attractive apart from the Sangatte workings, with views of Britain on fine days, and is a far better route to Boulogne than the awful N1.

Among new roads from Calais, the little D127 running south through farming hamlets seems lost. It runs first beside a branch of the Calais canal to Guines, Henry VIII of England's front-line headquarters when we controlled Calais. Turn into Guines' little square with the Town Hall down one side and, apart from the modern cars, you could imagine that you had slipped back to 1918. The shops, cafés and the little Lion d'Or inn seem to belong to another age. It is even called place Maréchal Foch. Continue along the D127, a most attractive road which passes the hilly, close-wooded Forêt de Guines. Here it is well worth parking and walking among the superb oaks, beeches, horn-beams and silver birches. Signposted along a path is La Colonne Blanchard, the memorial to Blanchard and the American doctor Jeffries whose balloon landed here on 7 January 1785 after making the first aerial Channel crossing.

The D127 continues to pass through attractive country. Turn left onto the D191 to Hermelinghen and Licques, where buildings from an old abbey (Prémontrés) are now the presbytery, *mairie* and school. Licques is famous for chickens and turkeys, and has a turkey fair just before Christmas. The road is very pretty all the way to Ardres.

This circuit from Guines to Ardres does mean that you miss Camp du Drap d'Or (Field of the Cloth of Gold) just off D231 — the very place where Henry VIII and François I had their sumptuous and disastrous summit meeting in 1520. But there is nothing to be seen now but a stone marking the spot by a cornfield.

Ardres is a delightful agricultural town with a central green, a few shops,

This hilly landscape near Ardres is typical of the farmland behind Boulogne and Calais

old mansions and inns — a touch of old France. Grand' Place, paved and surrounded on its three sides by ancient picturesque houses and a 17th-century chapel, is particularly attractive. On the edge of Ardres is a pleasure lake, with yachting, canoeing, pedalos and pleasant bar-cafés serving light meals.

Just after the slip road to the A26 motorway on the N43 towards St. Omer a little road left leads to Reques-sur-Hem. A smaller road left before you reach it goes to Château de Cocove, a huge 17th-century mansion with two slightly tilted wings, built by an admiral, owned by his descendants until recently and now owned by a wine merchant who supplies many hotels and most of the supermarkets in the Nord. He has restored it, made most of it into a good hotel and filled the cellars with more than 15,000 bottles of wine from *vin-de-table* to grand-crus clarets and burgundies. You can take your choice and take it away.

East from Recques is the Forest of Éperlecques, flanked on the eastern side by the river Aa, and Watten, with a hill overlooking the whole Aa valley. A marked forest track crosses it.

The D226 north-east from Watten is attractive. At Eckelsbrugge cross the D928 onto the D11.

The road continues to **Cassel**, a fascinating town which sits on the green,

The World's Biggest Picnic

In 1520 François I of France wanted to make an alliance with Henry VIII of England against the Emperor Charles V, who ruled most of what is now Germany, Burgundy, Flanders and the Netherlands and Spain and its colonies.

The English owned Calais and Guines. It was arranged that the kings should meet between Guines and Ardres. Both were flamboyant, ostentatious and prickly-proud. The meeting which began on 7 June was one great party at which each vied to outdo the other.

It was called *Le Camp du Drap d'O* — The Field of the Cloth of Gold. François hung his tents with gold-thread cloth and dressed his courtiers in the most expensive and sumptuous clothes. Horses were draped in gold cloth and some had golden shoes.

The painter Jean Bourdichon arranged his décor. He used 6,000 workmen to prepare the site.

All Henry's 5,000 courtiers were dressed in velvet, satin and gold. His camp was like a palace in crystal 'scintillating in the sun'.

Cardinal Wolsey, Henry's organiser, sent over among other items, 2,014 sheep, 700 conger eels, 26 dozen heron and 4 bushels of mustard. Balls, feasts and tournaments went on until 24 June. The kings jousted every day. They both brought their own choirs and held a combined open-air mass.

On 24 June the wind was too strong for jousting. So Henry and François wrestled. François threw Henry flat on his back. The wind then blew down Henry's Crystal Palace. He was furious.

They parted swearing eternal peace but Henry went straight to a meeting with Charles V and signed a treaty with him against France.

valleyed slopes of Mont Cassel, 178 metres above the plains of Flanders. Built round a huge irregularly shaped paved Grande Place where the old buildings have coats of arms over doorways leading to secretive courtyards, it has been fortified since the Romans made it the axis of seven important roads. Normans, French, Flemings, Spaniards and English have fought over it. From October, 1914 to June, 1915, General Foch and the British General Ruyter had headquarters there during the Battle of Yser when the Germans were advancing. Foch had his office and stayed in the 18th-century Hotel Schoelbeque.

There is a huge statue of Foch on horseback in a garden at the top of the town, beside the reconstruction of a 16th-century windmill. On a fine day you can see much of Flanders to the coast 30km away. There is another lovely view from the dining room of the 18th-century inn Le Sauvage in Grande Place.

The Musée d'Art, d'Histoire et de Folklore is housed in a fine 16th-century Renaissance building in Grande Place, Hotel de la Noble Court. Most of its items were destroyed in the German attack in 1940 and it has little of great interest, though there is some good Flemish furniture and wood panelling (open 1 June–30 September).

East of Cassel (6km) right by the A26 motorway is the typical little Flemish town of Steenvoorde, with trim painted houses under red-tiled roofs — a centre for dairy products. The giant carried in procession at fêtes is of Yan den Houtkapper, a woodcutter who made a hardwearing pair of wooden shoes for the Emperor Charlemagne, and was rewarded with a special breastplate.

On the outskirts of Steenvoorde are two old windmills, the well-preserved Moulin du Nord by the little D18 and Moulin Drieve on the D948 west of town.

The D916 leads to Hazebrouck (6km) which is 15km north-east of Aire-sur-la-Lys and 10km north of Nieppe forest. Hazebrouck is a fair-sized market town well known in the First World War as a communications centre because of its railway lines from Paris to Dunkerque and Lille to Calais. It has an Augustinian convent (1518–1616) with a small museum.

The most delightful village in the area is **Esquelbesq** on the river Yser, just off the D916 at Wormhout, north of Cassel. It is pure Flemish, with a paved main square, a huge 16th-century church with gables, decorated with coloured bricks, and low-built Flemish houses; neat, painted and with flowers in season. Its brick château has pointed turrets reflected in a moat and a massive, unusual eight-sided lantern rising to 45 metres.

Bergues, further north up the D916, is a superb old town, much admired by visitors to Dunkerque. It seems like a small copy of Bruges. It, too, is pure Flemish, its peaceful streets and canals keeping the atmosphere of another age. Yet it was built as a fortress for war in the Middle Ages, and there are still old walls, towers and beautifully carved doorways, with remnants of an 11th-century abbey.

The belfry, called the loveliest in France, was destroyed in 1944, so they have built a faithful copy in sand-coloured brick. Its octagonal belltower stands on a square tower 54 metres high. The belfry houses a carillon of 50 bells, which are played at 11 am on Mondays, on holidays and some Saturday evenings. Walk up the 171 steps and you see clearly Vauban's star-shaped fortifications of the 17th century, with four gates, and the yellow-ochre gabled houses reflected in the moat and canals. The French used the old walls for defence in 1940 and the Germans made a breach by bombing them with Stuka dive-bombers, then entering behind flame-throwers.

The municipal museum (closed Fridays) in place St. Martin is in a 17th-century almshouse, elaborately carved outside — the work of Wenceslaus Cöeburger.

The D3 road east to **Hondschoote** by the Canal de la Basse Colme is attractive. Hondschoote was once a very important town, centre of the Flemish serge industry, with 28,000 inhabitants. Now it has about 4,000 people, is quiet, neat and attractive. A series of fires destroyed its cloth industry. In one fire alone, started in fighting between Catholics and Huguenots in 1582, 17 streets with 900 places of manufacture were burned down. Persecution and strife under Spanish rule in the 17th century led to all

Thousands of windmills like this one once brought power to the farms of the North

the weavers deserting the town by 1650. Most fled to Bruges.

The Renaissance-style Town Hall is very attractive and the 16th-century church of St. Vaast with a tall tower is beautiful. In the Town Hall is a tableau tracing the Battle of Hondschoote in 1793 when the French Revolutionary army defeated the British and Austrians. Just outside the town to the north is Nordmolen, said to be the oldest windmill in Europe, built in 1127. It was still grinding corn as late as 1959.

The Second World War may have all but wiped out **Dunkerque**, but it certainly did not kill it. It is not a pretty place but it is vital — even dynamic. And it continues to grow as a port and industrial town. It is now the third largest port in France. Ferry passengers arriving from Britain very often find out nothing about Dunkerque itself because they land some way from the centre and usually skirt the town to reach the A25 motorway which starts 9km outside it.

The centre of the town around place Jean Bart is lively and pleasant and the huge sand beach at Malo-les-Bains, backed by many cafés and good fish restaurants, attracts the people of Lille and Britons on short-break holidays.

Malo is divided from Dunkerque itself by the Canal des Wateringues. Recently Malo has become more and more a very pleasant residential district. These were the sands from which nearly 350,000 British and French soldiers were taken off in 1940 under German bombing and artillery fire by ships of all shapes and sizes, from cruisers to pleasure boats sailed by amateur yachtsmen.

The superb sands stretch 10km to Bray-Dunes from where the promenade continues over the Belgian border to La Planne. Bray has a fleet of catamarans and holds summer regattas.

Dunkerque still has a sizeable fishing fleet. Kippers are a traditional speciality. During the happy Dunkerque Carnival, just before Mardi Gras, the Mayor throws kippers to the crowd from the balcony of the Town Hall.

Dunkerque's Musée des Beaux Arts in place Général-de-Gaulle was opened in 1973 in a heavy concrete building which looks like a Corbusier hangover. It has a good collection of paintings of the 16th to 20th centuries. A naval gallery shows the evolution of shipbuilding since the 7th century,

Dunkerque, 1940

When the British and French forces retreated to Dunkerque on 27 May 1940, the British command estimated that they could evacuate 45,000 men in two days, before the Germans overwhelmed them. Hitler was so convinced that his bombers, especially the Stuka dive-bombers, could stop any mass evacuation, that he saved his tanks for his drive to Paris and his invasion of Britain. But in Sheerness and along the Kent coast a great motley fleet gathered. 'A spontaneous movement swept the seafaring population of our south and south-east shores,' wrote Churchill in his *History of the Second World War*. 'Everyone who had a boat of any kind, steam or sail, put out for Dunkerque.'

The boats included lifeboats from liners in London docks, Thames tugs, yachts, fishing boats, lighters, barges and pleasure boats. Altogether 860 boats took part in the evacuation — 700 British and 160 Allied. Between 27 May and 4 June, 338,226 men were brought to Britain, both British and French. Two-thirds were taken from Dunkerque harbour by bigger boats. A third were taken by little boats from the sand beaches or the sea into which they had waded.

The beach and harbour were bombed constantly. But the beaches were brilliantly organised and very few men hiding in the dunes were lost. Many were bitter that the RAF was not protecting them, but it was. Though hopelessly outnumbered, the fighters from Britain kept up attacks on the German planes near their airfields or high above the clouds where the troops below could not see them. They broke up attack after attack and inflicted great losses on the Luftwaffe. Churchill said, 'This was a decisive clash.' He spoke of 'a great victory' in the air. It was a foretaste of the Battle of Britain.

British and French troops had held off the German attacks on a line from Gravelines to Bergues and along the canal to Nienport in Belgium. On the final day, 4 June, 4,000 British troops and several thousand French were fighting the rearguard. They fought until the Germans overwhelmed them in Dunkerque. Of 372 little ships sailed across by civilians 170 were sunk. They still kept crossing until the end.

with models of early ships. In the basement is a museum of Dunkerque's part in the Second World War.

Open since 1982 is the Contemporary Art Museum in Jardin des Sculptures (closed Tuesdays). The park is made up of grassy hills with modern sculptures at intervals. Inside the museum are works of modern Americans, and a whole room of the paintings of the Dutchman Karel Appel, known now for his wooden reliefs.

Dunkerque was built up from a fishing port in the 7th century and was disputed over centuries by the Spaniards, the French, the English and the

Dutch. England was actually given the port after 1658 in return for the help given by Cromwell's great Ironside regiments in the Netherlands fight for freedom from the Spanish Empire. When Charles II followed Cromwell, that spendthrift monarch sold Dunkerque to Louis XIV for 5 million livres to repay debts. Colbert, Louis's minister, told the military architect Vauban to fortify it. It became a corsair's lair.

Under the Treaty of Utrecht which Louis XIV was forced to sign after defeats by the English, Dunkerque's fortifications were destroyed under the control of English Commissaries, who virtually ruled Dunkerque until England's defeat in the American War of Independence.

In 1944, the German admiral Frisius, commanding the occupying forces there, had the civilian population evacuated, flooded the Moëres valley to the south-east as a barrier, and held the port until the German capitulation in May 1945.

To the west is **Gravelines**, a popular seaside resort with the people of Flanders. This old port where the Aa river reaches the sea was fortified in 1160. The sea surrounded the dunes on which the fishing hamlet called Les Huttes was built. For centuries Gravelines was the port of St. Omer. The old ramparts are very well preserved. The powder magazine of Vauban's castle, called The Arsenal, now houses a museum of engravings and prints (closed Tuesdays). The Varennes barracks of 1737 are used for municipal housing.

Gravelines is now a forward-looking town. It lost its fishing fleet to Boulogne but has turned the harbour into a good marina. It has a very good Social Cultural Centre with activities ranging from a nursery and baby clinic to a school of sailing and it has built the largest sport and leisure centre in the north of France (called Sportica) with a huge range of activities, including excellent indoor tennis courts, skating and ice-hockey on an artificial rink made of silicon, swimming pools, a 90-metre water slide and a basketball stadium.

9. Arras, Cambrai, Lille

Arras to Cambrai

Arras is busy, sometimes crowded, usually interesting and in places delightful. The squares are enormous, the old arcaded Flemish houses in Grand' Place and place des Héros are stunning, and the markets, famous for centuries, are as bustling and crowded as if supermarkets had never been invented and the open market were the only place to shop.

The elegant tall narrow houses round these squares are in red brick and old stone, with Flemish ornamental stepped gables and covered arcades whose colonnaded arches form a continuous gallery-walk all round the squares. Their style is 16th–17th century and some of them are from those years. The others were superbly rebuilt from the rubble left when Arras was devastated in the First World War. On many buildings are the heraldic coats of arms of crafts, trades and families. Grand' Place is cobbled and kept free of cars (there is a car-park underneath). It is one of the loveliest squares in Europe.

The Town Hall in place des Héros, originally 15th-century, has been rebuilt, too — exactly as it was, complete with the superb 75-metre belfry. It is well worth seeing the inside. The first and most unusual exhibits are two monumental giants called Colas and Jacqueline. They are paraded round town on fête days. Then there are photographs of what Arras looked like in 1918 after the bombardments. A glance at these will show you just what a remarkable job the rebuilders did to those old houses. Up the main stairs a fresco in La Salle des Fêtes shows life in Arras in the 16th century, including the 12th-century cathedral, demolished in 1799.

There are two ways of reaching the top of the belfry — by climbing 326 steps or by taking a lift from the vaults and climbing only the last 33 steep steps. The view over the rooftops to the cathedral is interesting. The cathedral is the old abbey-church of St. Vaast designed by the same architect as La Madeleine in Paris, in 1766. A colossal monumental staircase leads up to a classical façade. In fact, the huge building is rather like a majestic sober monument.

The abbey of St. Vaast was founded in the 7th century and housed the relics of the saint, the first bishop of Arras. It was restored by Cardinal Rohan in 1746 and again after the First World War. Its building is rather severe with formidable 50-metre cloisters used for exhibitions. Part of the abbey houses the Musée Municipal, with the theme of 'Arras, town of art'.

In the 14th and 15th centuries Arras was a great tapestry-producing centre.

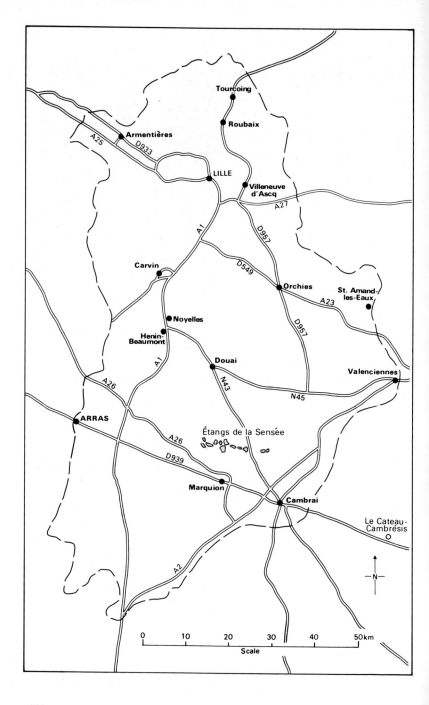

When the town was annexed by the Dukes of Burgundy in 1384, the tapestries became fashionable at the Burgundian court and they were also exported to England in return for the wool used to make them. By the 15th century the art was already dying. Tournai, now in Belgium, had taken the trade.

In the tapestry display in this museum there is only one made in Arras (15th-century). In fact, they are very rare. Yet the word 'arras' was used for any tapestry in England. Shakespeare had Polonius hiding 'behind the arras' in *Hamlet*. And *arazzi* is the Italian word for tapestries.

The art collection here is so varied as to be called miscellaneous. Much is interesting, nothing really great. There are some unusual statues from the 12th–15th centuries. Among the pictures are paintings by Corot and his friends, and watercolours by Dufy.

Beautiful Flemish-style central squares in Arras, with arcades and old shops, were restored superbly after being damaged in the First World War

In boulevard Charles de Gaulle near the old citadel is a memorial to British soldiers missing during the First World War and along a little road alongside is Mur des Fusillés, with a plaque to members of the French Resistance shot by the Germans against this wall in 1942.

Just off the road to Lens north from Arras is the village of Vimy. On the ridge nearby stands one of the most solemnly impressive war memorials in Europe, the huge memorial to the 75,000 Canadians killed in the First World War. Many were killed here fighting for this ridge with the British 3rd Army under General Allenby in 1917. Stone steps flanked by walls lead to two great stone pillars with carvings of Canadian soldiers at the top. The park in which the memorial stands was until fairly recently the one green stretch in a land of mines, slag-heaps and blackened brick miners' houses known as *cites* and *corons* stretching to the town of Lens. The Germans took Lens in October 1914 and worked the mines flat out for four years. When driven out, they systematically flooded all the mines in the area. But it was Europe's glut of steel and of coal starting in the 1960s which finally silenced the mines. Lens lost 5,000 of its 42,000 inhabitants in ten years. The last pit closed in December 1990. Lens has built zones for industry and artisans, and a sports stadium where the renowned team Racing Club de Lens plays. The French Government paid the redundant

Giants

The giants of Flanders were born in the 16th century when they were carried in religious processions. Usually they were of Goliath or St. Christopher. After the Revolution they became local folk heroes or people of local legend and were the heroes of carnivals, carried in procession, as they still are.

Lille has the most famous. Lydéric and Phinaert date from 1560 and are 17 metres high. The legend of these two goes back to AD 600. Phinaert was a brigand who lived in a château. He attacked the Prince of Dijon and his wife on their way to England. The prince was killed, his wife escaped and gave birth to a boy before being recaptured by Phinaert. The boy was baptised Lydéric by a hermit, who brought him up. When grown up, he killed Phinaert in single combat, married the sister of King Dagobert, took over Phinaert's Flanders forests and founded Lille. Phinaert and Lydéric are carried through the streets at Whitsun.

They have been joined since 1825 by La Belle Jeanne Mailloté, a gallant lady who led the women to drive out pillagers from Lille in the 14th century, and now also by a fat jolly giant Gambrinus, who loves beer.

A Scandinavian warrior named Reuze is the busiest giant. In Cassel he promenades on the first Sunday in March and with his wife on Easter Monday. He is in Dunkerque at Mardi Gras and the Sunday before. Dunkerque believes that he was a raiding Viking warrior who was wounded. Instead of killing him the locals nursed him to health, so he stayed to defend the town.

Bailleul's Mardi Gras giant is Gargantua — appropriately in a food-producing town. Hazebrouck's giant Roland appears on Trinity Sunday with his friends Tis-je, Tas-je and Toria. In Douai Gayant and his family of four take their walk on the Sunday after 5 July. Born in 1538, he claims to be the oldest giant in the Nord. He represents Jean Gélon who, in the 11th century, saved the town from a band of brigands. Arras has Colas and Jacqueline waiting in the town hall for fête days.

miners fully while they trained for new jobs. The old houses have been cleaned, gutted and modernised.

South from Arras the N17 has been relieved of much of its terrible traffic by the A1 motorway for some time now, but is still busy. Bapaume, the first big town, was absolutely flattened in the First World War. The Germans took it, abandoned it in March 1917, took it back a year later, and were finally driven out in August 1918 by the New Zealanders, part of the British 3rd and 4th Army force which drove 35 German divisions across the Somme battlefield, taking 34,000 prisoners. This whole area of northern

France, where the Germans had built the strong Hindenburg Line, lost centuries of heritage in four dreadful years.

The N39 south-east from Arras, the Cambrai road, is almost dead straight because it is of Roman origin. This was yet another First World War battle area, fiercely contested. The names are still there — Observation Ridge, Telegraph Hill. From little Monchy-le-Preux the Germans had a view right over the British lines. Now cereals and beetroot are grown round here and it is one of the most fertile areas of France.

Built in 1786, the Town Hall of Cambrai was completely reconstructed after destruction in the First World War

Cambrai, on the banks of the Escaut river which runs into the St. Quentin canal, is a market town. It has also been a textile town since the 14th century, making the fine linen called cambric mentioned by Shakespeare. Its linen handkerchiefs are famous. Cambrai has recovered after being badly damaged in both world wars. In the Battle of Cambrai in 1917 tanks were used for the first time. Its old ramparts have become pleasant boulevards and as it is mainly built in white limestone it is quite an attractive town. Its best old buildings are religious.

The Gothic cathedral, said to have been one of the finest in the world, was destroyed in the Revolution and replaced by the 18th-century abbey-church of Notre-Dame. Its tower was built in 1876. The cathedral has frequently been restored after various wars but has kept its neo-classical style. Inside is a monument to the great Fénelon who was Archbishop here. It was sculpted in 1826 by Jean-Pierre David, usually called David d'Angers after his birthplace.

There is a statue of Fénelon in white stone in the centre of a square across the road from the cathedral, and just outside the square is the Chapelle du Grand Séminaire, a Jesuit chapel until 1692. It has a very ornate baroque façade in the great Baroque Flamand (Flemish) style born in the superb old Bourse in Lille. Inside the chapel is a remarkable collection of religious art from the Middle Ages to the 19th century. On the corner of the square is a wooden house of the 16th century known as Maison Espagnole. The 17th-18th-century church of St. Géry, with a 76-metre tower, has a beautiful red and marble rood screen from 1635 and an enormous painting of the Entombment by Rubens.

The third great tower of Cambrai is the belfry, 70 metres high, all that is left of the 15th-century church of St. Martin. Two mechanical figures mark the hour by hammering in a bell. They are called Martin and Martine and have been there since 1512.

Fénelon

François de Salignac de la Mothe Fénelon was born in Château de Fénelon in Périgueux in 1651, one of eleven children. He was a student in Cahors and used to stay at the priory of Carennac where his uncle was Senior Prior. At 20 he went to a seminary in Paris and was ordained in 1675. His uncle died and in 1681 he became Commendatory Prior of Carennac in his uncle's place. Here he wrote *Télémaque*, the adventures of Ulysses' son, but did not have it published.

Then Louis XIV appointed him tutor to his grandson, the young Duke of Burgundy, and in this position Fénelon wrote several books including his *Fable* and *Dialogues of the Dead*. His book *Maximes des Saints* caused a fierce controversy and the Pope condemned it. In 1695 the King made him Archbishop of Cambrai. Then he published *Télémaque* which Louis XIV immediately took to be a satire on his court. Fénelon was restrained within his diocese. He spent the rest of his life looking after it and his reputation for kindness and understanding made him popular in Cambrai, although he was not so understanding with Protestants. He died in 1715 in a carriage accident.

In a fine 18th-century mansion in rue de l'Épée is the Musée Municipal, which contains a good collection of Dutch and Flemish works, including paintings by Ingres, Boudin, Utrillo and Maurice de Vlaminck, the eccentric and rebellious painter who chose the bold use of colour called Fauvism, of which Matisse was the greatest exponent. Vlaminck was a racing cyclist, then a violinist before he took to painting. There are sculptures by Rodin, Bourdelle and an inevitable bust of Fénelon by J-B. Lemoyne (18th-century).

It is understandable that Cambrai should be so proud of Fénelon, who was not only their archbishop but who also died there. But it is rather sad that I have found nothing to commemorate a man who was born there — Louis Blériot, one of the greatest airmen and aircraft designers. Not only was he the first man to cross the Channel in an aeroplane in 1909 but he designed monoplanes which were the pioneers of many later aircraft in France and Britain.

Cambrai was hotly disputed by the French and Burgundians for centuries and was finally taken for France after a siege by Louis XIV in 1677. It was captured by the Duke of Wellington in 1815, the Prussians in 1870, then by the German General Von Kluck in August 1914, after which it became the headquarters of Prince Rupprecht of Bavaria. The Germans occupied it again from May 1940 to 3 September 1944.

Along the N43, 22km south-east of Cambrai, is the little industrial town of **Le Cateau-Cambrésis**, Wellington's headquarters in 1815 and birthplace of Henri Matisse, the artist, in 1869. His family lived in the nearby village of

Bohain but he was born in his grandparents' house at 45 rue de la République, in Le Cateau.

In 1951 Le Cateau started a museum of contemporary art in Matisse's honour. He gave them a number of his works — sculptures, paintings, a tapestry, hangings, engravings and drawings. The museum was called after him. He died in 1954. In the 1970s his family gave further Matisse items and the museum was transferred to Palais Fénelon in rue Charles-Seyeoux (closed Monday, Tuesday except in July, August). The most interesting works are paintings he did in his younger days and a 1946 Gobelins tapestry, 'The Lute'.

Cambrai to Lille

North of Cambrai is a playground of waterways almost unknown outside the area. Called Étangs de la Sensée, they are named after the Sensée river, a tributary of the river Escaut, which runs from Cambrai north-east to Valenciennes. The Sensée canal from Douai runs through them and joins the modern Canal du Nord in the middle of the little lakes. From Lécluse to Wasnes-au-Bac there is a string of these lakes stretching across the countryside — mostly pretty, among high foliage and ringed with poplar trees. In summer families from Douai, Cambrai and Arras go there to picnic and spot the wild waterfowl, and most of the year the waterways are a fisherman's mecca. At Aubigny-au-Bac is a beach where there are pedalos and boats and people bring their canoes. Brunémont has a campsite, Lécluse has chalets for fishermen, Féchain has good fishing and Palluel has its devotees seeking peace. At Arleux, the biggest village, they grow garlic. The N43, which joins Cambrai to Douai, passes alongside Aubigny-au-Bac.

Douai is much maligned. We confess to avoiding it for years. It seemed to have everything stacked against it. Until recently capital of the coal-mining country, centre of chemical and metallurgical industries, it was totally wrecked in two world wars, and is now hemmed in by big main roads rumbling with lorries, and has a mind-bending one-way system. Now we know that it is a vital, likeable town, with an important university and a delightful 15th-century town hall belfry, in an ostentatious Gothic style, flaunting itself like an overdressed actress. 'So amusing, so mad, so alive,' said Victor Hugo in 1837. And Corot's painting of it is in the Louvre. The jingle of its 62 bells on each quarter and hour seems to be Douai's song of defiance to the two enemies that have tried to destroy this old Flemish town — wars and industry. The bells give special concerts each Saturday morning and on fête days, and on Monday evenings in mid-summer. You can climb the steep 190 step belfry stair for a view of the town (daily 1 April–31 August, on Sundays all the year).

The spirit of Douai lives in its annual carnival Le Cortège des Gayants. On the second Sunday in July five giants in the costume of the Middle Ages are carried throught the town by folkloric groups. These are Gayant, the father, 7.5 metres tall, made in 1538, Marie Caregon, his wife, 6.5 metres tall, and their

The belltower of Douai, built in 1390, has a carillon of 62 bells, and there are regular musical recitals

children Jacquot, Binbin and Filion. This starts a week of feasts, parties, concerts, ballets, folk dancing, organ recitals and carillon concerts from the belfry, finishing with a revue and firework display.

Around the Town Hall and off the Grande Place, rich in pavement cafés, are narrow streets with delightful 18th-century houses — giving the area an elegant 18th-century atmosphere. A warren of narrow streets open onto the quays of the river Scarpe which bisects the town.

The 16th–18th-century buildings of the Ancienne Chartreuse house the museum (closed Tuesdays) which contains some excellent paintings and bronzes. The Chartreuse itself, mainly 16th-century, is plain but beautiful. There are some superb Flemish works of art inside, including a series of 15th–16th-century altarpieces, a Brussels tapestry and some excellent panels, especially those by Jean Bellegambe, a local 16th-century artist. His wood works here are quite a revelation and his carved bronze Tripod of Bacchus is superb.

There are works by Veronese and Caracci and the Dutch paintings inevitably include a Van Dyck. In the French section David, Courbet and Delacroix are represented. Good late-19th-century works include those of Pissarro, Renoir and Sisley. The piece which draws the most public attention is a bronze by Rodin — 'The Prodigal Son'.

Due east of Douai and north-east of Cambrai, **Valenciennes** had a beautiful old town centre in wood until the Second World War. Its old ramparts have become boulevards. It has many factories now but was once called the Athens of the North because of its citizens' taste for art and the number of artists who lived there. In the 18th century it had a famous École des Beaux Arts, an Academy of Art and a Salon for display.

The Musée des Beaux Arts in boulevard Watteau is magnificent. Most famous of its native artists was Antoine Watteau, the great rococo painter who invented the *fêtes galantes* type of painting in which elegant people live in a dream world of music, pleasure and dalliance. You can see two outstanding examples here in his 'Country Pastimes' and 'Open-Air Concert', though the portrait of the father of his friend and fellow *fêtes galantes* artist Jean-Baptiste Pater, who also lived here, is quite different.

The sculptor Jean Carpeaux was born in Valenciennes. He revived French sculpture in the 19th century, and became notorious for his gorgeously brazen and erotic group 'La Danse' which was put outside l'Opéra in Paris in 1869, to be violated and covered in ink by puritanical Parisians. It is now in the Louvre. It would be splendid to see it back outside l'Opéra.

A large room is given to his sculptures, bronzes and to interesting plaster maquettes of nearly all his great works, including 'La Danse'. Another room is devoted to his lesser-known paintings and watercolours, mostly intended to help him in his sculptural compositions. There are works in the museum by Jean-Baptiste Pater, not as good as Watteau, and of two family imitators, Louis and François Watteau, nephew and great-nephew. A whole room is devoted to Rubens, including a magnificent 'Landscape With Rainbow'.

In the quiet, green place Watteau, by St. Géry's church with a 19th-century façade and lovely 13th-century interior, is a fountain with a statue of Watteau by Carpeaux, who was born round the corner at 39 rue de Paris.

St. Amand-Raismes Regional Park begins almost on the northern edge of Valenciennes — 10,000 hectares, of which 6,000 are forest. It has forest roads and footpaths, lakes, wild game, including boar and deer, a campsite, and sailing and boating on Étang d'Amaury, a lake of 100 hectares.

The spa of **St. Amand-les-Eaux** is on the Scarpe river and is known for its faïence pottery. It has an 82-metre-high belfry from 1624. You must climb 365 steps to reach the bell, but the view is rewarding. The bell is called Amanda, weighs 4,650 kg and was made in the 17th century.

The spa treatment establishment has some of the most radio-active waters in France, at a temperature of 26°C, and is used in treating rheumatic problems.

The remains of a 17th-century abbey in Grande Place are beautiful and inside is a fine collection of 18th-century pottery. The old Echevinage (entrance pavilion) with its belltower is a Flemish Renaissance masterpiece. Inside are paintings by the Watteau nephew Louis. It is a rewarding little town.

The D169 from Anzin, the suburb of Valenciennes across the Escaut river, leads through the forest to St. Amand-les-Eaux. Turn left onto the D955 and you can reach the D957 which runs into the D549 to the outskirts of Lille. If you do not want to use the motorway, this is a longer but more attractive route from Cambrai to Lille than going through Douai. It misses the Douai–Lens coalfields.

Lille is a great, sprawling industrial city, economic capital of Northern France and like all industrial capitals it has a dozen different faces, from ugly, noisy conglomerations and huge factory developments to beautiful old and modern buildings and good museums. The people of Lille work very hard, play very hard and eat very well. Its energy is exhausting, even to a bystander.

Its importance as a communications centre is international, for motorways converge here from Paris, Dunkerque, Ostend, Antwerp, Brussels and

Cologne and sometimes when you are leaving it seems difficult not to get onto one. Its railway junctions are some of the most important in Europe, including 'TGV LILLE-EUROPE'. It is hardly a holiday town, unless you want to combine business and pleasure by touring its great restaurants or by joining another half-million visitors to its huge annual International Fair in April. The Paris–Lille railway was operating as early as 1846.

Its industrial suburbs of Roubaix and Tourcoing northwards spread to the Belgian border. It makes tractors, turbines and diesel engines, has chemical, metal, cotton, linen and printing works, and is famed for biscuits, chocolate, sugar products, beer and spirits. It has built a vast new hospital complex and is a university city. The new buildings of the justly renowned Université des Sciences de Lille are at a highly planned new town, Villeneuve d'Ascq, 8km to the east.

Most of the things especially worth seeing are around the old quarter, with place Général-de-Gaulle at the centre. Lille had more right than most French towns to give the general's name to its main square. He was born there in 1890.

The most beautiful building is the 17th-century Flemish baroque Ancienne Bourse, which is made up of 28 houses side by side, with an arcaded gallery in a square around a big courtyard, so peaceful after Lille's noisy traffic. The carved decoration is magnificent, with colour typical of Flemish baroque. This was the age of 'pictorial stone-cutters', and you can see some lovely examples

Flowers are sold in Lille's 17th-century Ancienne Bourse, where fortunes were once made

of their work in the buildings which have survived Lille's very stormy history. Maison de Gilles de la Boé (1636) is covered with carving. The whole fronts of some houses were carved as if they were sculptured works of art. The row of houses called Rang de Beauregard (1687) opposite the Nouvelle Bourse in place du Théâtre is carved as one piece of sculpture.

The old Hospice St. Sauveur is another of these sculptured Flemish buildings with arcaded galleries and windows framed with decoration. In contrast, the modern Palais de Justice (1969) is a concrete and glass tower, though the carved wall of one room and fine contemporary tapestries add decorative relief.

Another superb building is the Hospice Comtesse, named after the Countess of Flanders, Jeanne de Constantinople, who founded it in 1237. It was rebuilt in the 15th century after a fire. The Salle des Malades has wooden vaults and fine 15th-century windows with broken arches.

There are several interesting churches in Lille, especially the vast Gothic St. Maurice, built between the 15th and 19th centuries, with five gables and a lacework spire, and inside a mass of tall columns.

Lille has had a turbulent history. The counts of Flanders owned it, then the dukes of Burgundy (under whom it mainly flourished). It became a Spanish possession, part of Spanish Flanders. Then it was annexed by France. The Noble Tour (1459) a truncated keep, survives from its original ramparts. It is now a memorial to the Resistance fighters of the Second World War, many of whom were shot by the Nazis. The Roubaix and de Grand gates (1610–22) were part of defences.

Louis XIV built the enormous Citadelle after he took Lille in 1667. It was built by the master, Vauban, and is one of his greatest masterpieces. Its shape is a regular pentagon with bastions and ravelins outer defences. For a fortress it is strangely beautiful. Two thousand workers took three years to build it with 60 million bricks dressed with stone. The entrance to the main fortifications is by a monumental decorated arch, Porte Royale. The citadel is still held by the army but you can visit it on Sundays in summer. Outside among the lawns where you can walk is a little zoo and children's playground.

Near the modern Town Hall with its 108-metre tower is Porte de Paris, a memorial arch by Simon Vollant, built in the late 17th century to the glory of Louis XIV, showing him being crowned by Victory. That was when he was winning victories in Flanders and Germany, before he ran up against two of the greatest generals in history — the Duke of Marlborough and Prince Eugène, the Austrian born in Paris who drove the Turks out of Hungary and to whom Louis had refused a commission. These two inflicted a series of such heavy defeats on him that he had to make a humiliating peace, losing most of his Netherlands conquests, and France was nearly bankrupt. But Lille remained French.

Lille was besieged and nearly starved eleven times, as well as suffering harshly from German occupation in both world wars. This may account for the love of good eating — almost a local tradition.

Lille is proud of its Symphony Orchestra and its Musée des Beaux Arts, housing one of the finest art collections in France. You need days to see it. Pictures range from the Flemish paintings of Jean Bellegambe, Bruegel the Elder and Bosch to the Italians (Titian and Veronese), from Rubens to Goya, and from the three Watteaus to the Impressionists.

The museum dates from 1792 when Louis Watteau, nephew of Antoine and an adopted citizen of Lille, persuaded the local council that the works seized from religious institutions during the Revolution should be seen by the people. Thus in one room are four enormous, beautiful but depressing altarpieces: Ruben's 'Descent from the Cross' and 'Martyrdom of St. Catherine', Jordaens' 'Temptations of the Magdalene' and Van Dyck's 'Christ on the Cross'.

There are oddities. The star of the show for a long time was the wax 'Head of a Woman'. Experts believed it was by Raphael, then by Leonardo da Vinci. Today they think it is a 17th-century work of the Flemish sculptor who worked in Rome, François Duquesnoy, though why that should detract from its artistic value is difficult to fathom.

Among the earlier works are two panels by the Dutch artist Dieric Bouts, who died around 1475, called 'Hell' and 'Paradise'. The 'Hell' panel has such gruesome scenes and fiendish devils that it must have frightened thousands of medieval peasants into treading the straight and narrow path. Ironically amusing is Goya's 'Time or the Elderly Woman' — grostesque old lady, heavily made up, staring in a mirror marked *Que tal?* (How are you?) with the winged figure of Time behind her. It was said that Goya intended people to recognise Queen Maria Luisa of Spain, which was naughty of him because he was court painter to her husband King Charles and had painted the usual flattering portraits of all the royal family.

Among the moderns are good paintings by Monet, Corot, Boudin, Sisley, Lépine, Jongkind, Fantin-Latour and Courbet.

It is an interesting, varied museum and deserves a new, better-lit and less depressing building. Depression is not characteristic of Lille — or of Flanders.

Part Three
Practical Information

Phone Number Changes

France's eight figure phone numbers become ten-figure numbers in autumn 1996. A two-figure prefix will be added to each number according to the first two figures of its present eight numbers. thus: 31.03.02.00 becomes **02**.31.03.02.00.

Present numbers starting	Now begin	Present numbers starting	Now begin	Present numbers starting	Now begin
20	03	47	02	75	04
21	03	48	02	76	04
22	03	49	05	77	04
23	03	50	02	78	04
24	03	53	05	79	04
25	03	54	02	80	03
26	03	55	05	81	03
27	03	56	05	82	03
28	03	57	05	83	03
29	03	58	05	84	03
31	02	59	05	85	03
32	02	60	03	86	03
33	02	61	05	87	03
34	02	62	05	88	03
35	02	63	05	89	03
37	02	65	05	90	04
38	02	66	04	91	04
39	02	67	04	92	04
40	02	68	04	93	04
41	02	69	04	94	04
42	04	70	04	95	04
43	02	71 ·	04	96	02
44	03	72	04	97	02
45	05	73	04	98	02
46	05	74	04	99	02

Paris and all Île de France numbers at present beginning (1) will instead begin **01**. These numbers at present start (1) 30, 34, 39, 40, 41, 42, 43, 44, 45, 46, 47, 48, 49, 53, 60, 64, 69.

This section is divided into two parts: Normandy (Chapters 4, 5 and 6) and Somme, Picardy, Pas de Calais (Chapters 7, 8 and 9).

Normandy

Tourist Offices (Offices de Tourisme and Syndicats d'Initiative)

NORMANDY — Comité Régional de Tourisme, 14 rue Charles Corbeau, 27000 Evreux (32.31.05.89).

ALENÇON — Maison d'Ozé, Alençon, 61000 Orne (33.26.11.36).

BAGNOLES-DE-L'ORNE — pl. République, Bagnoles, 61140 Orne (33.37.85.66).

BAYEUX – Pont St. Jean, Bayeux, 14400 Calvados (31.92.16.26).

CABOURG — Jardins du Casino, Cabourg, 14390 Calvados (31.91.01.09).

CAEN — pl. St. Pierre, Caen, 14000 Calvados (31.86.27.65).

CHERBOURG — 2 quai Alexandre III, Cherbourg, 50100 Manche (33.93.52.02).

DEAUVILLE — pl. Mairie, Deauville, 14800 Calvados (31.88.21.43).

DIEPPE — Quai du Carénage, 76200 Seine-Maritime (35.84.11.77).

EVREUX — 1 pl. Gén-de-Gaulle, Evreux, 27000 Eure (32.24.04.43).

FALAISE — bd de la Libération, Falaise, 14700 Calvados (31.90.17.26).

OUISTREHAM — Jardins du Casino, Riva-Bella, Ouistreham, 14150 Calvados (31.97.18.63).

ROUEN — 25 pl. Cathédrale, Rouen, 76000 Seine-Maritime (35.71.41.77).

ST. LÔ — Place du Gén. de Gaulle, St. Lô, 50000 Manche (33.05.02.09).

Recommended Hotels and Restaurants

A = Very expensive, B = Expensive, C = Moderately expensive, D = Moderate, E = Inexpensive.

ALENÇON: 61000 Orne, **Petit Vatel** (restaurant), 72 pl. Cdt-Desmeulles (33.26.23.78). Excellent modern and regional dishes. Meals B–D. Balzac's 'Gourmands of Alençon' would look no further.

LES ANDELYS: 27700 Eure, **Chaîne d'Or**, 27 rue Grande (32.54.00.31). Classic old coaching inn. Meals B–D. Rooms C–E. Gained Michelin star, 1996

ARGENTAN: 61200 Orne, **Renaissance**, 20 av. 2e-Division-Blindée (33.36.14.20). Reliable, meals with individuality. Meals B–E. Rooms C–E.

ARROMANCHES: 14117 Calvados, **Marine**, quai Canada (31.22.34.19). Simple hotel right on landing beach. Regional cooking. Good shellfish. Meals B–E. Rooms D. Shut mid-Nov–mid-Feb.

AVRANCHES: 50300 Manche, **Croix d'Or**, 83 rue Constitution (33.58.04.88). Old posting inn, rustic furniture; cosy bedrooms. Meals D. Rooms C–D. Shut mid-Nov–mid-March.

BAGNOLES-DE-L'ORNE: 61140 Orne, **Manoir du Lys**, 3km on D335, D235 (33.37.80.69). Delightful old manor renowned for Norman cuisine. Meals C–D. Rooms A–C.

BAYEUX: 14400 Calvados, **Lion d'Or**, 71 rue St. Jean (31.92.06.90). Old coaching inn. Well run. Good value meals. Excellent wine cellar. Meals B–D. Rooms C–D.

LA BOUILLE: 76530 Grand Couronne, Seine-Maritime, **St. Pierre** (35.23.80.10). On banks of the Seine. Delightful inn, superb cooking; book. Meals–Rooms C–D.

BRETEUIL-SUR-ITON: 27160 Eure, **Mail**, rue Neuve-de-Bémécourt (32.29.81.54). Restful 18th-century house with beams, nice garden, good cooking. Meals C. Rooms C–E.

BRICQUEBEC: 50260 Manche, **Vieux Château** (33.52.24.49). Good regional meals. Meals C–E. Rooms D–E.

BRIONNE: 27800 Eure, **Vieux Donjon**, rue Soie (32.44.80.62). Small, with flowery courtyard. Imaginative dishes. Meals B–E. Rooms D–E.

CABOURG: 14390 Calvados, **Pullman Grand Hotel**, promenade Marcel Proust (31.91.01.79). Ghosts of the 1920s. Luxurious and dear. Inventive and classical dishes. Meals B. Rooms A.

CAEN: 14000 Calvados, **Daniel Tuboeuf**, 8 rue Buquet (31.43.64.48). Modern décor, excellent cooking, with imagination, at reasonable prices. Meals B–D.
Le Dauphin, 29 rue Gemare (31.86.22.26). Norman country cooking; nice but small bedrooms in old priory. Meals B–E. Rooms C–D.
Manoir d'Hastings, at Bénouville 10km north-east by the new Pegasus Bridge (31.44.62.43). Superb Norman and 'modern regional' cooking. Gorgeous expensive bedrooms; in ancient priory. Meals A–B. Rooms A. Book.

CARTERET: 50270 Manche, **La Marine**, 11 rue de Paris (33.53.83.31). Outstanding shellfish. Well run. Meals A–B. Rooms B–C.

CAUDEBEC-EN-CAUX: 76490 Seine-Maritime, **Normandie**, 19 quai Guilbaud (35.96.25.11). Traditional Logis. Regional cooking, good value. Meals C–E. Rooms D–E.

CHERBOURG: 50100 Manche, **Le Faitout**, rue Tour-Carrée (33.04.25.04). Jolly bistro, old family dishes (*pot-au-feu*). Sensibly priced wines. Meals C–E.

CLÉCY: 14570 Calvados, **Moulin du Vey** (31.69.71.08). Delightful converted water mill by lovely river Orne. Good imaginative cooking. Meals B–D. Rooms C–D.

CONCHES: 27190 Eure, **Toque Blanche** (restaurant), 18 pl. Carnot (32.30.01.54). Norman cooking with *trou normand* in old building served in Norman costume. Meals B–D.

DEAUVILLE: 14800 Calvados, **Ciro's**, sur Les Planches (31.88.18.10). Famous restaurant on the promenade. Meals A–C.
Le Spinnaker, 52 rue Mirabeau (31.88.24.40). Modernised Norman dishes. Prices moderate for Michelin star. Meals B–C.

DIEPPE: 76200 Seine-Maritime, **Marmite Dieppoise**, 8 rue St. Jean (35.84.24.26). Still the best of Dieppe's many fish restaurants. Meals C–E.
Hotel Europe, bd de Verdun (35.90.19.19). New comfortable B & B hotel, all rooms with sea view; useful. Rooms C. Breakfast E.
Restaurant St. Jacques, 12 rue Oranger (35.84.52.04). Inventive dishes. Excellent cuisine. Meals B–E.
Arcades, l'Arcade de la Bourse (35.84.14.12). On harbour front. Simple. Good value. Meals B–D. Rooms D–E.

EU: 76260 Seine-Maritime, **Pavillon Joinville**, route du Tréport (35.86.24.03). Former royal hunting lodge; very attractive rooms and grounds. Meals B–C. Rooms A–C.

FALAISE: 14700 Calvados, **Fine Fourchette** (restaurant), 52 rue Georges-Clemenceau (31.90.08.59). Classic cooking, good choice. Meals B–E.

GRANVILLE: 50400 Manche, **Bains**, **Restaurant Potinière**, 19 rue Clemenceau (33.50.17.31). Modernised grand hotel with sea views. Lovely fish. Meals B–E. Rooms B–D.

LE HAVRE: 76600 Seine-Maritime, **Hotel Bordeaux**, 147 rue L. Brindeau (35.22.69.44). Town centre; totally renovated. No restaurant. Rooms C–D.
Nice-Havrais (restaurant) at Ste. Adresse, 76310 Seine-Maritime, 6 pl. F.-Sauvage (35.46.14.59). Lovely sea views, excellent cooking, especially fish. Meals B–E.

HONFLEUR: 14600 Calvados, **Cheval Blanc**, quai Passagers (31.81.65.00). Historic hotel overlooking old harbour. Rooms B–C. Next door is Honfleur's best restaurant **Assiette Gourmande** (31.89.24.88). Famous chef Gérard Bonnefoy, careful, clever cooking. Meals A–D.
Auberge de la Source, Barneville-le-Bertran, 6km SW (31.89.25.02). Pleasant country hotel. Very good fish. Meals C–D (weekends only except 1 June–31 August). Rooms D–E.

LYONS-LA-FORÊT: 27480 Eure, **La Licorne** (32.49.62.02). Fine old inn. Classical cooking. Meals B–C. Rooms B–C.

MESNIL-VAL: 76910 Criel-sur-Mer, Seine-Maritime, **Vieille Ferme** (35.86.72.18). 17th-century farmhouse. Lovely dishes. Meals C–E. Rooms C. We love it.

MONT-ST. MICHEL: 50116 Manche, **Terrasses Poulard** (33.60.14.09). Lovely hotel, superb rooms; book. Large popular restaurant. Meals C–E. Rooms A–D.

ORBEC: 14290 Calvados, **France**, 152 rue Grande (31.32.74.02). 18th-century post-house inn, friendly, good value. In lovely countryside. Meals C–E. Rooms D–E.

OUISTREHAM-RIVA BELLA: 14150 Calvados, **Normandie**, 71 av Michel-Cabieu (31.97.19.57). Popular restaurant for Norman cooking and shellfish. Meals D–E. Rooms D.

PONT-AUDEMER: 27500 Eure, **Auberge du Vieux Puits**, 6 rue Notre-Dame-du-Pré (32.41.01.48). 17th-century house in charming gardens, antique furnishings, beams. Fine cooking. Meals B–C. Rooms C–D .

ROUEN: 76000 Seine-Maritime, **Dieppe et Restaurant Le Quatre Saisons**, pl. Bernard-Tissot (35.71.96.00). Charming old house with modern comforts. Regional cooking. Meals C–D. Rooms B–C.
Les Nymphéas, 9 rue Pie (35.89.26.69). Our young favourite from La Bouille, Patrick Kukurudz, is a new star of Rouen. Great cooking with Norman prejudice. Order the menus. Meals A–D.

ST. GATIEN-DES-BOIS: 14130 Pont l'Évêque, Calvados, **Le Clos St. Gatien** (31.65.16.08). Lovely old black and white farm beside forest. Meals D–E. Rooms E.

ST. JEAN-LE-THOMAS: 50530 Sartilly, Manche, **Bains** (33.48.84.20). Excellent little seaside hotel. Delightful Norman cooking (closed October–end March). Meals C–E. Rooms D–E.

ST. LÔ: 50000 Manche, **Le Marignan**, pl. Gare (33.05.15.15). Good classical-regional cooking. Meals A–E. Rooms D–E; good wines.

ST. MARTIN-AUX-CHARTRAINS: 14130 Pont l'Évêque, Calvados, **Auberge de la Truite** (31.65.21.64). Good modern cooking by chef-patron. 8km from Deauville. Meals B–E.

ST. VAAST-LA-HOUGUE: 50550 Manche, **France et Fuchsias**, rue Maréchal-Foch (33.54.42.26). Covered in climbing fuchsias. Fish from quayside, vegetables from own farm. Bedrooms vary. Meals B–E. Rooms C–E.

TRELLY: 50660 Manche, **La Verte Campagne**, Hameau Chevalier (33.47.65.33). Farmhouse with a Michelin star (see text). Excellent Norman orientated dishes. Meals A–D. Rooms C–E.

VARENGEVILLE: 76119 Seine-Maritime, **La Terrasse**, 3km at Vasterival (35.85.12.54). Good value. Meals D–E. Rooms D–E.

VERNEUIL-SUR-AVRE: 27130 Eure, **Hostellerie du Clos**, 98 rue Ferté-Vidame (32.32.21.81). Elegant, well-run Grande Epoque manor house. Meals B–C. Rooms A.

VILLEDIEU-LES-POÊLES: 50800 Manche, **St. Pierre et St. Michel**, 12 pl. République (33.61.00.11). Friendly inn used by locals. Excellent value cheap meals. Meals D–E. Rooms D–E.

VIRONVAY: 27400 Louviers, Eure, **Les Saisons** (32.40.02.56). Attractive chalet hotel. Good meals. Meals B–D. Rooms A–B.

Events

LES ANDELYS: mid-September — Fair.

BAGNOLES-DE-L'ORNE: end April–end October — Casino galas and horse events.

BERNAY: end March–early April — Flower Fair.

BEUVRON-EN-AUGE: November — Cider Festival.

BRICQUEBEC: 30 July–1 August — Fête of St. Anne (Cavalcade).

CAUDEBEC-EN-CAUX: July — Church Organ Recitals. September — Best Cider Contest.

CAEN: March — Spring Fair. September — Caen Fair.

CHERBOURG: Whitsun — International Yacht Rally.

DEAUVILLE: mid-July–end August — International horse-racing, show-jumping, polo. End August, mid-September — Yearling Sales.

DIEPPE: mid-June — Sea Festival. Mayday and September — International Kite-flying Championships. August — Summer Fair. September — Herring Fair.

DOMFRONT: early July — Beer and Folklore Festival.

ÉTRETAT: early May — Fêtes Normandes.

EU: end May — Carnival.

EURE DÉPARTEMENT: mid-May–mid-June — Eure en Fleurs — 150 displays through Département.

EVREUX: 6 December — St. Nicolas Fair.

FÉCAMP: early July — International Folklore Procession, and Blessing of the Sea.

FORGES-LES-EAUX: mid-June — Vintage and Veteran Car Rally.

GISORS: end August — Flower Festival.

GRANVILLE: Sunday before Mardi Gras — Carnival. Last Sunday in July — Pardon of the Sea, Torch Pilgrimage. Mid-August — Summer Carnival.

LE HAVRE: regattas through summer. Early July — Sea Festival. Mid-August — Grand Flower Show.

HONFLEUR: Whitsun — Procession of Fishermen and Blessing of the Sea.

LA HAYE-DE-ROUTOT: 16 July — St. Clair Bonfire.

LE TRÉPORT: mid-July — Sea Festival. End May — Mussel Fair.

LISIEUX: end September — Pilgrimage of Ste. Thérèse.

LYONS-LA-FORÊT: early May — Forest Game Festival. Whitsun — Craft Festival. End June — St. Jean Bonfire. Mid-October —- Feast of St. Denis.

MONT-ST. MICHEL: early May — St. Michel's Religious and Folk Festival. End June–early July — Festival of the Mont. July — Great Pilgrimage. Last Sunday in September — Fête of St. Michel.

MORTAGNE-AU-PERCHE: mid-March — International Boudin (Black Pudding) Contest. End August — Dog Fair.

MORTRÉE: July — Music Soirées in Château d'O.

NEUFCHÂTEL-EN-BRAY: November — Fair St. Martin.

PACY-SUR-EURE: mid-November — Autumn Fair.

PIN-AU-HARAS: 1st & last Sundays in September and dates in October — Horse Competitions, Processions and Presentations.

ROUEN: end May — Festival of St. Joan of Arc.

ST. CHRISTOPHE-LE-JAJOLET: last Sunday in July and 1st Sunday in October — Pilgrimage of Blessing the Motor Cars.

STE. MÈRE-ÉGLISE and STE. MARIE-DU-MONT: 6 June — Commemoration of D-Day Landings.

ST. LÔ: May — Horse Trials and Contests.

ST. VALERY-EN-CAUX: mid-July — Sea Festival.

VERNON: end May — Cherry Fair.

VIMOUTIERS: 3rd weekend in October — Apple Fair (with cider and calvados).

(See also Box in Chapter 3 for information on markets.)

Museums

L'AIGLE: Musée Juin 44: Bataille de Normandie (33.24.19.44). Open Easter to All Saints' Day. Closed Mon.

ALENÇON: Musée des Beaux-Arts et de la Dentelle (33.26.61.25). Open all year. Closed Mon.

ARGENTAN: Le 'Point d'Argentan' (33.67.12.01). Pm except Sun and holidays.

ARROMANCHES: Musée du Débarquement (31.22.34.31). Open all year.

BARENTON: Maison de la Pomme et de la Poire (33.59.56.22). Open April–end Sept.

BAYEUX: Tapisserie de la Reine Mathilde (31.92.05.48). Open all year.
Musée Baron Gérard (31.92.14.21). Open all year.
Musée Memorial de la Bataille de Normandie (31.92.93.41). Open all year (Nov–Feb weekends only).

BEC-HELLOUIN: Musée Automobile (32.44.86.06). Closed Wed and Thurs in winter.

CAEN: Musée des Beaux-Arts (31.85.28.63). Closed Tues and public holidays.
Musée de Normandie (31.86.06.24). Open as Beaux-Arts.
Musée de la Poste et des Techniques de Communication (31.50.12.20). Closed Sun and Mon.
Musée-Mémorial (31.06.06.44). Open all year.

CAUDEBEC-EN-CAUX: Musée de la Marine de Seine (35.96.27.30). Closed Tues except Jul, Aug. Nov, Dec open Sat and Sun pm only.

CHERBOURG: Musée de la Guerre et de la Libération (33.20.14.12). Closed Tues low season and public holidays.
Musée Thomas-Henry (33.44.40.22). Closed Tues and public holidays.

CLÉCY: Musée du Chemin de Fer Miniature (31.69.07.13). Open daily Easter–end Sept. Sun pm only rest of year.

CLÈRES: Musée de l'Automobile et Militaire (35.33.23.02). Open all year.

COURSEULLES-SUR-MER: Parc à Huitres. Open all year.

DIEPPE: Musée (35.84.14.76). Closed Tues, end Sept–early June.
Musée de la Guerre et du Raid du 19 aout 1942. Open early April–end Sept.

EVREUX: Musée (32.39.34.35). Closed Sun morning, Mon.

FÉCAMP: Musée de la Bénédictine (35.28.00.06). Open end Mar–mid-Nov.

GRANVILLE: Aquarium (33.50.19.10). Open end Mar–mid-Nov.

LE HAVRE: Musée des Beaux-Arts André Malraux (35.42.33.97). Closed Tues and public holidays.

HONFLEUR: Musée de la Marine. Open mid-June–mid-Sept.
Musée Eugène Boudin (31.89.16.47). Closed Tues and Jan, Feb.

LISIEUX: Exposition 'Le Carmel de Ste. Thérèse'. Open Palm Sun–early Oct.

Diorama de Ste. Thérèse (31.62.06.55). Open all year. Closed Sun and public holidays.

LISORES: Ferme-musée Fernand Leger (31.63.53.13). Closed Wed. Nov–Mar open only weekends and holidays.

LIVAROT: Conservatoire des Traditions Fromagères (31.63.45.96). Open daily April–Oct, Wed–Sun rest of year.

LOUVIERS: Musée Municipal. Closed Tues.

LE MOLAY-LITTRY: Musée de la Mine (31.22.95.14). Closed Wed.

MONT-ST. MICHEL: Musée de la Mer (33.60.23.90). Closed Jan.
Musée Historial du Mont (33.60.14.45). Open end Mar–mid-Oct.
Musée Historique (same as Musée de la Mer).

MORTAGNE-AU-PERCHE: Musée Percheron (33.25.25.87). Open Aug–Oct, Sat, Sun, Mon pm.

ORBEC: Musée Municipal (31.32.82.02). Open weekend pm, Easter–Oct. Closed Tues. Also open weekday pm in July, Aug.

OUISTREHAM-RIVA-BELLA: Musée du Débarquement 'No. 4 Commando' (31.97.00.39). Open daily June–Sept, Sat and Sun, Palm Sunday–end May.

ROUEN: Musée des Beaux-Arts (35.71.28.40). Closed Tues and Wed am.
Musée Jeanne d'Arc (35.88.02.70). Open daily May–mid-Sept. Closed Mon rest of year.
Musée Corneille (35.71.63.92). Closed Tues, Wed am.
Musée Flaubert. Closed Mon, Sun and holidays.
Musée des Antiquités. Closed Thurs.
Musée d'Histoire Naturelle. Closed Mon, Tues.
Secq des Tournelles. Closed Wed am, Tues.

RY: Musée des Automates (35.23.61.44). Open Easter–Oct, Mon, Sat, Sun and holidays.

ST. LÔ: Musée des Beaux Arts (33.57.57.01). Closed Tues, am in winter.

STE. MÈRE-ÉGLISE: Musée des Troupes Aéroportées (33.41.41.35). Open daily Feb–mid-Nov. Weekends only mid-Nov–mid-Dec.

STE. OPPORTUNE-LA-MARE: Maison de la Pomme. Open April–Oct Sun pm, daily July–Aug.

TROUVILLE: Aquarium. Open Easter–Oct.

UTAH BEACH: Musée du Débarquement (33.71.53.35). Open daily April–Oct.

VALOGNES: Musée Regional du Cidre (33.40.22.73). Open June–Sept. Closed Sun am, Wed.

VENDEUVRE (CHÂTEAU DE): Musée du Mobilier Miniature (31.40.93.83). Open Easter–All Saints' Day Sun pm and holidays. Daily June–Sept.

VERNON: Musée A.G. Poulain (32.21.28.09). Open pm. Closed Mon and some holidays.

VILLEDIEU-LES-POÊLES: Musée du Cuivre et Maison de la Dentellière (33.61.00.16). Open daily June–Sept.
Fonderie de Cloches (33.61.00.56). Closed Sun and Mon, Oct–May.
Atelier du Cuivre (33.51.31.85). Closed Sun, Mon and holidays Sept–June.

VILLEQUIER: Musée Victor-Hugo (35.56.78.31). Closed Tues, some holidays, also Mon, Oct–April.

VIMOUTIERS: Musée du Camembert (33.39.30.29). Closed Mon am, also Sat pm and Sun, Sept–May.

Châteaux and Historic Buildings

LES ANDELYS: Château Gaillard (32.54.41.93). Open mid-Mar–mid-Nov. Closed Wed am, Tues.

BAILLEUL: Château (35.27.77.87). Open Easter–All Saints' Day, weekends and holidays. Open daily except Mon June–Sept.

BALLEROY: Intérieur du Château (31.21.60.61). Open daily April–Oct except Wed and 1st May.
Musée des Ballons (31.21.60.61). Open as Château.

BARFLEUR: Phare de la Pointe de Barfleur (33.23.10.56). Visits spring holiday–Sept daily. Rest of year Sun and school holidays.

BEAUMESNIL: Château (32.44.40.09). Visits May–Sept, Fri pm, Sat, Sun, Mon.

BEC-HELLOUIN: Abbaye (32.44.86.09). Closed Tues, Sun am and holidays am. Open for concerts 5 or 6 times a year.

BLAINVILLE: Château. Visits July, Aug.

BRICQUEBEC: Château (33.52.21.13). Visits July, Aug. Closed Tues and last weekend in July.

CAEN: Bâtiments conventuels de l'Abbaye aux Hommes (31.84.81.25). Open all year except some holidays.
Bâtiments abbatiaux de l'Abbaye aux Dames (31.43.86.60). Visits all Sat, pm rest of week.

CANY: Château (35.97.70.32). Open July–Sept except Fri and 4th Sun in July.

CLÉCY: Manoir de Placy (31.69.75.06). Open Sun pm, Easter–All Saints' Day, every pm July, Aug.

CLÈRES: Parc Zoologique (35.33.23.08). Open mid-Mar–end Nov.

COQUAINVILLIERS: Distillerie du Moulin de la Foulonnerie (31.62.29.26). Open every day April–mid-Sept. Rest of year Mon–Fri.

CREULLY: Château (31.80.37.64). Open July, Aug.

DOMFRONT: Hôtel de Ville (33.38.65.36). Closed Sun, holidays, Mon am, Sat pm.

FALAISE: Château (31.90.17.26). Closed Sun am, Mon, Tues, Nov–Palm Sunday.

FONTAINE-HENRY: Château (31.80.00.42). Open Easter–Nov some afternoons.

GIVERNY: Maison de Claude Monet et son Jardin (32.51.28.21). Open April–Oct except Mon and Easter.

HAMBYE: Abbaye (33.61.76.92). Open Feb–Dec except Tues, and Wed am low season.

HARCOURT: Château. Open pm Mar–Nov except Tues.

JUMIÈGES: Abbaye (35.37.24.02). Open all year.

MIROMESNIL: Château (35.04.40.30). Open May–Oct pm except Tues.

MONT-ST. MICHEL: Abbaye (33.60.14.14). Open all year.

MORTAIN: Abbaye Blanche (33.59.00.21). Open June–Sept except Sun am and Tues.

NACQUEVILLE: Château (33.03.27.89). Open Easter–Sept except Tues and Fri.
O: Château (33.35.34.69). Open every pm except Tues and Feb.

PIN-AU-HARAS: Haras. Open all year.

PIROU: Château (33.46.34.71). Open all year except Tues.
Son-et-Lumière end July–early Aug 10.30 pm.

ROUEN: Cathédrale Notre-Dame. Visits to crypt, ambulatory and tombs during summer holidays, Easter and weekends and public holidays.
Beffroi (35.71.28.40). Open Palm Sunday–Oct except Tues, Wed am and some holidays.
Hôtel de Bourgtheroulde. Open banking hours and Sat, Sun and holidays pm.
Tour Jeanne d'Arc (35.98.55.10). Open all year except Thurs and some holidays.
Église St. Godard. Open all year.

ST. CHRISTOPHE-LE-JAJOLET: Château de Sassy (33.35.32.66). Open pm Palm Sunday–All Saints' Day.

ST. LÔ: Haras (33.57.14.13). Visits mid-July–mid-Feb.

ST. WANDRILLE: Abbaye (35.96.23.11). Visits to cloisters pm and Sun and holiday am.

THURY-HARCOURT: Parc et Jardins du Château (31.79.65.41). Open July–Oct every pm. April–June Sun and holidays pm.

VARENGEVILLE: Parc des Moustiers (35.85.10.02). Open Mar–Nov except Sun am.
Chapelle St. Dominique (35.85.13.19). Open Whitsun–Sept.
Manoir d'Ango (35.85.12.08). Daily Mar–Nov. Rest of year weekends and holidays.

VASCOEUIL: Château (35.23.62.35). Open afternoons Easter–All Saints' Day.

VERNEUIL-SUR-AVRE: Tour de l'Église de la Madeleine (32.32.17.17). Open 1st Sunday of month April–Nov.

Somme, Picardy, Pas de Calais

Tourist Offices

NORD-PAS DE CALAIS — Comité Régional du Tourisme, 26 pl. Rihour, 59800 Lille (20.57.40.04).

PICARDIE — Comité Régional du Tourisme, 11 Mail Albert Ier, BP 2616 Amiens, 80000 Somme (22.92.26.39).

SOMME — Comité Départemental du Tourisme, 21 rue Ernest-Cauvin, 80000 Amiens (22.92.26.39).

AMIENS — Office de Tourisme, rue Chapeau des Violettes, Amiens, 80000 Somme (22.91.79.28).

ARRAS — Hôtel-de-Ville, Arras, 62000 Pas-de-Calais (21.51.26.95).

BOULOGNE — quai de la Poste, Boulogne, 62200 Pas-de-Calais (21.31.68.38).

CALAIS — 12 bd Clemenceau, Calais, 62100 Pas-de-Calais (21.96.62.40).

CAMBRAI — 48 rue de Noyon, Cambrai, 59400 Nord (27.78.36.15).

DUNKERQUE — Beffroi, Dunkerque, 59140 Nord (28.66.79.21).

LILLE — Palais Rihour, 59800 Lille (20.30.81.00).

ST. OMER — bd Pierre Guillain, St. Omer, 62500 Pas-de-Calais (21.98.08.51).

LE TOUQUET — Palais de l'Europe, Le Touquet, 62520 Pas-de-Calais (21.05.21.65).

Recommended Hotels and Restaurants

ABBEVILLE: 80100 Somme, **L'Escale en Picardie** (restaurant), 15 rue Teinturiers (22.24.21.51). Superb fish. Also shellfish bar for a quick snack. Meals B–D.

AIRE-SUR-LA-LYS: 62120 Pas-de-Calais, **Trois Mousquetaires**, **Château de la Redoute** (21.39.01.11). One of the friendliest and nicest family-run hotels in France, in 19th-century château with grounds and trout lake. Outstanding classical-regional cooking, excellent value. Meals B–E. Rooms B–D.

AMIENS: 80000 Somme, **Le Prieuré**, 17 rue Porion (22.92.22.47). In 16th-century former priory under the cathedral. Talented cooking. Meals C–E. Rooms C–D.

ARDRES: 62610 Pas-de-Calais, **Grand Hotel Clément**, espl. Mar-Leclerc (21.82.25.25). Elegant, part of scene of Ardres. Coolen family have served fine meals since 1917. Meals A–C. Rooms B–C.

ARRAS: 62000 Pas-de-Calais, **La Faisanderie** (restaurant), 45 Grand' Place (21.48.20.76). Dearest and very best in Arras. Superb cooking in lovely old house. Meals A–C.

BERGUES: 59380 Nord, **Tonnelier**, near church (28.68.70.05). Good value. Regional bourgeois cooking. Meals C–E. Rooms D–E.

BOLLEZEELE: 59470 Wormhout, Nora, **Hostellerie St. Louis**, 47 rue Église (28.68.81.83). In an 18th-century château but not quite a 'château hotel'. Friendly,homely, good cooking and value. Meals B–D. Rooms C–E.

BOULOGNE: 62200 Pas-de-Calais, **Métropole**, 51 rue Thiers (21.31.54.30). Pleasant, well kept 'B & B' hotel with charming garden. Excellent situation. Rooms C.
La Matelote, 80 bd Ste. Beuve (21.30.17.97). Tony Lestienne still serves best fish in the area. Meals B–D.
Rest. de Nausicaa, bd Ste. Beuve (21.33.24.24). Lunch only. In Nausicaa entrance. Tony Lestienne directs. Meals D–E.

CALAIS: 62100 Pas-de-Calais, **George V**, 36 rue Royale (21.97.68.00). Modernised. Good food. Meals B–E. Rooms C–E.
Le Channel, 3 bd de la Résistance (21.34.42.30). Wonderfully consistent value over years. Meals C–E.

CAMBRAI: 59400 Nord, **Château de la Motte Fénelon**, square Château (27.83.61.38). Delightful white 19th-century house in big park. Peaceful. Meals B–D. Rooms A–C.

DUNKERQUE: 59140 Nord (Dunkerque is badly off for good restaurants, so see Malo-les-Bains below — almost a suburb — and Tétegham).

ÉTAPLES: 62630 Pas-de-Calais, **Pêcheurs d'Étaples**, quai de la Canche (21.94.06.90). Fish restaurant, run by fishermen's co-operative. Good views. Superb fish and value. Meals C–E.

HARDELOT-PLAGE: 62152 Neufchâtel, Pas-de-Calais, **Parc**, 111 ave François I (21.33.22.11). Very pleasant new hotel with sports facilities in park. New chef offers innovations to traditional dishes. Very good value. Meals C–D. Rooms B.

HAZEBROUCK: 59190 Nord, **Auberge de la Forêt**, at La Motte-au-Bois, 5km south on D946 (28.48.08.78). Logis in heart of Nieppe forest. Good value. Meals B–D. Rooms D–E.

HESDIN: 62140 Pas-de-Calais, **La Chope**, 48 rue d'Arras (21.86.82.73). Logis. Lovely family cooking, mostly Flemish, brightly refurbished. Meals D–E. Rooms D–E.

HESDIN-L'ABBÉ: 62360 Pont-de-Briques St. Étienne, Pas-de-Calais, (4km NE of Hardelot), **Château Cléry**, on N1 (21.83.19.83). Newly converted 18th-century château. Rooms B–C. No restaurant.

LILLE: 59800 Nord. (So many good restaurants that a functional hotel is best for overnights.) **Mercure Royal**, 2 bd Carnot (20.51.05.11). *Fin de siècle* hotel beautifully refurbished rooms. B–C.
La Porte de Gand, at Porte de Gand (20.74.28.66). Robert Bardot, artist and superb chef, has left his Le Flambard to open new restaurant in an historic monument. Lower prices, dishes simpler, down to one Michelin star. Meals B–C.
Le Club, 16 rue Pas (20.57.10.10). All good — food, service, wine list. Meals B–D.

LUMBRES: 62380 Pas-de-Calais, **Moulin de Mombreux** (21.39.62.44). Delightful streamside watermill with very comfortable hotel rooms built in sympathetic style in garden. Delicious cooking. Meals A–C. Rooms A–B.

MALO-LES-BAINS: 59240 Dunkerque, Nord, **Au Bon Coin**, 49 av Kleber (28.69.12.63). Famous for fish. Outstanding value in weekday menu. Five modernised bedrooms. Meals C–E. Rooms E.

MONTREUIL-SUR-MER: 62170 Pas-de-Calais, **Château de Montreuil** (21.81.53.04). Christian Germain is one of France's best young chefs. Lovely house. Meals A–B. Rooms A. Regained Michelin star, 1996.
Darnetal, place Darnetal (21.06.04.87). Warm, happy, unusual décor; modern classic cooking. Simple old-style rooms. Meals C–E. Rooms D–E.

PONT DE BRIQUES: 62360 Pas-de-Calais, **La Rivière**, 17 rue Gare (21.32.22.81). 5km from Boulogne, outstanding lightened Norman cooking; bedrooms refurbished. Meals A–D. Rooms E.

RECQUES-SUR-HEM: 62890 Pas-de-Calais, **Château de Cocove**, off N43, 7km from Ardres (21.82.68.29). Huge 18th-century château. View of fine park from dining room. Old-style cooking. Meals B–D. Rooms B–D. Large wine cellar for take away sales.

ST. OMER: 62500 Pas-de-Calais, **La Bretagne**, 2 pl. Vainquai (21.38.25.78). Good value meals, three restaurants. Meals B–E. Rooms C–D.

ST. QUENTIN: 02100 Aisne, **Grand Hotel et Restaurant Président**, 6 rue Dachery (23.62.69.77). Brilliantly modernised hotel with superb young chef and outstanding pastry cook. Meals A–C. Rooms A–C.

TÉTEGHEM: 59229 Nord (6km SE of Dunkerque) **La Meunerie** (28.26.14.30). Old-mill restaurant with beautiful inventive dishes embracing Flemish. Superb pâtisserie. Nine luxury rooms. Meals A–B. Rooms A–B.

LE TOUQUET: 62520 Pas-de-Calais, **Pérard restaurant**, 67 rue de Metz (21.05.13.33). Next to his famous fish shop, Serge Pérard's restaurant has been made more comfortable. Magnificent fish and shellfish; fish soups are bought by renowned Paris restaurants. Meals C–D.
Café des Arts, 80 rue Paris (21.05.21.55). Good, imaginative but not chi-chi dishes in art déco room. Meals B–C.

VALENCIENNES: 59300 Nord, **L'Alberoi** (Buffet-Gare) (27.46.86.30). Railway buffet has lost its Michelin star but still sells the best meals in town. Meals B–D.

LE WAST: 62142 Colembert, Pas-de-Calais, **Château des Tourelles** (21.33.34.78). Logis in old manor. Very good value. Meals C–E. Rooms D.

WIMEREUX: 62930 Pas-de-Calais, **Atlantic**, digue de Mer (21.32.41.01). Predictable but good regional dishes, with fish from Boulogne. Get a sea-view room. Shut in winter. Meals C–D. Rooms C–D.

Events

ABBEVILLE: early June — Fête; Fair.

AMIENS: early May — International Jazz Festival; Carnival.

ARRAS: June — Rose Festival. June Summer Fete. End August — Fête.

BAILLEUL: February — Carnival.

BOULOGNE: June — Summer Fête. July — Opal Coast Festival (with Berck, Calais, Étaples, Hardelot, Le Portel). 2nd week July — Fishermen's Festival. August — Pilgrimage to Cathedral.

CASSEL: April — Carnival.

DOUAI: June, July — Concerts of Chimes. July — Fête de Gayant (giants)

DUNKERQUE: February/March — One of the biggest Mardi Gras Festivals in Europe, lasting a month. July — Opal Coast Festival. Mid-August — Pilgrimage to Notre-Dames-des-Dunes; Sea Festival.

FORT-MAHON-PLAGE: Easter — Land-Yacht Races.

HAZEBROUCK: February — Carnival.

LICQUES: Just before Christmas — Turkey Fair.

LILLE: Easter — Easter Fair (2 weeks). April — International Fair. June — Fête. September — Festival of the Ancienne Bourse. Massive Jumble Sale. December–early January — Winter Fair.

ST. OMER: Late May — Fête du Chapeau-Vert.

LE TOUQUET: April — International Show-Jumping. August — Flower Festival; Music Festival.

WIMEREUX: May — Shellfish Fête. August — Mussel Fête.

(See also Box in Chapter 3 for information on Markets.)

Museums

AMIENS: Musée de Picardie (22.91.36.44). Closed Mon.

ARRAS: Musée des Beaux-Arts (21.21.26.43). Open daily except Tues. Closed Sun am off season.

CALAIS: Musée de la Guerre. Open May–Sept.

CAMBRAI: Musée Municipal (20.81.38.03). Closed Tues.

DOUAI: Musée Municipal (La Chartreuse) (27.87.17.82). Closed Tues.

DUNKERQUE: Musée des Beaux-Arts (28.66.21.57). Closed Tues.

LILLE: Musée des Beaux-Arts (20.57.01.84). Closed Tues.

ST. OMER: Hotel Sandelin et Musée (21.38.00.94). Closed Mon, Tues.

ST. QUENTIN: Musée Antoine Lécuyer (23.64.72.44). Closed Sun am, Tues.

VALENCIENNES: Musée des Beaux-Arts (27.46.21.09). Closed Tues.

Châteaux and Historic Buildings

AMIENS: Parc Zoologique de la Hôtoie. Closed Nov–Easter.

ARRAS: Hôtel de Ville et Beffroi. Closed Sun pm, Mon am and holidays.

BOULOGNE: Colonne de la Grande Armée. Closed Tues, Wed and Oct.

DOUAI: Beffroi. Visits Sun pm all year. Weekdays April–Aug. Sun am July, Aug. Concerts Sat and holidays 10.45 am; recitals 9 pm Mon June–Sept.

HESDIN: Hôtel Ville. Visits weekdays, and Sun am in summer.

LILLE: Citadelle (20.30.81.00). Visits Sun in summer.

MONTREUIL-SUR-MER: Citadelle. Closed Tues and mid-Oct–mid-Nov.

Index